SOFT AND EMPTY HARD GELATINE CAPSULE TECHNOLOGY

C. P. Deodhar

NIRALI PRAKASHAN
The Way to Excellence

SOFT AND EMPTY HARD GELATINE CAPSULE TECHNOLOGY

First Edition : **August 2011**

© : **Sarita C Deodhar**

The text of this publication, or any part thereof, should not be reproduced or transmitted in any form or stored in any computer storage system or device for distribution including photocopy, recording, taping or information retrieval system or reproduced on any disc, tape, perforated media or other information storage device etc., without the written permission of copyright holder with whom the rights are reserved. Breach of this condition is liable for legal action.

Every effort has been made to avoid errors or omissions in this publication. In spite of this, errors may have crept in. Any mistake, error or discrepancy so noted and shall be brought to our notice shall be taken care of in the next edition. It is notified that neither the publisher nor the copyright holder or seller shall be responsible for any damage or loss of action to any one, of any kind, in any manner, therefrom.

Published By :
NIRALI PRAKASHAN
Abhyudaya Pragati, 1312, Shivaji Nagar,
Off J.M. Road, PUNE – 411005
Tel - (020) 25512336/37/39, Fax - (020) 25511379
Email : niralipune@pragationline.com

Printed By :
Repro Knowledgecast Limited,
Thane

DISTRIBUTION CENTRES

PUNE
Nirali Prakashan
119, Budhwar Peth, Jogeshwari Mandir Lane
Pune 411002, Maharashtra
Tel : (020) 2445 2044, 66022708
Fax : (020) 2445 1538
Email : bookorder@pragationline.com

MUMBAI
Nirali Prakashan
385, S.V.P. Road, Rasdhara Co-op. Hsg. Society Ltd.,
Girgaum, Mumbai 400004, Maharashtra
Tel : (022) 2385 6339 / 2386 9976,
Fax : (022) 2386 9976
Email : niralimumbai@pragationline.com

DISTRIBUTION BRANCHES

NAGPUR
Pratibha Book Distributors
Above Maratha Mandir, Shop No. 3, First Floor,
Rani Jhanshi Square, Sitabuldi, Nagpur 440012,
Maharashtra, Tel : (0712) 254 7129

BENGALURU
Pragati Book House
House No. 1,Sanjeevappa Lane, Avenue Road Cross,
Opp. Rice Church, Bengaluru – 560002.
Tel : (080) 64513344, 64513355,
Mob : 9880582331, 9845021552
Email:bharatsavla@yahoo.com

JALGAON
Nirali Prakashan
34, V. V. Golani Market, Navi Peth, Jalgaon 425001,
Maharashtra, Tel : (0257) 222 0395
Mob : 94234 91860

KOLHAPUR
Nirali Prakashan
New Mahadvar Road,
Kedar Plaza, 1st Floor Opp. IDBI Bank
Kolhapur 416 012, Maharashtra. Mob : 9855046155

CHENNAI
Pragati Books
9/1, Montieth Road, Behind Taas Mahal, Egmore,
Chennai 600008 Tamil Nadu, Tel : (044) 6518 3535,
Mob : 94440 01782 / 98450 21552 / 98805 82331
Email : bharatsavla@yahoo.com

RETAIL OUTLETS
PUNE

Pragati Book Centre
157, Budhwar Peth, Opp. Ratan Talkies,
Pune 411002, Maharashtra
Tel : (020) 2445 8887 / 6602 2707, Fax : (020) 2445 8887
Pragati Book Centre
Amber Chamber, 28/A, Budhwar Peth,
Appa Balwant Chowk, Pune : 411002, Maharashtra,
Tel : (020) 20240335 / 66281669
Email : pbcpune@pragationline.com

Pragati Book Centre
676/B, Budhwar Peth, Opp. Jogeshwari Mandir,
Pune 411002, Maharashtra
Tel : (020) 6601 7784 / 6602 0855
Pragati Book Centre
917/22, Sai Complex, F.C. Road, Opp. Hotel Roopali,
Shivajinagar, Pune 411004, Maharashtra
Tel : (020) 2566 3372 / 6602 2728

PBC Book Sellers & Stationers
152, Budhwar Peth, Pune 411002, Maharashtra
Tel : (020) 2445 2254 / 6609 2463

MUMBAI
Pragati Book Corner
Indira Niwas, 111 - A, Bhavani Shankar Road, Dadar (W), Mumbai 400028, Maharashtra
Tel : (022) 2422 3526 / 6662 5254
Email : pbcmumbai@pragationline.com

www.pragationline.com   info@pragationline.com

A Note About the Author...

The Author of the Book, Late C. P. Deodhar was known in the Pharmaceutical World as 'Capsule Deodhar'. He is called the 'Father of Indian Hard Gelatin Capsule' as he is the one who manufactured the first hard gelatine capsule in India. This was in the year 1956. The capsule till then was a total Foreign product, being imported, empty as well as filled, by the then multinational companies operating in India.

On taking his M.Sc. Degree in Biochemistry in the year 1954, Mr. Deodhar, aspiring to do basic research work in medicine, got seized with the idea of manufacturing hard gelatine capsule. The capsule technology that time was a very closely guarded secret, being the world monopoly of two American Companies viz. M/s Eli Lilly and Co. and M/s Parke, Davis and Co. Mr. Deodhar, undaunted by the challenges posed, carried on innumerable experiments in this ill-equipped make-shift laboratory with untiring zeal, patience and perseverence and ultimately succeeded in producing the first capsule made by hand on plastic dipping mould in the year 1956.

He thereafter got fabricated under his supervision a semi-automatic capsule manufacturing plant, with the help of an Engineering Company, and after trial runs, started commercial production in October 1958. The constant struggle for improvements in process technology, and quality of capsules produced as well as for increase in the machine output was going on. Besides experiencing acute financial constraints, he was facing multiple problems on production front, which he had to attend single handedly, without guidance from any source. The production was going on and in the year 1961, he approached Govt. of India for putting a ban on import of capsules. Government agreed and the import of capsule was banned since that year. Then there was no looking back.

However, he was not at all satisfied with the quality of capsule produced on semi-automatic plant and realized that his cherished dream of producing capsules, a good quality one, measuring up to International standards in every respect, hygienically very safe to consume and suitable for filling operations on all types of filling machines can only be realized, if production is done on a fully automatic capsule manufacturing machine. He therefore approached Homi Mehta Group in the year 1962 for necessary assistance. Homi Mehta Group took over his capsule manufacturing activity and reposing faith in his competency and the capsule technology developed by him, imported two automatic capsule manufacturing plants. After erecting the plants, production started in a year 1964 in a big way. However, since the process technology was not made available along with the machines, efforts and experiments were constantly going on for improvements in the process and the machine, facing challenges on so many fronts like bacterial contamination, colours, machine settings, various machine parts which were required to be outsourced in the absence of machine workshop, grease, air-conditioning etc. besides marketing of the capsules produced and attending problems faced by the pharmaceutical companies on their filling machines.

Aspiring all the time to produce better and better quality capsule, he joined in the year 1977, Associated Capsule Group, who were then producing capsules on semi-automatic machines alongwith one fully automatic plant fabricated in their own workshop. Their full-fledged workshop was a great incentive for him to join them. Mr. Ajit Singh and Mr. Jasjit Singh, the Chairman and Managing Directors of the Group were equally charged with the dream of producing the best quality capsule. Their technical expertise, professional management, very progressive outlook and excellent business acumen, coupled with the vast technical expertise and rich experience of Mr. Deodhar gave a tremendous impetus to the capsule manufacturing industry and ACG Worldwide now is one of the largest capsule manufacturing and marketing groups of the world with exports being made to more than 80 countries in the world. Mr. Deodhar thus could see his dream realized in his life-time.

After working for one than 50 years in the Capsule Industry, Mr. Deodhar retired from the active field at the age of 76. He then shifted to Pune to pursue another passion of his life viz. teaching. Here he joined Poona College of Pharmacy. The well-equipped laboratory here was a great incentive for him to carry out his further experiments in capsule. He joined the College in August 2006. Seeing that there is a considerable gap in academics and industry, he decided to work in the direction of bridging that gap to the extent possible. Also seeing that there is no proper and complete information available on capsule and the relative technology, he set-up on the task of putting in writing his vast knowledge and experience in the field. He thus started work on the book **'Soft and Empty Hard Gelatine Capsule Technology'**. He completed the soft capsule part of it and the first 10 chapters of the hard capsule part. Destiny however, did not allow him to see the book completed by him and he left this world on 2nd October, 2008, after a very brief illness.

It was essential that the work he had started, about which he was so passionate, should get completed and should be made available to the public. We set upon the task of completing his work and approached his friends and colleagues for necessary assistance. They willingly agreed to the request out of love and respect for Mr. Deodhar and gave write-ups on the remaining topics of the book. The book thus could be completed and presented in this form.

SARITA C. DEODHAR

Acknowledgements ...

Profuse thanks are due to Mr. Somesh Sathe, the Managing Director of Arbestool and Tooltronics India. His companies are engaged in Soft Capsule Manufacturing and they not only manufacture the machines but also provide technical know-how here in India as well as abroad. Late Mr. Deodhar received extensive help from Mr. Sathe, while working on the soft capsule part of the book. The hour long deliberations with him and the prompt supply of relevant material and catalogues helped Mr. Deodhar to a considerable extent in writing on soft capsule. We are very grateful to Mr. Sathe for taking keen interest in the work and extending his valuable assistance.

For Hard Gelatine Capsule Technology part of the Book - which was Mr. Deodhar's main domain, the first and foremost thanks are due to Mr. Ajit Singh and Mr. Jasjit Singh, the Chairman and Managing Directors of ACG Worldwide. Mr. Deodhar worked with them for nearly 30 years and it is here that he could see his dream of Indian capsule being very well accepted all over the world fulfilled. In the book he has drawn liberally on the data and material available in the catalogues of ACG Worldwide and we are very thankful to them, for having given their consent to it.

Thanks are also due to Dr. Prasad Kanitkar of Pfizer and Co., Mr. Raghavan Srinivas, a senior consulting engineer and the colleagues of Mr. Deodhar in ACG Worldwide, viz. Mr. P.H. Deshmukh, Vice President; R&D, Mr. Sharad Kulkarni, Vice President; Operations at Shirwal Plant, Mr. S.V. Powale, G.M. Corpn. Q. A at Kandivli and Mr. Bhupesh Lad, DGM at P+am.

While Dr. Kanitkar gave a write up on 'Pharmacehtical Requirements of the Quality Attributes of Filled Capsules - Ch. 13', Mr. Raghavan and Mr. Kulkarni provided write-ups on 'Packaging of Filled Capsules - Ch. 12', Mr. Deshmukh, besides giving all the help to Mr. Deodhar while he was working on the book, also gave a write-up later on 'Finishing Operations - Ch. 11'. It is only because of the self-less assistance extended by all these that it became possible to get the book completed.

Thanks also have to be given to Mr. Jeevan Deshpande, Mechanical Draftsman, who worked with Mr. Deodhar patiently for long hours and gave all the drawings and sketches made to Mr. Deodhar's satisfaction.

Last but not the least thanks are due to our publisher Mr. Dinesh Furia and Mr. Jignesh Furia of Nirali Prakashan who had taken keen interest in the book from the very beginning, gave all the help required and patiently waited to receive the complete manuscript in hand. His excellent team of Assistants Mrs. Manasi Pingle, Mr. Akbar Shaikh and Miss Chaitali Takle had been extremely helpful and co-operative all throughout. I am immensely thankful to all of them.

It is only with the blessings of Almighty and the willful assistance of friends, relatives and well-wishers that this book could get completed and I remain to be indebted to them all.

SARITA C. DEODHAR

Contents ...

SOFT CAPSULE TECHNOLOGY

1. Description and Identification Attributes of Soft Gelatin Capsule   1.1 – 1.8

1.1	Description of Soft Gelatin Capsule	1.1
1.2	Important Features of Soft Gelatin Capsule	1.1
1.3	Identification Attributes of Soft Gelatine Capsules	1.1
	1.3.1 Shapes and Sizes of Capsules	1.2
	1.3.2 Types of Capsules	1.4
	1.3.2.1 Seam and Seamless	1.4
	1.3.2.2 Extra Hard, Hard, Medium and Soft	1.4
	1.3.3 Colours	1.5
	1.3.3.1 Plain Transparent	1.7
	1.3.3.2 Coloured Transparent	1.7
	1.3.3.3 Opaque White	1.7
	1.3.3.4 Coloured Opaque	1.7
	1.3.3.5 Combination or Bicoloured	1.7
	1.3.4 Flavour (Flavoured Soft Capsules)	1.8
	1.3.5 Printed Matter	1.8
	1.3.6 Colour of Printing Ink	1.8

2. Shell Composition and Manufacturing of Gelatin   2.1 – 2.8

2.1	Shell Composition	2.1
2.2	Gelatin	2.1
	2.2.1 Acid Bone Gelatin	2.3
	2.2.2 Limed Ossein or Limed Hide	2.3
2.3	General Specifications of Type A and Type B Gelatin used in the Manufacturing of Soft Gelatin Capsules	2.5
	2.3.1 Bloom Strength	2.6
	2.3.2 Viscosity	2.6
	2.3.3 Microconstituent Iron	2.7
	2.3.4 Microbial	2.8

3. Soft Capsule Fill Materials   3.1 – 3.8

3.1	Liquids or Solutions	3.1
	3.1.1 Water Immiscible Liquids	3.1
	3.1.2 Water Miscible Liquids	3.1
3.2	Suspensions of Solids in Liquids	3.2
3.3	Formulation of Fill Materials	3.2
3.4	Basis of Determination of Capsule Size for Liquids and Suspensions	3.2
	3.4.1 Determination of Capsule Size for Liquid Formulations	3.4
	3.4.2 Determination of Capsule Size for Formulations in Suspension Form	3.4
3.5	Base Adsorption (B.A.)	3.6

4. History and Production of Soft Gelatin Capsule   4.1 – 4.12

4.1	Introduction	4.1
	4.1.1 Plate Process	4.1
	4.1.2 Rotary Die Process	4.2

		4.1.3	Seamless Soft Gel Process	4.2
			4.1.3.1 Limitations of Fill Materials	4.4
		4.1.4	Accogel Process	4.4
		4.1.5	The Reciprocating Die Process	4.4
		4.1.6	The Procap Process	4.4
	4.2	Production of Soft Shell Capsule on Rotary Die Machine		4.4
		4.2.1	Air-Conditioning	4.7
		4.2.2	Preparation of Gel Mass	4.8
		4.2.3	Processing of Fill Material	4.8
			4.2.3.1 Liquids	4.8
			4.2.3.2 Suspensions	4.9
		4.2.4	Production on Rotary Die Machine	4.10
		4.2.5	Cleaning and Drying of Capsules	4.12
		4.2.6	Visual and Diametrical Sorting	4.12
		4.2.7	Quality Control	4.12
		4.2.8	Bulk Printing	4.12
		4.2.9	Bulk Packing / Bottle Packing / Blister Packing	4.12
5.	**Effects of External Weather Conditions on Soft Gelatin Capsule**			**5.1 – 5.4**
	5.1	Introduction		5.1
	5.2	The Chemical Compositon of Shell		5.3
	5.3	Relationship of Moisture Content of Capsule with the Condition of Air Surrounding It and the Chemical Composition of Capsule		5.3
	5.4	Recommended Atmospheric Conditions for Transportation and Storage		5.4
6.	**Disintegration, Dissolution, Bioavailability and New Developments in Soft Capsule Technology**			**6.1 – 6.4**
	6.1	Disintegration		6.1
	6.2	Dissolution		6.1
	6.3	Bioavailability		6.2
	6.4	New Developments in Soft Capsule Technology		6.3
	6.5	New Applications		6.3
	6.6	Alternative Raw Materials to Gelatin		6.4

HARD GELATINE CAPSULE TECHNOLOGY

1.	**Historical Development of Two-Piece Empty Hard Gelatin Capsule**		**1.1 – 1.6**
	1.1	Introduction	1.1
	1.2	Development of Capsule Technology	1.1

	1.2.1	Dipping Moulds	1.1
	1.2.2	Chemical Composition of Solution Used for Dipping	1.2
	1.2.3	Air Conditioning (A.C.)	1.2
	1.2.4	Capsule Making Machines	1.2
		1.2.4.1 Stacker Machine	1.3
		1.2.4.2 Colton Machine	1.4
1.3		Development of Capsule Technology in India	1.5
1.4		HPMC and Pullulan Capsules	1.6

2. Identification Attributes of Two-Piece Empty Hard Gelatin Capsule   2.1 – 2.28

2.1		Description of Empty Hard Gelatin Capsule	2.1
2.2		Important Features of Hard Gelatin Capsule	2.1
2.3		Identification Attributes of Capsule	2.2
	2.3.1	Size (Capacity)	2.2
	2.3.2	Type (Configuration)	2.5
		2.3.2 (1) Plain Capsules	2.5
		2.3.2 (2) Locking Capsules	2.6
		2.3.2 (3) Pre-Lock Capsule	2.18
		2.3.2 (4) Tamper Evident Capsule (Coni-Snap Supro Capsules)	2.20
	2.3.3	Shape	2.20
	2.3.4	Embossed Matter	2.21
	2.3.5	Colour Scheme and Colour HUE (of coloured capsules)	2.22
	2.3.6	Printed Capsules	2.26
	2.3.7	Form of Printing	2.27
	2.3.8	Colour of Printing Ink	2.28
	2.3.9	Flavour (Flavoured Hard Gelatin Capsules)	2.28

3. Raw Materials Used in the Manufacture of Two-piece Empty Hard Gelatin Capsules   3.1 – 3.10

4. Manufacture of Two-Piece Empty Hard Gelatin Capsule   4.1 – 4.16

4.1	Introduction	4.1
4.2	Manufacture of Hard Gelatin Capsules	4.2
4.3	Preparation of Stock Gelatin Solution	4.3
4.4	Aging of Gelatin Solution	4.4
4.5	Preparation of Gelatin Solution for Dipping and Feeding	4.4
4.6	Production of Empty Hard Gelatin Capsule on Fully Automatic 'Colton' type Hard Gelatin Capsule Making Machine	4.5
	4.6.1 Dipping Moulds or Pins (Basic Design)	4.5
	4.6.2 Pin Bars	4.6
	4.6.3 Colton Type Capsule Manufacturing Machine	4.7

		4.6.4	The Manufacturing of Capsule is Subdivided into the Following Steps	4.7

        4.6.4   The Manufacturing of Capsule is Subdivided into the Following Steps   4.7
                4.6.4.1 Lubrication of Dipping Moulds   4.9
                4.6.4.2 Dipping of Pin Bars   4.9
                4.6.4.3 Distribution of Picked Up Gelatin Film Uniformly on Pins and Setting of Film   4.11
                4.6.4.4 Drying   4.11
                4.6.4.5 Striping, Cutting and Joining   4.12
                4.6.4.6 Coarse Sorter   4.14
                4.6.4.7 Off Machine Drying   4.14
                4.6.4.8 Electronic/Manual Sorting   4.14
                4.6.4.9 Final Packing   4.15
    4.7   Quality Control   4.15

5. Printing of Empty Capsules   5.1 – 5.14
    5.1   Introduction   5.1
    5.2   History of Capsule Printing   5.1
    5.3   History of Printing of Capsules in India   5.2
    5.4   Capsule Printing Process   5.3
    5.5   Capsule Printing Machines   5.4
    5.6   Printing Ink   5.9
    5.7   Print Defects   5.11

6. Pharmacopoeial and Industrial Standards of Empty Hard Gelatin Capsules   6.1 – 6.14
    6.1   Introduction   6.1
    6.2   Pharmacopoeial Standards   6.1
        6.2.1   Identification   6.2
        6.2.2   Average Weight   6.2
        6.2.3   Disintegration   6.3
        6.2.4   Microbial Limits   6.3
        6.2.5   Loss on Drying   6.4
    6.3   Industrial Standards   6.4
        6.3.1   Indian Pharmacopoeial Standards   6.4
        6.3.2   Additional Microbial Standards   6.4
        6.3.3   Efficacy as a Container for Medicament   6.5
        6.3.4   Presence of All Relevant Identification Attributes   6.5
        6.3.5   Maintaining the Visual Defects Affecting Accuracy and Uniformity of Dosage less than the Values Specified under AQL by Empty Capsule Manufacturer and the Control on Individual Weight of Empty Capsule for better Evaluation of Fill Weight   6.5
        6.3.6   Smooth Performance on Various Machines of Capsule Usage   6.6
                6.3.6.1 Strength and Flexibility, and Absence of Brittleness   6.6
                6.3.6.2 Good Flowability   6.9
                6.3.6.3 Proper Fit for Its Performance   6.10
                6.3.6.4 Free from Visual Defects Causing Stoppage of

			Capsule Usage Machines	6.11
		6.3.6.5	Free from Defects, which have Potential to Cause Problems in Capsule Usage Machines	6.11
		6.3.6.6	Aesthetic Appeal	6.12
	6.4	Capsule Defects		6.13

7. Drugs of different Medicinal Systems in Different Physical Forms Filled in Hard Gelatin Capsules — 7.1 – 7.2

8. Formulation of Drug (Powder or Granule Form) for Capsule Filling Machines — 8.1 – 8.10

- 8.1 Introduction — 8.1
- 8.2 Formulation of Drugs — 8.2
- 8.3 Fillers or Diluents — 8.2
- 8.4 Properties of Formulated Drug Required for Smooth Performance on Capsule Filling Machine — 8.3
  - 8.4.1 Non-Hygroscopicity — 8.3
  - 8.4.2 Homogeneity — 8.4
  - 8.4.3 Uniform Density — 8.4
  - 8.4.4 Flowing Behaviour — 8.4
  - 8.4.5 Cohesiveness — 8.5
  - 8.4.6 Compressibility — 8.5
  - 8.4.7 Lubrication — 8.5
  - 8.4.8 Non-Stickiness — 8.5
  - 8.4.9 Filled Capsules Facing Problem During Rejoining and Locking — 8.6
- 8.5 Properties of Formulated Drug Required for Improving Disintegration Time (D.T.) and Dissolution — 8.7
- 8.6 Requirements of Formulation for Empty Capsule — 8.9
- 8.7 Conclusion — 8.10

9. Different Mechanisms Used on Capsule Filling Machines to Operate Capsules for Filling Drugs — 9.1 – 9.14

- 9.1 Introduction — 9.1
- 9.2 Rectification of Capsules — 9.4
- 9.3 Opening the Capsule and Separating Cap and Body — 9.12
- 9.4 Filling the Drug into the Opened Body — 9.14
- 9.5 Joining the Filled body with Cap and Locking the Capsule — 9.14
- 9.6 Ejecting the Filled Capsule — 9.14

10. Filling Machines — 10.1 – 10.28

- 10.1 Introduction — 10.1
- 10.2 Auger Fill Machines — 10.2
  - 10.2.1 Principle — 10.2
  - 10.2.2 Calculation of the Volumetric Capacity to Determine the Capsule Size

	for Filling the Unit Drug Dosage	10.2
10.2.3	Historical Development	10.3
10.2.4	Description and Working of Machine	
	(Working on the same Filling Principle)	10.5
	10.2.4.1 Machine Parts Handling Capsules	10.7
	10.2.4.2 Machine Parts Handling Powder	10.7
	10.2.4.3 Powder Filling Process	10.10
10.2.5	Weight Control	10.11

10.3 Dosator-Piston Machine 10.11
    10.3.1 Dosator-Piston Machine Intermittent Type 10.12
        10.3.1.1 Principle 10.12
        10.3.1.2 Calculation of Volumetric Capacity to Determine the
                Capsule Size for Filling the Unit Drug Dose 10.12
        10.3.1.3 Historical Development 10.13
        10.3.1.4 Description and Working of Machine
                (Working on Dosator-Piston Intermittent type Filling Principle) 10.13
                10.3.1.4 (A) Machine Parts Handling Capsule 10.14
                10.3.1.4 (B) Machine Parts Handling Powder 10.14
                10.3.1.4 (C) Working of the Machine (Powder Filling Process) 10.16
        10.3.1.5 Powder Filling Device 10.18
        10.3.1.6 List of Few Machine Manufacturers (Intermittent Machines) 10.19
    10.3.2 Rotary Machines 10.21
        10.3.2.1 Principle 10.21
        10.3.2.2 Calculation of Volumetric Capacity to Determine the
                Capsule Size For Filling the Unit Drug Dose 10.21
        10.3.2.3 Historical Development 10.21
        10.3.2.4 Working of Rotary Machine
                (Working on Dosator-Piston Rotary Type Filling Principle) 10.22
                10.3.2.4 (A) Machine Parts Handling Capsule 10.23
                10.3.2.4 (B) Machine Parts Handling Powder 10.23
                10.3.2.4 (C) Working of the Machine 10.23
        10.3.2.5 Weight Control 10.26
        10.3.2.6 List of Manufacturers of Rotary Machines .. 10.27

11. Finishing Operations   **11.1 – 11.10**

11.1 Capsule Cleaning and Polishing 11.1
11.2 Capsule Sorting 11.3
11.3 Capsule Band Sealing 11.5
11.4 Weighing of Capsules and Check Weighing Machines 11.8
    11.4.1 Sample Automatic Check Weighing Machine 11.9

11.4.2 100% Check Weighing Machine	11.9
12. Packaging of Filled Capsules	**12.1 – 12.16**
12.1 Introduction	12.1
12.2 History of Packaging	12.1
12.3 Focus on Quality	12.2
12.4 Types of Packaging	12.4
12.4.1 Major Types of Packaging Materials	12.5
12.4.2 Closures and Containers	12.5
12.4.3 Package Development Considerations	12.6
12.5 Packaging of Filled Capsules	12.7
12.5.1 Introduction	12.7
12.5.2 Importance of Packing in Pharmaceutical Manufacture	12.7
12.5.3 Functions of Packaging Containment	12.7
12.5.4 Material Characteristics	12.7
12.5.5 Testing and Stability	12.8
12.6 Packaging Materials for Blister Packing of H. G. Capsules	12.9
12.6.1 Main Considerations When Selecting Blister Packing Materials	12.9
12.6.2 Forming Films	12.9
12.6.3 Lidding Material	12.11
12.7 Packaging Machineries	12.13
12.7.1 Basic Operations Involved in Packing	12.13
12.7.2 Types of Packing	12.13
12.7.2.1 Bulk Packing in Glass/HDPE Bottles	12.13
12.7.2.2 Strip Packing Machine	12.14
12.7.2.3 Blister Packing Machine	12.15
13. Pharmaceutical Requirements of the Quality Attributes of Filled Capsules	**13.1 – 13.10**
13.1 Introduction	13.1
13.2 Average Weight	13.2
13.3 Disintegration	13.2
13.4 Loss on Drying	13.3
13.5 Microbial Limits	13.4
13.6 Disintegration Time	13.6
13.7 Content Uniformity	13.7
13.8 Dissolution	13.8
13.9 Conclusion	13.10

PART I

SOFT CAPSULE TECHNOLOGY

1.

HISTORICAL DEVELOPMENT OF TWO-PIECE EMPTY HARD GELATIN CAPSULE

1.1 INTRODUCTION

Two piece empty hard gelatin capsule has a history of more than 150 years. It was invented by PARISIAN PHARMACIST MR. C. LEBHUY. He was granted a patent on 20th Oct 1846 (French Patent 4435). It was stated in the patent that the capsules were made by dipping process. The dipping moulds used were silver plated metal cylinders about 4 to 5 cms long. For producing cap (lid) and body (container) the dipping moulds of different diameters were used. The diameters of the moulds were such that after the cap and body shells were produced, they would join smoothly to form a capsule. The capsules were made by dipping the moulds into decoction of starch or tapioca, the consistency of a bouillie, which was sweetened with little sugar and with 'fish silver'. In the subsequent patent he had taken on the composition of solution for dipping the moulds, the use of gelatin was included.

1.2 DEVELOPMENT OF CAPSULE TECHNOLOGY

The development of capsule technology had taken place mainly in the areas of
  (i)   Dipping moulds
  (ii) Chemical composition of solution used for dipping
  (iii) Air conditioning
  (iv) Capsule making machines

1.2.1 Dipping Moulds

Dipping moulds of various materials were made to produce capsules. They were wood, iron rods, plated iron moulds, lead, brass, plastic and stainless steel. Finally the industry is now using the dipping moulds made from special free cutting stainless steel rods or from stainless steel (material) which can be heat treated after the moulds are made from them. The hardened moulds are used to minimize their wear during use (i.e. during stripping of dried capsule shells from the dipping moulds)

1.2.2 Chemical Composition of Solution used for Dipping

Various edible polymers were tried as a main component of the composition. They were starch, carrageen, gelatin, HPMC and Pullulan. HPMC polymer is made from cellulose and pullulan polymer is made by fermentation process from starch. The capsule made from HPMC and pullulan polymers are called vegetarian capsules as these polymers are of vegetable origin. This is a recent development.

Many other chemicals were added in small quantities into the polymer solution to get capsules which would be stable, look good, attractive and perform well on all types of capsule filling and packing machines. In early days substances like gums, sugars etc were added to improve the elasticity and strength. But they are not being used now. Presently additives in use are :

(i) Preservatives.
(ii) Plasticizers.
(iii) Edible colours and pigments.
(iv) Process performance aids.

(this part is given in details in the chapter no three)

For capsules which are made from HPMC and pullulan, gelling agents like gellan gum, carrageenan etc. are added. Without them these capsules are difficult to manufacture.

1.2.3 Air Conditioning (A.C.)

In olden days, the production of capsules was a non-continuous operation. For continuos production of capsules it is essential to have air of specific constant temperature and humidity in the production areas. It is difficult to have such specific conditions in any production area all the time, all the year round as changes in temperature and humidity do naturally take place time wise i.e. daytime and nighttime as also seasonwise. Therefore in those days, the capsules were produced only when the weather conditions in the production areas were favourable. To overcome this problem, air-conditioning the production areas was the only solution.

M/s Eli Lilly and Co. of U.S.A., was the first capsule manufacturing company, who installed 'air-conditioning' system in the year 1912 for the production of capsule and thereafter they started producing capsule continuously 24 hours a day, all the year round.

1.2.4 Capsule making Machines

Upto 1913, capsules were produced on semi-automatic capsule making machines. Cutting and joining operations were manually done. The efforts were on to develop the fully automatic machine for manufacture of capsules from the year 1900 onwards.

1.2.4.1 Stacker Machine

The first fully automatic machine was developed by Mr. B.W. Scott of M/s Arthur Colton and Co. (Detroit U.S.A.) in the year 1913 for M/s Eli Lilly and Co. U.S.A. (Ref. U.S. Patent No. 1,07,459). This machine was called "STACKER" machine. The production rate on this machine was 8000 capsules per hour. It became easy for M/s Eli Lilly and Co. to make capsules 24 hours a day and all the year on this machine because of their successful implementation of A.C. system for capsule making.

In the starting it was possible on this machine to make only single coloured capsule as there was only one single dipping tank to dip cap and body pin bars together. After few years, the machine was modified to accommodate two dipping tanks, one for dipping body pin bars and the other one for dipping cap pin bars. To make this possible, the machine was modified by adding the devices to separate the cap and body pin bars for dipping operation.

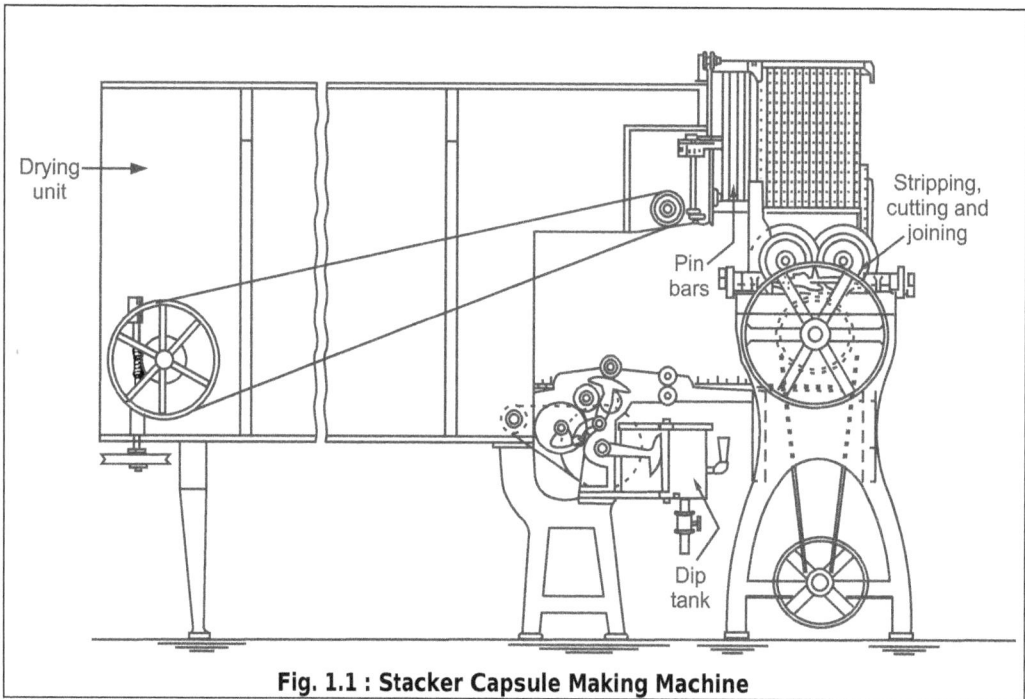

Fig. 1.1 : Stacker Capsule Making Machine

Another interesting part of this machine was that, pin bars were held stationary in the inverted position and dip tanks were raised upto them. The automatic capsule making machine made it possible to make capsules untouched by hands. This was important from the point of view of making capsule ideally suitable for pharmaceutical use.

1.2.4.2 Colton Machine

In 1931, Mr. Arthur Colton got a patent for his newly developed high output capsule making machine, (U.S. patent No. 1,787,777). This machine was called COLTON 750 machine. It had pairs of 750 bars as against 175 pairs of bars in STACKER machine. The machine was approximately 40' long, having 6' width and 5' height. It had a capacity to produce 30,000 capsules per hour. This machine was divided into two parts through which cap and body bars passed separately but synchronously. It was provided with two dipping tanks for dipping separately cap and body pin bars. Therefore it was possible to produce bi-coloured capsules right from the beginning without any difficulty. Mr. Colton was producing capsules on several of such machines with minimum man power. It was said that production of four machines was managed by one person at a time. Finally he sold all these machines to M/s Parke Davis and Co. Detorit U.S.A.

Around 1940/45 M/s Eli Lilly & Co. got two Colton machines and they started capsule production on them. Till then M/s Eli Lilly were producing capsules on STACKER machines.

The quality of capsules produced on fully automatic capsule making machines was far superior to the capsules made on semi-automatic capsule making machines. The net result of this was that the operations of semi-automatic machines were closed down and the capsule market became monopoly of two American companies namely M/s Eli Lilly and Co and M/s Parke Davis and co. of U.S.A. who were operating fulling automatic machines for production of capsules. This situation remained for quite a long period. Both these companies modified their machines and improved the process for higher out put and better product. It is said that both these companies are producing empty capsules around 1,00,000 per hour per machine and the capsules perform well on automatic capsule filling machines whose production rate is more than 1,80,000 capsules per hour. Both these companies have expanded their activities and started producing empty capsules in different countries in the world. Around 1991/92, the capsule division of M/s Eli Lilly and Co. changed hands. It was sold to M/s Shionogi of Japan. M/s Shionogi have their capsule manufacturing operations at three different locations in the world, viz. Japan, Europe and U.S.A.

In 1963, the name of the capsule division of Parke Davis and co was changed to CAPSUGEL. Few years back, the management of M/s Capsugel was taken over by M/s Pfizer U.S.A.

Fig. 1.2 : First Invented Colten Machine

In U.S.A. and Canada, few pharma companies entered in the field of manufacturing of capsules. They were S.K. and F. (now known as S.K. and B), Roche, R.P. Scherer (U.S.A) and R.P Scherer (Canada). All these companies were in this field for a short period of time.

There are countries in the eastern part of the world who entered in the field of manufacturing of capsules from 1960 onwards. They are Japan, Korea, Singapore, India, China and others. In some of the countries as mentioned above M/s Capsugel (Ex M/s Parke Davis and Co) is already producing capsules; but other than M/s Capsugel, other manufactures are also engaged in this activity.

As this book is written in India, a short review of development of capsule technology in India is given below.

1.3 DEVELOPMENT OF CAPSULE TECHNOLOGY IN INDIA

In India, Mr. C.P. Deodhar, a biochemist, initiated the work in the year 1954 to make empty hard gelatin capsule and he succeeded in producing the first hard gelatin capsule by using plastic dipping moulds in the year 1956. He developed the first semi-automatic machine with the help of one engineering company and started commercial production of capsules on that semi-automatic machine in the year 1958 in Mumbai (Bombay). This activity was started under the name of C and S laboratories whose name was subsequently changed to Pharmaceutical Capsule Laboratories. This company under the management of H.M. Mehta and co. imported two fully automatic Colton 750 capsule making machines from U.S.A. in the year 1963 and started production of capsules on them in the year 1964.

M/s Gelikap in Baroda and M/s Associated capsule in Mumbai brought the machines and technology of making capsules from Italy in the year 1963 and 1964 respectively.

Around 1974, M/s Associated Capsules manufactured indigenously the fully automatic capsule making machine to make empty capsules in India. This machine was similar to the machine made by M/s Arthur Colton (Colton 750). Associated Capsule made lot of developments in the capsule making machine, in the process technology and slowly expanded their capsule making machine manufacturing capacity from one machine in 1974 to around 50 machines (indigeneously manufactured) in the year 1995. Today they are the leading capsule manufacturer in India and second larger producers of capsules in the world. This company not only makes the capsules, but also makes capsule filling, sealing, polishing, sorting, (empty and filled), weighing and blister packing machines of international standards. Their capsules and machines are being exported and they are well received in the international markets.

1970 onwards, besides Associated Capsules, many other companies were producing capsules on semi-automatic and automatic machines. Exact reasons were not known, but around 91-92 there was a heavy recession in the capsule market in India and it continued for 2 to 3 years, as a result of which by 1995, all the semi-automatic capsule makers had to close down their manufacturing activity. Even the few manufactures who were producing capsules on fully automatic capsule making machines were forced to close down.

As it stands today, besides Associated Capsule Group there are other companies who are making automatic capsule making machines, dipping moulds, capsule filling and packing machines etc. in the country. There are 8 to 10 capsule manufactures of empty capsules, other than Associated capsules, producing capsules on fully automatic machines. The number of machines run by these manufactures are ranging from one to twenty machines. It is a matter of pride that India is now self sufficient in all the spheres of gelatin capsule manufacturing activity including the raw materials required.

It is said that India produces over 50 billions of capsules a year.

This figure was indicated in the year 2006.

1.4 HPMC AND PULLULAN CAPSULES

HPMC (Hydroxypropyl Methylcellulose) and PULLULAN capsules. (also known as veg. capsules)

Many neutraceutical products are filled in HPMC capsules. Other than Shionogi and Capsugel companies, there are few other companies who manufacture these capsules in the world by dipping process.

Around 1997-98, Associated Capsules started experiments to make capsules from HPMC. Now the quality of these capsules has reached the international standards and the company is now exporting these capsules also all over the world.

There is another company in India named Natural capsule, who also manufacture HPMC capsules. They named their product as 'Natural Capsule'.

■■■

2.

SHELL COMPOSITION
AND
MANUFACTURING OF GELATIN

2.1 SHELL COMPOSITION

The capsule shell is mainly composed of gelatin, plasticizer and water. Other than these, it may contain preservatives, synthetic and natural edible colours. To get the sweet taste, some times sugar is added. To aid solubility and reduction in aldehydic tanning of gelatin, Fumaric acid is added. It is used within the permissible range prescribed by Food and Drugs Administration U.S.F.D.A. or respective drug authority of the respective country.

The plasticizers of pharmaceutical grade like glycerine, sorbitol, propylene glycol are used. Any one of the plasticizer is used alone or in combination.

The main component of the shell being gelatin, it is detailed below :

2.2 GELATIN

Two types of gelatins are described in U.S.P./N.F. They are Type A and Type B. Type 'A' gelatin is manufactured from 'Pig skin' and 'Bone' (Animal). The iso-ionic point of A type gelatin produced from 'Pig skin' is pH 7 to 9. The iso-ionic point of A type gelatin produced from 'Bone' is pH 5.5 to 6. The stocks are treated with acid and thereafter acid is washed. The gelatin is produced by extraction process from the acid removed materials.

Type 'B' gelatin is processed from Bones and hides by Alkali process. The iso-ionic point of this gelatin is pH 4.8 to 5.2. The manufacturing of Type A and Type B gelatin is given in the following flow diagram.

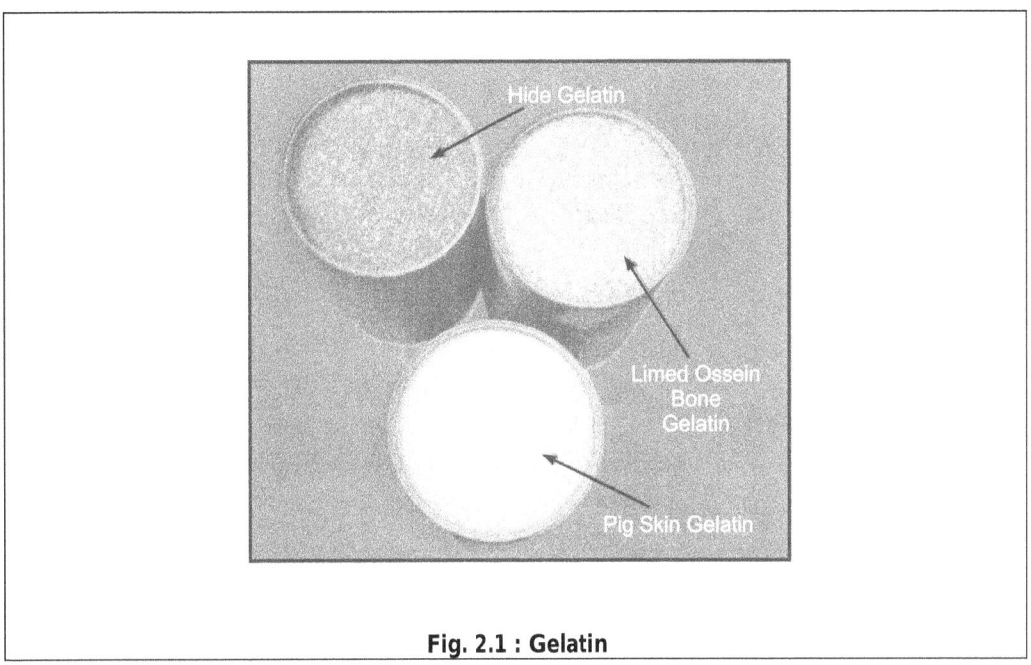

Fig. 2.1 : Gelatin

Manufacturing of Type A and Type B Gelatins by using Different Sources and Processes :

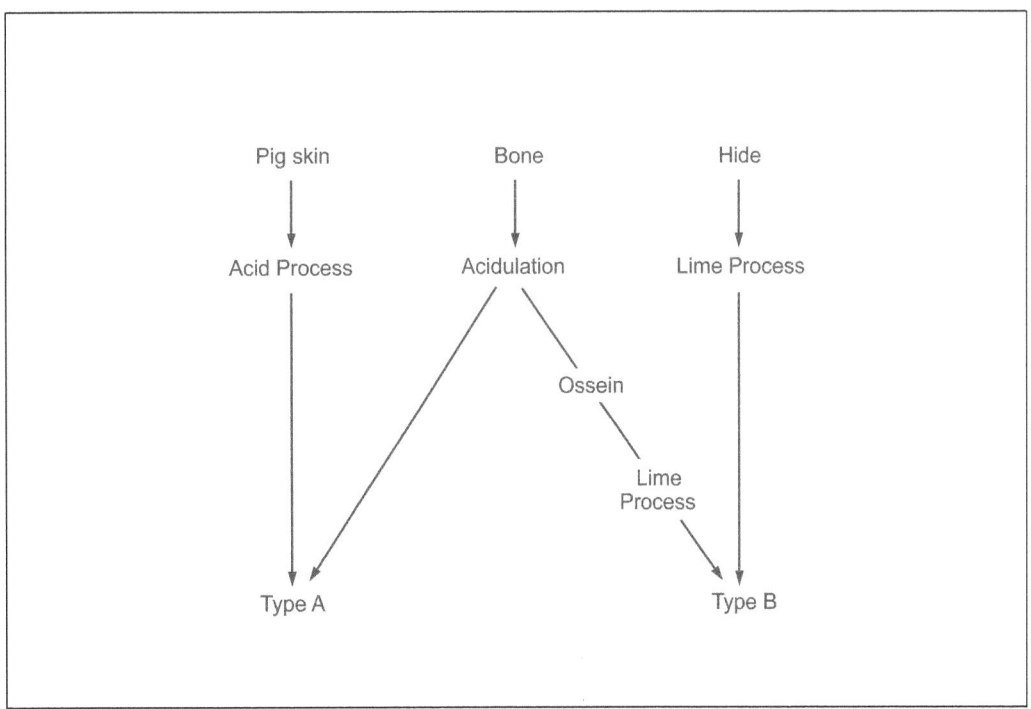

2.2.1 Acid Bone Gelatin

Flow Diagram of Manufacturing of Type A Gelatin
(Acid Process) Pig Skin, Hide[*] and Ossein

Product	Process Operations	Remarks
Skin or Hide	Cleaning, size reduction, washing ↓	Grease, adhering contaminants are removed by washing. Cutter or choppers reduce the piece size.
Bone	Acid treatment ↓	Raw materials are soaked in diluted mineral acid such as hydrochloric for 24 to 48 hours.
	Washing ↓	The pretreated collagen is washed for suitable ionic conditioning.
Gelatin solution	Extraction ↓	Placed in stainless steel extraction vats, the pretreated collagen is converted into gelatin by hot sterile water. Several extractions are performed sequentially.
	Filtration ↓	See same steps as in limed ossein process chart.

2.2.2 Limed Ossein or Limed Hide

Flow Diagram of Manufacturing of Type 'B' gelatin
(Alkali Process)

Product	Process Operations	Remarks
Degreased bones	Sieving	Dissolution of the mineral part of the bones by means of acids such as hydrochloric or phosphoric. The bone after removal of mineral part is called "ossein".
Dicalcium phosphates ossein	Acidulation ↓	
1. Ossein 2. Hide is used as another raw material to make 'B' type gelatine.	Liming ↓	For removal of impurities and hydrolysis of collagen, ossein is immersed for 8 to 12 weeks in a bath of lime milk. Similar treatment is given to hide. Liming on-wards, hide

---

[*] Hide is also used for producing Type A gelatin.

		is being treated in the same way as ossein.
Pre-treated ossein	Washing	The lime is eliminated by washing and the ossein is brought to an acid pH for extraction of gelatin.
	↓	
Gelatin solution	Gelatin extraction	Placed in stainless steel extraction vats, pre-treated collagen is converted into gelatin by hot sterile water. Several extractions are performed sequentially.
	↓	
	Filtration	Coagulated substances and impurities in suspension are eliminated.
	↓	
	Deionization	Minerals are removed from gelatin by means of resin exchangers.
	↓	
	Concentration	The gelatin solution is concentrated through a multi-stage evaporator.
	↓	
	Sterilization	The gelatin is sterilized by steam injection method.
	↓	
Gelatin gel	Setting and Drying	The gelatin is set by chilling; the extruded gel is dried by conditioned and filtered air to water content of 10 to 12%.
	↓	
Dried gelatin	Grinding and Sieving	The dried gelatin is ground and sieved to standard particle sizes.
	↓	
Ground dried gelatin	Storage and Sampling	The ground gelatin is packed into multi-layer bags or fibre drums. A sample of each bag or drum is taken for analytical testing and quality control.
	↓	
	Blending	Using the analytical data of each extraction the gelatin is blended according to the specifications of each customer and each country's regulations.
	↓	
	Packaging and Sampling	The gelatin blend is packed in bags or drums and final tests are performed to meet customer's specifications for

	↓	a consistent quality.
	Shipment	Bags and drums are loaded in containers for shipment.

The industrial production of gelatin consists of a series of steps involving multiple chemical, physical and bacteriological processes requiring critical controls.

Using the analytical data of gelatin made from each extraction, the final blend is made by mixing gelatins from various extracts to meet the customer's specifications.

At the same time, manufacturer has to abide by the 'Food and Drug rules' of the country, (where the product is manufactured) while manufacturing gelatin.

The manufacturers of gelatin give the broad specifications of the gelatins used for the manufacturing of soft capsules.

2.3 GENERAL SPECIFICATIONS OF TYPE A AND TYPE B GELATIN USED IN THE MANUFACTURING OF SOFT GELATIN CAPUSLES

Table 2.1 : General Specifications of Gelatin used in Soft Capsule

Physical Test	Limed Ossein	Acid Ossein
B.S. Bloom of 6.67% (con.) w/w at 10°C expressed in grams	150 – 175	175 – 195
Viscosity of 6.67% (con.) w/w at 60°C *mPaS	3.6 – 4	2.7 – 3.2
Moisture % Max.	13.00	13.00
Ash % Max.	2.00	1.00
pH	5.0 – 6.0	5.0 – 6.0
Iso-ionic point pH	4.7 – 5.3	6.0 – 8.0
Clarity (45% soln. in 30% glycerol)	Clear No precipitate	Clear No precipitate
Particle size		
% passing 10 U.S. mesh	100	100
% passing 60 U.S. mesh max.	5	5
Sulphur dioxide ppm max.	60	60
Hydrogen peroxide ppm max.	60	60
Iron ppm max.	30	30
Heavy metals ppm max.	50	50
Arsenic ppm max.	0.8	0.8
Microbiological standards		
Total count organisms per g max.	1000	1000
Salmonellae in 10 g.	Absent	Absent
Coliforms in 0.1 g.	Absent	Absent

| *E. coli* in 10 g. | Absent | Absent |

*mPaS means milli pascal per second

1 mPaS = 10 millipoises

Although gelatin manufacturers have provided broad specifications of soft capsule grade gelatin, the individual capsule manufacturer has his own specifications which are based on the requirements of the formulations to be encapsulated.

Some important tests are detailed below.

2.3.1 Bloom Strength

The test was invented by Mr. O.T. Bloom in the year 1925, thereafter it is called "Bloom" strength test.

The bloom strength is a force (expressed in grams) required to depress the surface of gelatin gel [made up of 6.67% (conc.) w/w gelatin in water, gel matured at $10°C \pm 0.1°C$ for 17 hours (17 ± 1 hour)] by a distance of 4 mm, using a flat bottom plunger 12.7 mm in diameter (B.S. 757, 1975). The force is applied in the form of stream of lead shots and the weight of lead shots in grams is termed as the Bloom strength. New versions of bloom strength measuring instruments are available and are used in the industry. One version is known as "Boucher Electronic Jelly tester" and another is known as "Texture Analyser".

The price of the gelatin is mainly decided on the basis of Bloom Strength Value. Higher is the bloom strength, higher is the price.

The gelatin having high bloom strength, when used in the manufacturing of capsule gives improved physical stability to the product. Second advantage is that it gives better strength to the capsule. Therefore for manufacturing bigger sizes of capsules (over 50 minim) the gelatin of high bloom strength is used.

It is an industrial practice to use only high bloom strength gelatin (180 to 200 bloom) wherever it is necessary. Otherwise medium bloom strength material (150 to 180) is used to save the cost for manufacturing standard products.

2.3.2 Viscosity

Viscosity of gelatin is determined on a 6.67% (conc.) w/w of gelatin in water at 60°C (± 0.1°C) by using Ostwald or pipette type viscometers. The value of viscosity measured in this way, is expressed in mPaS or in millipoise.

The gelatin used for soft capsule, can have the viscosity (of 6.67% conc. w/w at 60°C) ranging from 2.5 mPaS (25 millipoise) to 4.5 mPaS (45 millipoise). But individual manufacturer of capsule, sets the value of viscosity of gelatin in narrow band. Suppose the value of specified viscosity is 40 millipoises, then the viscosity value lying between 38 to 42 millipoises is acceptable to the manufacturer of capsules.

Viscosity is a measure of the molecular chain length and determines the manufacturing characterization of the gelatin film required for capsule making. Therefore it has its own importance.

The gelatin solution used for forming the ribbon on drums of soft gelatin capsule machine has to be maintained at some specific viscosity value. This viscosity can be achieved by using different gelatins of different viscosity specifications, by changing their concentrates in water.

Suppose one wants to make gelatin solution of 10,000 cps viscosity at 60°C for forming a ribbon on drum of soft capsule making machine, by using gelatin having its viscosity specification as (6.67% (conc.) w/w gelatin in water at 60°C) 40 millipoise, then the concentration of gelatin in water required may be 35% w/w. If same viscosity solution of 10,000 cps is to be made by using gelatin having its viscosity specification as (6.67% conc. w/w at 60°C) 20 millipoises, then the concentration of gelatin in water required will be much more than 35% (conc.) w/w. In other words in the second gelatin solution of 10,000 cps viscosity, the gelatin concentration will be much more than that of the first solution or water will be less in second solution than the first. The solution made from the gelatin of low viscosity specification, will be much useful to cast the ribbon to fill hygroscopic materials, as the ribbons will have low moisture content. Therefore, hygroscopic materials will get less chance to attract water from the ribbon. This will help to obtain better stable product in capsules.

2.3.3 Microconstituent Iron

Iron contents suggested in specification of gelatin for soft capsule as "not more than 30 ppm", but in reality no capsule manufacturer accepts the gelatin having Iron content more than 15 ppm. Concentrations above 30 ppm level often cause discolouration.

Discolouration may often result from the combination of high iron and reducing agents in capsule fill material (e.g. ascorbic acid).

With the use of modern technology for manufacturing gelatin, gelatin with low iron content is easy to manufacture and supply. Commercially such gelatin is readily available.

2.3.4 Microbial

Gelatin at high moisture content is an excellent material for the micro organisms to grow, therefore microbiological testing of gelatin is a must. Other than the specifications given under the heading of general specifications, it calls for absence of pseudomonas, staphylococcus and mould and yeast. Total plate count of NMT is 100 organisms per gram, although general specification specifies total plate count of NMT as 1000 organisms per gram.

■■■

3.

SOFT CAPSULE FILL MATERIALS

All over the world the major production of soft gelatin capsules is made on Scherer type rotary die capsule making machines. The materials filled on this type of machine are described below. In general, fill materials in soft gelatin capsule are (i) Liquids or solutions and (ii) suspensions of solids in liquids.

3.1 LIQUIDS OR SOLUTIONS

3.1.1 Water Immiscible Liquids

They are hydrocarbons, chlorinated hydrocarbons, ethers, esters, alcohols and high molecular weight organic acids. The capsulation of water immiscible liquids is the simplest dosage form of soft gelatin capsule and usually requires little or no formulation.

3.1.2 Water Miscible Liquids

They are limited to polyethylene glycols and non-ionic surface active agents such as polysorbates. Small amount of other water miscible liquids may be encapsulated, if they are not volatile and are suitably diluted.

Water soluble components like glycerin and propylene glycol cannot be used as major constituents of the capsule content. They have softening effect on gelatin shell. Due to their presence in the formulation, capsule becomes more susceptible to the effects of heat and humidity. As minor constituents (upto 5% of the capsule content) water and alcohol can be used as co-solvents to aid in the preparation of solutions for capsulation.

It is important to note that the following materials cannot be encapsulated. Water, low molecule weight water soluble volatile organic compounds, alcohols, ketones, acids, amines and esters. These materials readily migrate through gelatine shell.

Aldehydes, having tanning effect on gelatin, and liquids having acidic pH below 2.5 and alkalies pH above 7.5 should be avoided. Gelatin shell readily gets affected by acid substances filled inside the shell. The alkaline fills, cause a tanning of gelatin and retard shell solubility.

3.2 SUSPENSIONS OF SOLIDS IN LIQUIDS

Drug powders which are insoluble in a solvent can be encapsulated in a suspension form. Particle size of drug powder is of importance and should be less than 50 microns or finer. As a rule, finer the particle size better it is. In general, most organic or inorganic solids may be encapsulated in this manner. However, limitations do exist for some compounds due to their solubility in water and the resultant effect on gelatin shell. Included in this group are strong acids, alkalies and their salts.

The substance like ASPIRIN, is very unstable in presence of water. If filled in soft gel, will get decomposed by the water present in the gelatin shell. However this problem has been recently resolved and soft gelatin capsules with ASPIRIN are now available.

3.3 FORMULATION OF FILL MATERIALS

The drugs which are to be encapsulated require formulation so that the capsules made with that formulation will meet the requirements of capsule making machine, F.D.A., and customers. They are mainly as follows :

1. Capsule shell must be safe for human consumption.
2. Capsule should be easy to swallow.
3. It must be free from odour.
4. It should have uniform shape and size.
5. It should have uniform appearance and colour.
6. It must be easy to fill on the machine.
7. Seam of the capsule must be properly sealed.
8. It should not have any visual defects.
9. Medicines filled inside must have required fill weight within narrow tolerance limits. It must be uniform from capsule to capsule.
10. The composition of filled medicament assay should remain uniform from capsule to capsule.
11. The bioavailabilty of the filled medicament must meet the specified standards.
12. It should have long expiry date.

3.4 BASIS OF DETERMINATION OF CAPSULE SIZE FOR LIQUIDS AND SUSPENSIONS

With the view to fulfil the needs mentioned above, the pharmacist formulates the drug. But suggested formulation needs to be tested by manufacturing the trial lot of capsules on soft capsule making machine. To carry out the trials, die roll is required. To make a die roll, the volume (expressed in c.c. or size) of the formulation, required to be filled per capsule is essential. Without this data, die roll cavities cannot be designed and manufactured or cannot be selected from the die-rolls available with the manufacturer of capsule.

For calculating the "volume" or 'size' two things are required :

(i) The quantity in 'grams' of formulation required to be filled per capsule and

(ii) The density of the formulation at room temperature.

Pharmacist who has formulated the drug, gives the weight required to be filled per capsule based on analytical report of the formulation of experimental lot and the density is found out experimentally.

Once these two things are known, the volume of formulation to be filled per capsule is calculated from following equation :

$$\frac{m}{v} = d$$

$$\therefore \frac{m}{d} = \text{Volume}$$

where, m = mass of formulation to be filled per capsule, expressed in grams.
d = density of the formulation.
v = volume in c.c./minim required to be filled per capsule is calculated from the equation.

Once the volume is calculated a pair of suitable die rolls is made with the cavities. One pair of matching cavity in the pair of die rolls will accommodate the calculated volume of medicament plus the total gelatin shell thickness per capsule or the die roll from the stock which will meet the volume requirement. (Pair of die rolls is shown in Fig. 3.1).

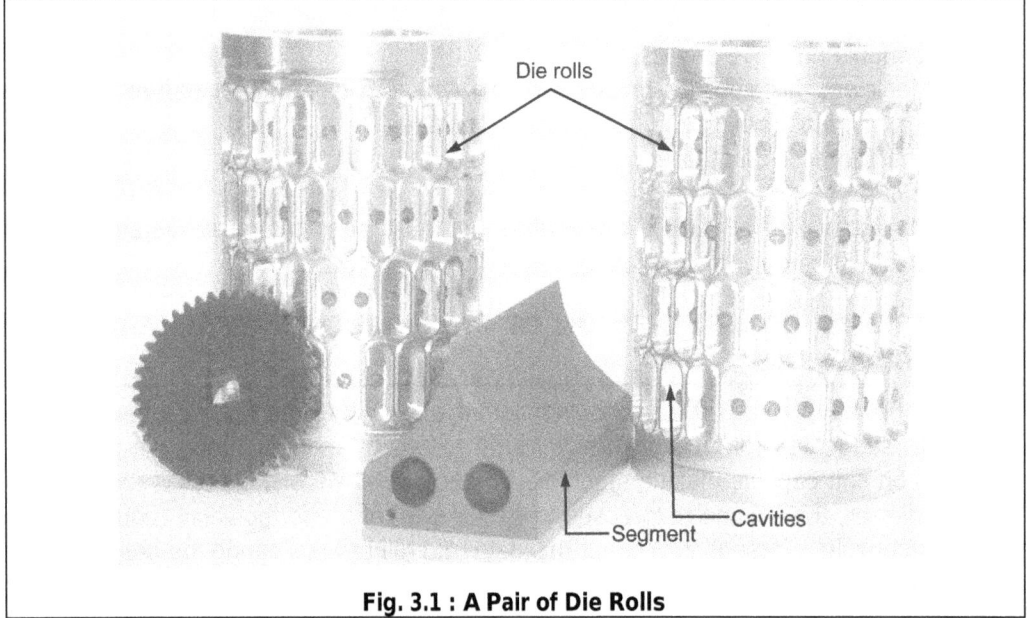

Fig. 3.1 : A Pair of Die Rolls

Normally the cavity of the die roll is made slightly bigger in volumetric capacity than the calculated volume, where the new die roll is to be manufactured for trial. Many modifications in formulations and trial runs are required on machine till the satisfactory formulation is ready for production.

It is a general rule in soft capsule industry that smaller the capsule size better it is. Therefore, the pharmacist who formulates the drug keeps this in mind before formulating the drug.

3.4.1 Determination of Capsule Size for Liquid Formulations

The capsule size for formulations in liquid state and which are easy to flow by 'GRAVITY' are easy to calculate by using the following formula :

$$\frac{m}{v} = d$$

$$\therefore \quad \frac{m}{d} = v$$

where,   m = mass of liquid formulation required to be filled per capsule (It is given by the formulator).

d = density of liquid formulation (to be found out experimentally).

v = volume of the formulation mass in c.c. required to be filled per capsule is calculated from the equation.

Very viscous liquids which are not flowing by gravity or cannot be sucked by pump, cannot be filled on soft capsule machine, unless they are brought to such a physical state that they can flow easily by gravity or can be sucked by pump. This state of fluidity is possible to achieve by diluting the viscous liquid by means of suitable low viscosity liquids which are compatible with each other. To keep the size of capsule under control, the liquid (which is used for dilution) is added in minimum quantities to form a homogeneous mixture. The size of capsule for such mixture is calculated in the same way as discussed earlier.

3.4.2 Determination of Capsule Size for Formulations in Suspension Form

Drug powders in dry form can be filled into soft gel on "Accogel machine". This machine is used by only one American company, named "Lederle Laboratories". Therefore, it is not available to other pharmaceutical companies to fill their drugs in dry powder form.

On Scherer type rotary die soft capsule machine, the drug in dry powder form as such cannot be filled. To fill drug powder, on such machine, it is essential to convert the drug powder into flowable state by dispersing it in liquid. This can be achieved, by making the suspension of drug powder into water or in oil, or non-ionic base materials. As the water suspension cannot be filled in soft gel capsules, the only option is to make the suspension in oil or in non-ionic base materials. This option is used in the drug industry to fill the drug powder in the soft gel.

The quantity of liquid required to make suspension of drug powder, depends on solid's particle size, shape, its physical state (fibrous, amorphous or crystalline) its density, its moisture content and its oleophilic or hydrophilic nature.

The most commonly used oils for making suspensions are mineral oils, soyabean oil, non-ionic surface active agents (polysorbates) polyethylene glycols 400 and 600 either alone or in combination.

For determining the correct size of capsule for filling suspension, (1) weight of the suspension required to be filled in per capsule and (2) the density of the suspension is required.

For working out this data, the analysis of the suspension sample is required. Before taking the sample for analysis, the sample has to be :

(i) Homogeneous

(ii) Non-sedimenting

(iii) Free from air bubbles.

(iv) Easy to flow by gravity.

(v) Easy to pump, which is fitted on capsule making machine for filling suspension.

Unless the sample satisfies all the above requirements, it cannot be taken for analysis. If these requirements are not met, the results of the analysis will be erroneous. Therefore size of capsule cannot be worked out. To meet the requirements mentioned above, sample has to undergo many processes and addition or deletion of additives.

The suspension has to be filled into the gelatin shell by the pump fitted on capsule making machine. To make the pumping operation smooth, it is required to bring down the particle size of the powder to 80 μ and less. It is normally achieved by using the micronizing equipments. Smaller particle size helps to keep the sendimentation rate low in suspension form.

For making a proper suspension, thorough wetting of all the particles in suspending liquid is necessary. It is achieved by using wetting agents.

For non-ionic base suspension formulations, the addition of wetting agents may or may not be required. But for vegetable oil base formulations, wetting agents are required. The most popular wetting agent used in industry is "SOYA LECITHIN" (natural product) at a concentration of 2% to 3% of the weight of oil. It is surface active and oil soluble. It is safe for human consumption and it is used in food and drug industry.

To maintain the homogeneity of suspension, the suspending agents are used. The concentration of suspending agents depend on type of formulation. The most widely used suspending agents for oil base suspensions are mixtures of waxes. In non-oily base suspensions they are polyethylene glycols 400 and 600. The suspending agents are soluble in liquids which are used for making suspensions.

The suspending agents provide lubricity to the formulation and it helps in soothening the capsulation operations. There are many other types of suspending agents used in the formulation. They are discussed in the later part of this chapter. When the suspension is stirred to mix up the additives, the air gets entrapped. To remove the entrapped air bubbles from the suspension, it is kept under vacuum.

The consistency of the suspension should be such that it can easily flow by gravity or can be easily sucked by pump. If this does not happen, one can adjust this with the help of liquid used for suspension. This is a machine requirement.

Finally to keep the fill volume low, the quantity of liquid used for making suspension has to be kept minimum. But it should not be at the cost of compromising the basic requirements.

To make such suspension, the first step is to calculate the amount of liquid required to suspend one gram of drug powder. This is expressed in soft capsule industry by the term "BASE ADSORPTION". Base Adsorption helps to work out the size (volume) of capsule.

3.5 BASE ADSORPTION (B.A.)

The term Base Adsorption is defined as "the number of grams of liquid base required to produce a capsulable mixture when mixed with one gram of solid".

$$\text{Base Adsorption} = \text{B.A.} = \frac{\text{Weight of base}}{\text{Weight of solid}}$$

From Base Adsorption, it is easy to calculate the volume (size) of flowable suspension, in terms of one gram of drug powder, provided the density of the suspension is known. The volume is calculated by the equation :

$$v = \frac{1 + \text{B.A.}}{d}$$

where B.A. = base adsorption

d = density of suspension

v = volume in c.c. of mixture (suspension) required to fill 1 gram equivalent of solid

The procedure followed in the laboratory to work out the base adsorption :

"A practical procedure for determining base adsorption and for judging the adequate fluidity of a mixture is as follows. Weigh a definite amount (40 g is convenient) of the solid into a 150 ml tared beaker. In a separate 150 ml tared beaker, place about 100 g liquid base. Add small increment of the base to the solid, and using a spatula, stir the base into the solid after each addition, until the solid is thoroughly wetted and uniformly coated with the base. This should produce a mixture that has a soft ointment like consistency. Continue to add liquid and stir until the mixture flows steadily from the spatula blade when held at 45 degree angle above the mixture. The flow is even and continuous and not in "globs". Attention should be given to the nature of the "cut-off " quality of the mixture. As the mixture tends to stop flowing, proper cut-off is exhibited when the stream contracts rapidly upwards towards the spatula blade, rather than "stringing out" in intermediate flow.

The following example will show the calculation of "base adsorption ".

30 grams of niacinamide requires 18 grams of an oil (This value depends upon the nature of the powder and the specific oil used) to provide a flowable mixture. To find out the base adsorption the following formula is used :

$$\text{B.A.} = \text{Base adsorption} = \frac{\text{Weight of base}}{\text{Weight of solid}} \qquad ...(1)$$

Weight of the base (oil) is 18 grams.

Weight of the solid (niacinamide) = 30 grams.

Therefore base adsorption is equal to $\frac{18}{30}$ = 0.6 i.e. one gram of dry niacinamide powder will require 0.6 gram of oil to form a flowable mixture. The other meaning of base adsorption is that, to fill one gram equivalent of dry niacinamide in the form of flowable mixture will be one gram of niacinamide plus 0.6 grams of oil. That is equal to 1.6 grams of flowable mixture. The flowable mixture hereafter is described as mixture.

The above mixture is homogenized and deaerated (under vacuum in a desicator) and the specific gravity (density) of the mixture is measured at room temperature. From density of mixture one would calculate, 1 c.c. volume of mixture will weigh how much. In above case, the measured density of the mixture is 1.28 gram/c.c. Therefore, 1 c.c. volume of mixture will weigh 1.28 gram. It means 1.28 grams of mixture is composed of 0.8 gram of niacinamide plus 0.48 gram of oil and its volume is 1 c.c.

As 1.6 grams of mixture is to be filled in capsule to get one gram equivalent of drug niacinamide, the volume of mixture requires to be filled will be $\frac{1.6}{1.28}$ = 1.25 c.c. This can also be calculated by using Base adsorption formula.

$$\left[\begin{array}{c} \text{c.c. of volume required} \\ \text{to fill 1 gram equivalent of NIACINAMIDE} \end{array}\right] = \frac{1 + \text{B.A.}}{\text{density}}$$

B.A. in this case is 0.6.

Density of the mixture in this case is 1.28 gram/1 c.c.

$$\left[\begin{array}{c} \text{Volume in c.c. of mixture required} \\ \text{to filll 1 gram} \\ \text{equivalent of dry niacinamide} \end{array}\right] = \frac{1 + 0.6}{1.28} \text{ c.c.} = \frac{1.6}{1.28} = 1.25 \text{ c.c.}$$

Minims Per Gram

Instead of expressing the volume in terms of c.c. (cubic centimetres), volume can be expressed in terms of minims. (1 c.c. = 16.23 minims). Therefore, the volume of mixture, to fill 1 gram equivalent of Niacinamide, in terms of minims will be

$$1.25 \text{ cc} \times 16.23 = 20.3071$$

$$\cong 20 \text{ minims.}$$

This is expressed as "MINIMS PER GRAM". i.e. mixture of 20 minims volume is required to fill one gram equivalent of Niacinamide powder.

■■■

4.
HISTORY AND PRODUCTION OF SOFT GELATIN CAPSULE

4.1 INTRODUCTION

The capsules were invented by a French Pharmacist Mr. Mothes in 1834. His aim was to develop a dosage form to accurately dispense liquids which had a bad odour and/or taste and therefore difficult to swallow. He made the dosage form, that is the capsule by dipping the moulds in the gelatin solution. The moulds were small round pouches made up of soft leather tied to a small long necked metal funnel by waxed string. The moulds were made firm by filling them with Mercury, before they were dipped in gelatin solution and removed. The pouch shaped gelatin films formed on the dipping moulds were removed manually and dried. To facilitate the easy removal of film, the mercury was emptied from the pouches. The capsules made by the above process were filled with the liquids by hand and sealed with the drop of gelatin. The capsules made by the above process had poor fill accuracy and poor yields. To make capsules by the above process was time consuming and therefore uneconomical.

The capsules made by the above process were used to fill medicinal substance called "oleoresin of copaiba". When taken by mouth as such, it was very nauseating. It was used in the treatment of venereal disease.

4.1.1 Plate Process

With the passage of time, plate process was evolved. This was a batch process operation. In this process, gelatin sheets of desired dimensions were made from gelatin and glycerin solution. Single sheet of gelatin was placed on the bottom plate of mould. Medication was added to the indentations. Second sheet of gelatin was placed on top of the medication and the top mould plate was kept over it so as to match the cavities of both the mould plates. Pressure was applied to both the mould plates. Due to pressure, gelatin sheets got sealed having medication filled between the two sheets forming the capsules.

Fish oil, Vit. A, Vit. D are filled on this machine. But due to the drawback of over exposure of the medication to atmosphere during manufacturing process, manufacturers are not in favour of using this machine. Practically, therefore, no machine is in operation in the world today.

4.1.2 Rotary Die Process

R.P. Scherer Corporation of Detroit (U.S.A.) invented in 1933, continuous operating soft capsule machine, known as rotary die machine. The process used to make capsules on this machine is called "Rotary Die Process". Over a period of time lots of modifications have taken place in this machine and the process. Today the capsule manufactured by Rotary Die Process is looked upon as of Industrial Standards.

R.P. Scherer was not selling these machines to Pharmaceutical Companies. Therefore, pharma companies had to give the raw materials to R.P. Scherer to manufacture their product in soft capsules. Therefore soft capsule manufacturing activity became a "contract manufacturing activity".

When rotary die soft capsules making machine similar to Scherer machine became available in the market, few pharmaceutical manufacturing companies started making capsules in house. Inspite of this, even today soft capsule manufacturing activity is mainly considered as contract manufacturing activity.

The first Scherer type rotary die machine was developed and manufactured in India in 1952 by M/s Capsulation services for their own use. In 1978 M/s Tooltronics (India) started manufacturing Scherer type rotary die machines in India. They are supplying these machines in India and all over the world. This company also supplies the process technology.

There are few other companies in U.S.A and in Europe who manufacture rotary type soft capsule manufacturing machines.

Advantages of Rotary Die Process:
(i) It achieves a fill accuracy of 97 to 99% of the target.
(ii) Yield is in the range of 98 to 99%.
(iii) Many varieties of oils and suspensions in oils can be filled.

Today, the soft capsule means, capsule made on "Scherer" type rotary die machine.

4.1.3 Seamless Soft Gel Process

The process and the machine for manufacturing the seamless soft gelatin capsules are unique.

This machine is manufactured in Holland. It is known as GLOBEX MACHINE. More than 200 machines are in operation all over the world.

The seamless soft gelatin capsules are manufactured on GLOBEX MARK I and GLOBEX MARK II machines. The capsules are produced by drop formation and therefore they do not require seaming operation, hence these capsules are called seamless capsules. The basic principle used is that the free falling liquids have a tendency to form spherical droplets due to surface tension. In this machine, gelatin solution and fill material are free falling liquid. The working of the machine is shown in the diagram given below.

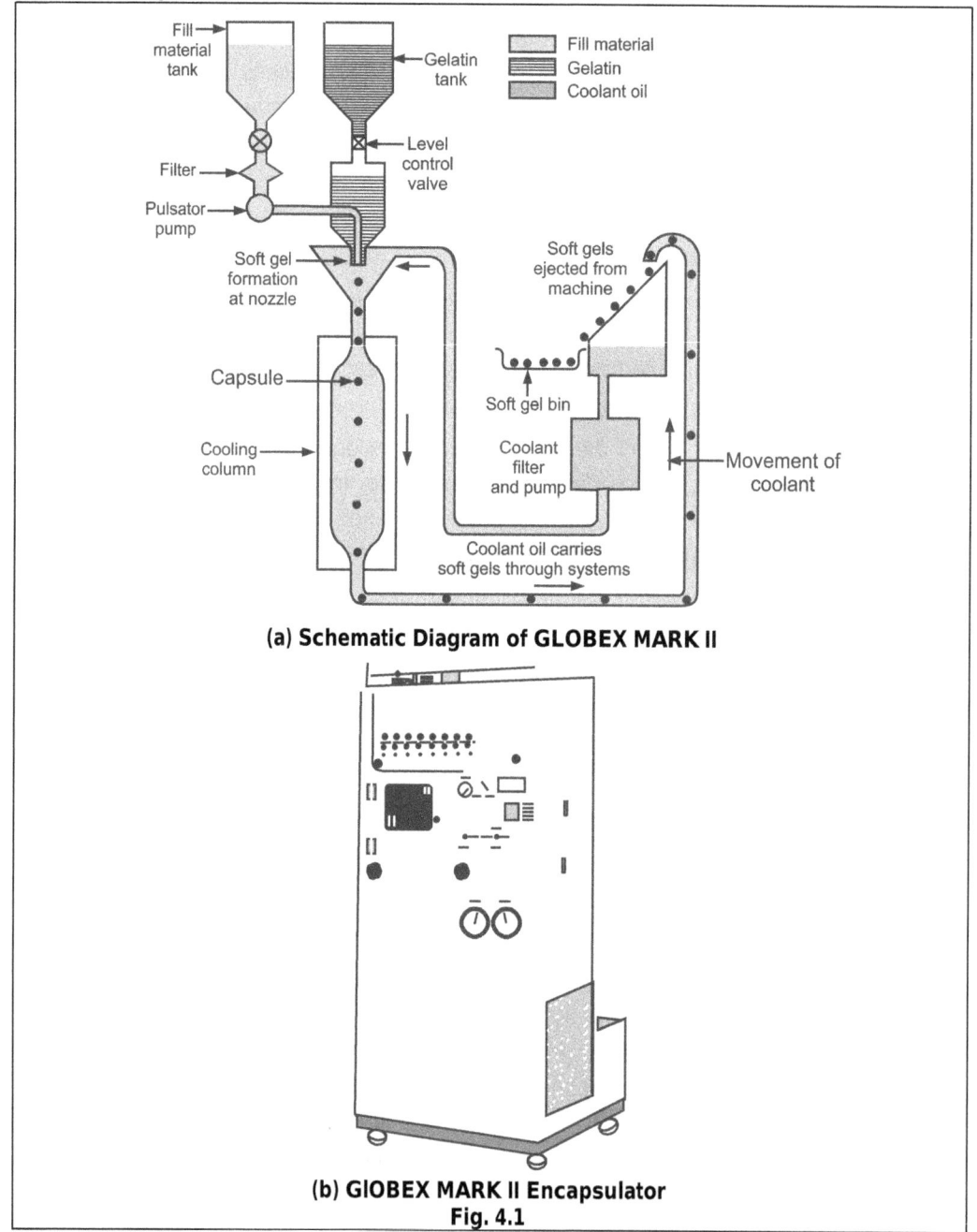

(a) Schematic Diagram of GLOBEX MARK II

(b) GlOBEX MARK II Encapsulator

Fig. 4.1

4.1.3.1 Limitations of Fill Materials

Not all fill materials are suitable for encapsulation by this process. The process limits the fill materials to hydrophobic liquids with specific gravities between 0.9 to 1.2 and viscosities between 1 to 130 cps of $30°C$. It is not possible to encapsulate aqueous or hydrophilic liquids of any kind on this machine.

Due to limitations of fill materials, this machine has not become popular. In India; one or two machines were in operation till few years back.

4.1.4 Accogel Process

It was developed in 1948 by M/s Lederle Laboratories. This process is similar to Scherer Process. On this machine dry powders, slugs and pelleted formulations are filled in. In India, this machine was in operation at M/s Lederle Laboratories at Balsar (Gujarat State). Few years back, the production operations on this machine at Balsar were closed down.

4.1.5 The Reciprocating Die Process

It was developed in 1949 by the Norton Company. This process is similar to Scherer process except that the soft gels are formed, sealed and cut out by vertically positioned reciprocating dies. These dies first form open shells in gelatin ribbons which are filled with fill material. As these shells pass through the dies again, the dies seal and cut out the soft gels. On this machine, semisolids and pelleted materials are filled. No such machine is in operation in India or elsewhere overseas today.

4.1.6 The Procap Process

The machine was invented in 1980 by Mr. Sydney Chasman. The patent was granted to him on 4th February 1986. (U.S. Patent No. 4,567,714). The machine is known as PROCAPS MACHINE. One piece soft gelatin capsules containing powder slugs are manufactured on it.

4.2 PRODUCTION OF SOFT SHELL CAPSULE ON ROTARY DIE MACHINE

The production of soft gelatin capsules on Scherer type rotary die machine is described below.

The production of soft gelatin capsule consists of 8 steps. They are as follows :
1. Preparation of gel mass.
2. Processing of fill material.
3. Production on rotary die machine.
4. Cleaning and drying of capsules.
5. Visual sorting and sorting on diameter sorting machine.
6. Quality control.
7. Bulk printing.
8. Bulk packing/Bottle packing/Blister packing.

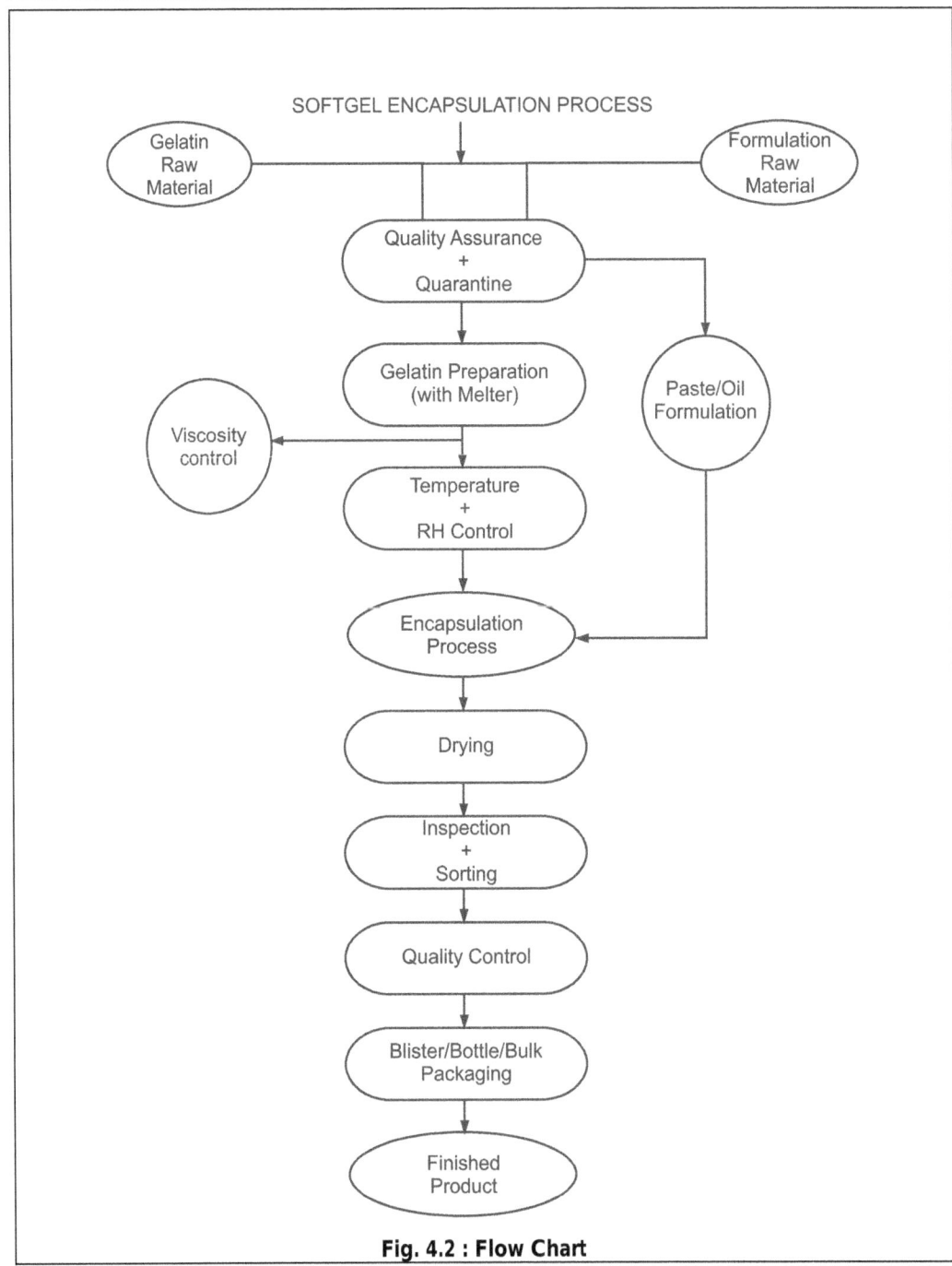

Fig. 4.2 : Flow Chart

Source : From Tooltronics, India.

The flow diagram of production process is given below :

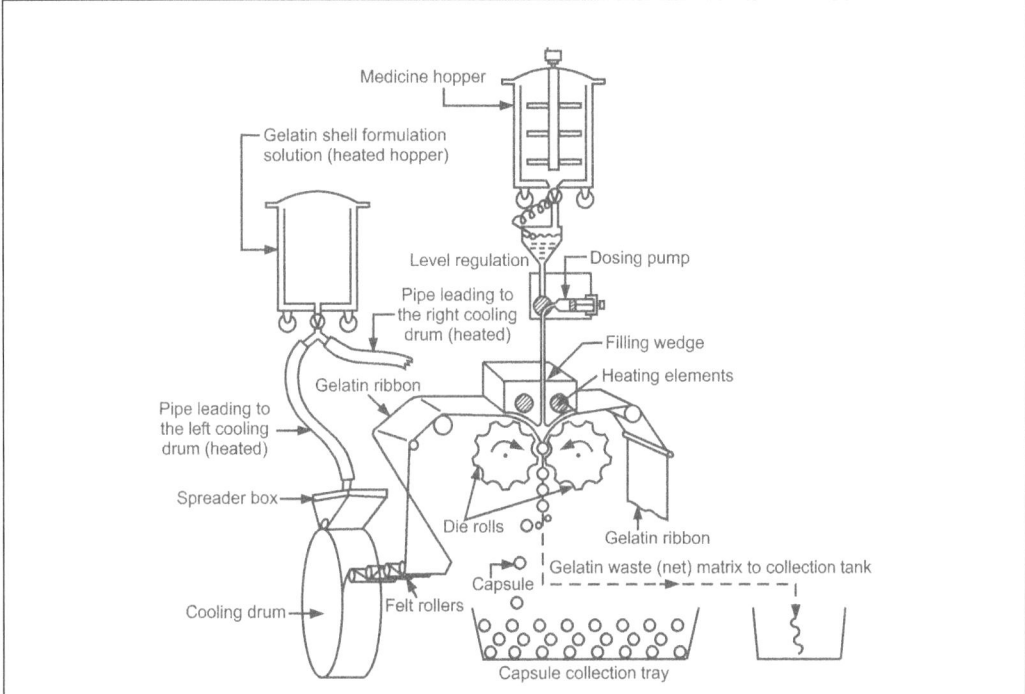

(a) Outline of the Rotary Die Method with the Courtesy of Tooltronics (Schematic Diagram)

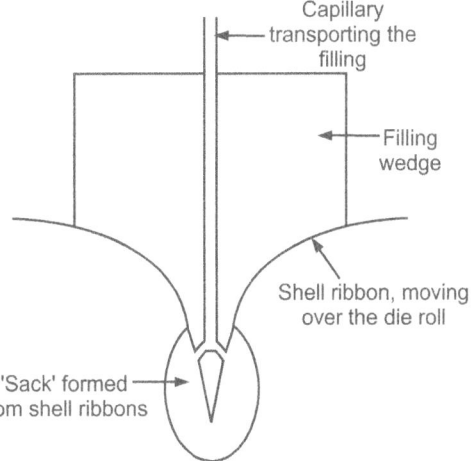

(b) Wedge Construction (The material is emptied to the sides well above the tip of the wedge; the shell ribbons 'wipe' the wedge tip clean and hence contamination of the sealing area by the tip is prevented.)

Fig. 4.3

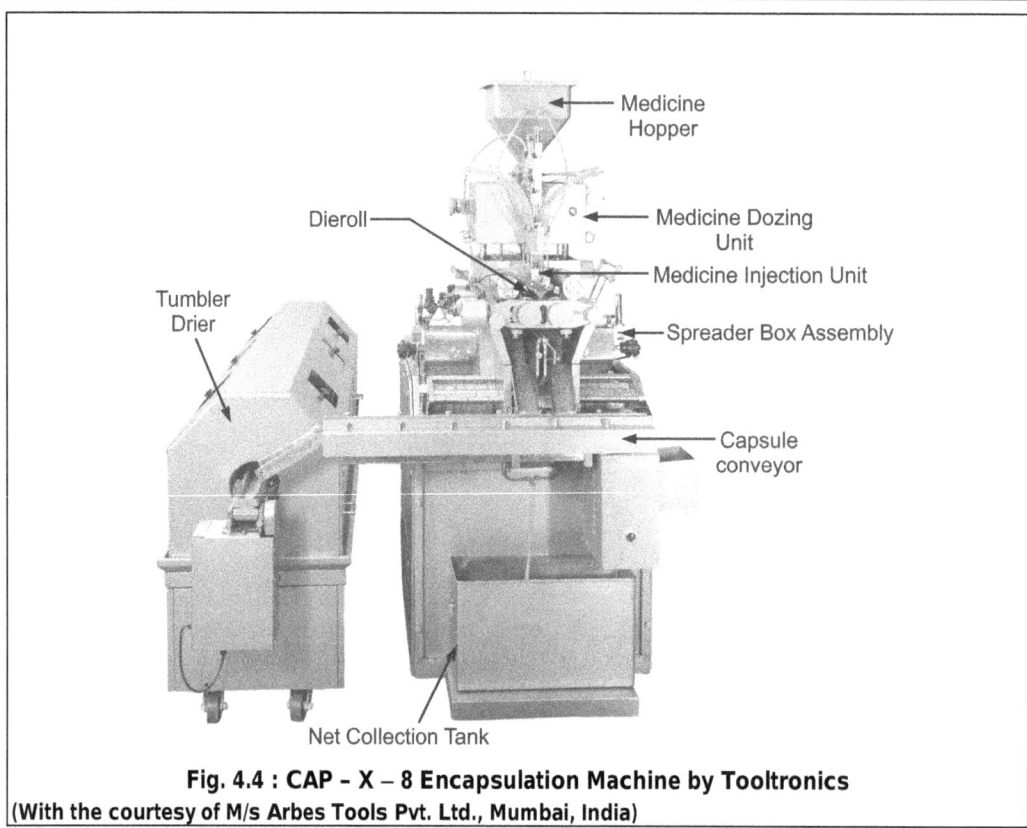

Fig. 4.4 : CAP – X – 8 Encapsulation Machine by Tooltronics
(With the courtesy of M/s Arbes Tools Pvt. Ltd., Mumbai, India)

The pharmacist who is incharge of soft gelatin capsule manufacturing unit has to meet the requirements imposed by Food and Drug Administration authority, as well as quality requirement of capsule by the customers. Therefore, he must have thorough knowledge of capsule manufacturing process as well as soft capsule as a product.

4.2.1 Air-Conditioning

Air-conditioning is required :

1. To get clean atmosphere in the operational area,
2. To maintain the proper physical state of gelatin film during production,
3. For drying the capsule,
4. To hold the low moisture content of "shell and fill" to get better stability to the product.

The dry bulb temperature and % relative humidity (R.H.) of the air maintained in operational area are 20° to 22°C and less than 40% R.H. respectively. In drying area it is maintained at 20°C to 22°C dry bulb temperature and 20% to 25% R.H.

Now-a-days, even "gel mass preparation room" is also air conditioned.

4.2.2 Preparation of Gel Mass

Gel mass is prepared by adding water and plasticizers such as glycerine or sorbitol or propylene glycol or combination of plasticizers to dry gelatin flakes. According to the requirement of hardness or softness of capsule, the quantity of plasticizer is decided. This mixture is mixed in a suitable mixer until a full hydrated fluff has been achieved. The fluff is then transferred to a S.S. water jacketed melter, fitted with heater and thermostat. It is heated under vacuum, until a clear gel is obtained. The gel is transferred and kept into electrically heated water jacketed holding tanks fitted with temperature controller and kept at 60°/65°C. The gel mass now can be used directly for encapsulation to produce transparent plain capsules. If coloured or opaque capsules are to be produced, colouring agents, opacifying agents are added to the gel mass by means of a high speed mixer. Flavouring agent is added to the gel mass to make flavoured capsules. But this is optional. Some manufacturers prefer to add preservatives in gel mass but it is done with the permission of user. This gives better microbial stability to the gel mass. The gel mass is checked for viscosity, pH, clarity, colour and consistency as well as moisture content. This is required to ensure that gel runs properly on the capsulation machine.

4.2.3 Processing of Fill Material

Area where processing of fill materials take place is mainly fitted with the following type of equipments.

1. Accurate weighing balance with printing facility.
2. Jacketed stainless steel tanks of required capacity for holding the batches of mix.
3. Mixer for handling for the initial blending of solids with liquid base.
4. For milling / or homogenizing – the equipment used such as homoloid mill, stone mill, hoper mill etc.
5. A special equipment is designed to expose thin layers of the mixed material continuously to a vacuum of 29" of Hg to remove the entrapped air.

4.2.3.1 Liquids

Liquid mixtures containing volatile liquids or liquid surface active agents as main constituents of the formulation, may be deaerated at temperature below 60°C for a period required to achieve the desired results.

If two miscible liquids are to be filled together, they are mixed thoroughly and then they are encapsulated.

4.2.3.2 Suspensions

Suspensions require more processing steps than liquids. More processing steps are essential to achieve uniformity of fill weight and uniformity of contents from capsule to capsule.

Drug powders of fine particle size are used. The powders are normally micromized and their size is less than 50 µ. As a thumb rule, lesser the particle size, better it is. The advantage of using powder of fine particles is that when properly suspended in oil, the suspension is easy to pump to deliver the dose into the gelatin film.

To form a proper suspension, wetting of the powder in the oil is a must. To achieve this, Soya Lecithin is added to the oil. It is soluble in oil. The concentration of Soya Lecithin used is 2 to 3% by weight of oil. It is a surface active agent and therefore helps in wetting the powder.

Another advantage of fine powder is that in the suspension state, the sedimentation rate of the powder goes down. The suspending agents are added in the formulations for further lowering down the sedimentation rate.

The list of typical suspending agents is given below :

Table 4.1 : List of Suspending Agents and their Concentrations

Type	Concentration of oily base (%)	Type	Concentration of non-oily base (%)
White wax NF	5	Polyethylene glycol 4000 and 6000	1 – 15
Paraffin wax	5		
Animal Stearates	1 – 6	Solid non-ionics	10
Aluminium monostearate@ NF	3 – 5	Solid glycol esters	10
Wax mixture*	10 – 30	Acetylated monoglycerides	5
Ethocel (100 cp)@	5 – 10		

*Part hydrogenated soyabean oil, 1 part yellow wax, NF; 4 parts vegetable shortening (melting point 33 to 38°C) used to 10% on the adsorption oil and at 30% on any filler oil required.
@used with volatile organic liquids such as butyl chloride, toluene, tetrachlorethylene : benzene.

(**Courtesy :** J.P. Stanley – Formerly Technical Director R.P. Scherer Corporation)

After the initial blending of solids with the base liquids is completed, the mixture is passed through mill/homogenizer. The purpose of this operation is to ensure the break-up of solids agglomerates, and that all particles are wet with the liquid carrier so as to obtain a 'SMOOTH and HOMOGENEOUS' mixture.

After milling operation, deaeration operation is carried out. The air which is entrapped during mixing and milling has to be removed from the suspension. This step is essential because (1) the entrapped air gives weight variation in fill weight and (2) the oxygen present in the entrapped air can interact with the fill materials, thereby affecting the potency of the drug.

To carry out the deaeration, special equipment is used. In this equipment, thin layer of suspension is exposed to vacuum of 29" for a short period of time. During deaeration, entrapped air is removed.

The suspension produced by carrying out the above steps is used for producing soft capsules as it has now become :
1. Smooth and homogeneous
2. Easy to fill
3. Air free
4. Such that the ingredients have been uniformly distributed from top to bottom.

Before using the suspension for production, the sample of the suspension (processed) is normally checked for :
1. % of ingredients used
2. Specific gravity
3. Homogeneity of suspension
4. Moisture content
5. Air entrapment

When the capsules are produced with such suspension, the capsules will be :
1. Uniform in weight
2. Having good uniformity of contents, and
3. Stable.

4.2.4 Production on Rotary Die Machine

Soft gelatin capsules are produced on rotary die machine which is fed by two tanks with materials. One tank contains molten gelatin at temperature of 60°C to 65°C and the other contains fill material at room temperature. The molten gelatin flows down by two heated pipes through two heated spreader boxes onto two separate large air-cooled casting drums, where flat solid ribbons of gel get formed. Two tone soft gels may be produced by utilizing two separate tanks of different colours of gelatin, each supplying one of the ribbon casting drums. The thickness of the ribbon is normally maintained in between 0.6 mm to 0.8 mm in a narrow band. The thicker shells are used on products requiring greater mechanical strength. The ribbons are fed through a special medium chain triglyceride oil (MCT) bath, over guide roles and then down between the wedge and the die rolls. (Few years back, mineral oil was used instead of medium chain triglyceride oil). The application of medium chain triglyceride (MCT) to the gelatin ribbons is essential, otherwise gelatin ribbons can stick to the parts through which they are passing. Since gelatin capsules are made from the ribbons, MCT remains on the surface of the capsules. Oil on the surface of capsules is removed after they are produced.

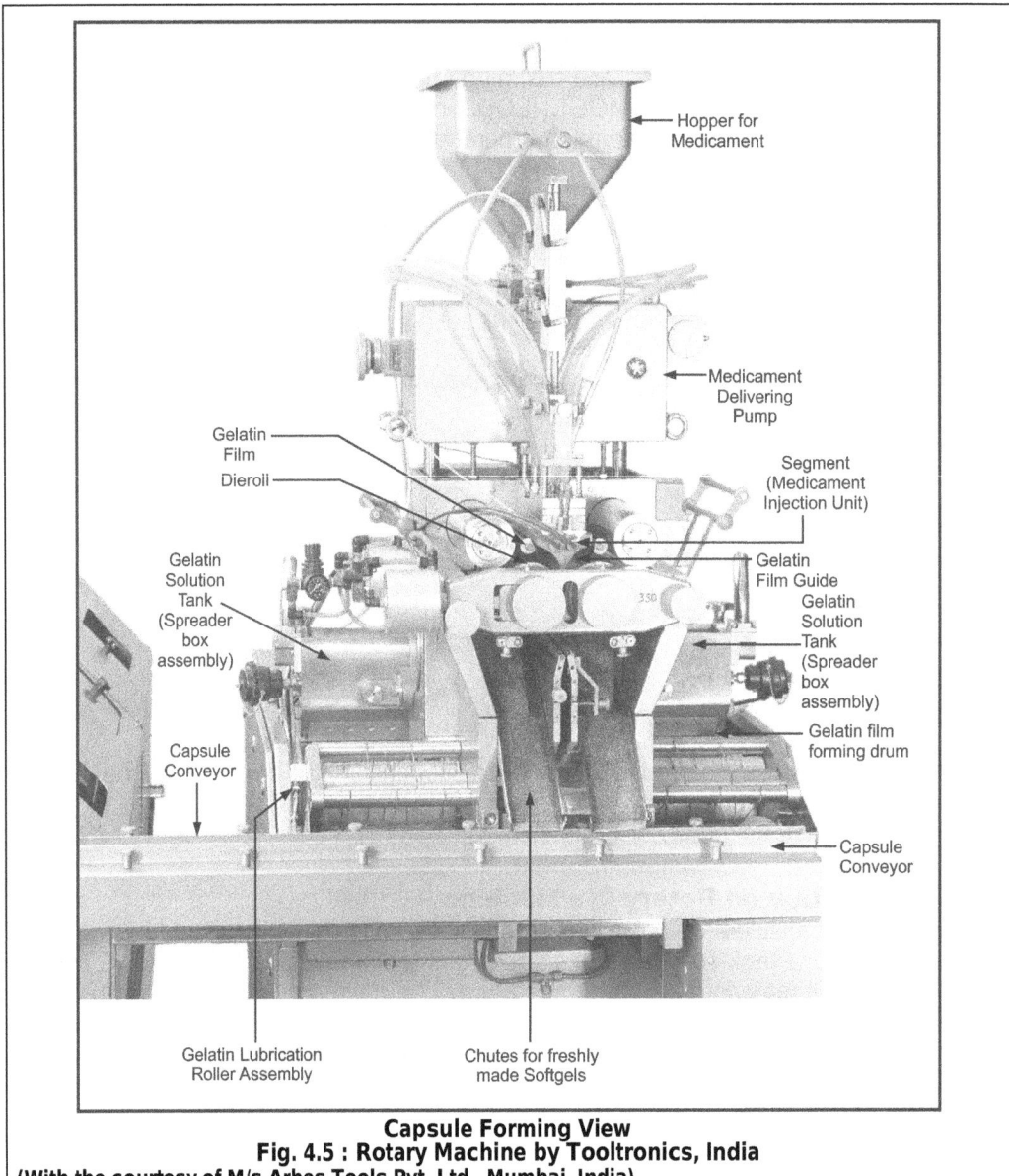

Capsule Forming View
Fig. 4.5 : Rotary Machine by Tooltronics, India
(With the courtesy of M/s Arbes Tools Pvt. Ltd., Mumbai, India)
Source : From Tooltronics, India.

Fill material (liquid and/or suspension) in the other tank flows under gravity through a tube leading to a positive displacement pump. Accurately metered volumes of the liquid fill material are injected from the wedge (heated at 37 to 40°C) into the space between gelatin ribbons as they pass between the die rolls. The combination of die size and injection volumes determines the soft gel size. The injection of fill material forces the gelatin to expand into the pockets of the dies which form the shape of the capsules.

The ribbon continues to flow past the heated wedge and is pressed between the rotating die rolls, where the soft gel halves are sealed together by application of heat and pressure. The soft gels are cut out automatically from gelatin ribbon by the dies. During manufacture, capsule samples are taken at certain time frequency for seal thickness and fill weight checks. The seals are measured under microscope and the machine is set to get required seal thickness. The fill weight checks are made by weighing first the weight of freshly prepared capsule and cutting it open, and then washing out the contents from the shell and empty shell weight is checked again. The difference gives the weight of fill material. If required, adjustment in pump stroke can be made to get the proper fill weight.

4.2.5 Cleaning and Drying of Capsules

Before the use of MCT, the gelatin ribbons were fed through MINERAL Oil [See production of rotary die machine Fig. 4.4 (b)]. Like MCT, mineral oil also used to remain on capsule surface after manufacture. To remove the oil from the surface of capsules, they were passed through naptha solvent. This was known as a 'naptha wash'.

Now-a-days after manufacture of capsules, instead of giving a naptha wash, capsules are cleaned in rotating dryer with the help of lint free oil absorbent cloth approved by U.S.F.D.A.

After external cleaning of special oil (M.C.T. oil), capsules are automatically transferred into a rotating dryer. The dryer consists of series of baskets which are timed to open at prescribed intervals. They are subjected to dry air during tumbling action. During this drying process 60 to 70% of the water that is to be removed gets removed. Then the capsules are spread on trays and all capsules are allowed to come to equilibrium with forced air conditions of 20 to 30% relative humidity at $22°C \pm 1°C$., When capsules are subjected to these conditions, the moisture of shell comes to 6% to 10%. It depends on the composition of shell and time of exposure. Kathabar systems are normally used to get the desired conditions of air used for drying the capsules.

4.2.6 Visual and Diametrical Sorting

Capsules are visually inspected on conveyor belt. The damaged and foreign capsules are removed manually. Thereafter they are sorted on diameter sorter which allows to pass any capsules within ± 0.05 mm of the theoretical diameter of the capsule under sorting. In this process of sorting, underfilled or over filled capsules get discarded automatically.

4.2.7 Quality Control

Capsules are checked for fill weight, uniformity and contents, thickness of films, seal etc. and all other tests given in the pharmacopoeia.

4.2.8 Bulk Printing

According to the order of the customer, capsules are printed on capsule printing machine and sorted for print defects. Now-a-days, printing inks are available in different colours, hence the printing of capsules with different colours is possible.

4.2.9 Bulk Packing / Bottle Packing / Blister Packing

This is being done as per the customer order.

The materials used for packing soft capsules should be such that it will protect the capsules from external heat and humidity and sturdy enough to stand the rough handling during transportation.

■■■

5.

EFFECTS OF EXTERNAL WEATHER CONDITIONS ON SOFT GELATIN CAPSULE

5.1 INTRODUCTION

The soft gelatin capsules, in packed or in naked conditions, exposed to adverse atmospheric weather conditions are likely to get damaged. The damage may manifest in the form of shrunk, dishaped, swollen, oil coming from seam, discoloured capsules etc.

Normally, the capsules ready for packing are rarely kept in uncontrolled atmospheric conditions. They are immediately packed either in bulk or in blisters and/or in bottles in controlled atmospheric conditions. However, there is a chance for packed capsules to get exposed to uncontrolled atmospheric conditions. Knowing this well, the capsule manufacturer selects good packing materials, which would withstand rough handling, provide effective insulation against heat and act effectively as moisture barrier. He securely packs good, tested and approved capsules and dispatches to chemists godown/shops with proper care. He also gives them the standing instructions as to how they should be stored and handled. But he does not have any control on conditions confronted by packed capsule containers during their transportation by various means and through different climatic conditions. He has no control on storage conditions in warehouses situated at airports, lorry depots, railway sidings, wharfs, docks or customs quarantine areas. The retail chemists may not have proper facilities for storage. The storage place may not have air-conditioning facility. The good packing materials used for packing capsules cannot protect the packed capsules from excessive rough handling and exposure to uncontrolled atmosphere conditions for a long period of time. Therefore, damage to capsules in packed condition is possible during transportation and storage.

The adverse atmospheric conditions are excessive fluctuations in surrounding atmosphere at high temperature and/or humidity for long periods and excessive heat (radiation heat emanating from direct heat sources, such as sun rays, boilers, steam pipers etc.) for long duration. Exposure to high temperatures can cause damage in relatively short period of time. Capsules melt and fuse together. At times oil comes out from seam and the external surface of capsules get oily.

The temperature and relative humidity of the air surrounding the capsule, chemical composition of shell and their relationship with moisture content of capsule is given in the schematic diagram.

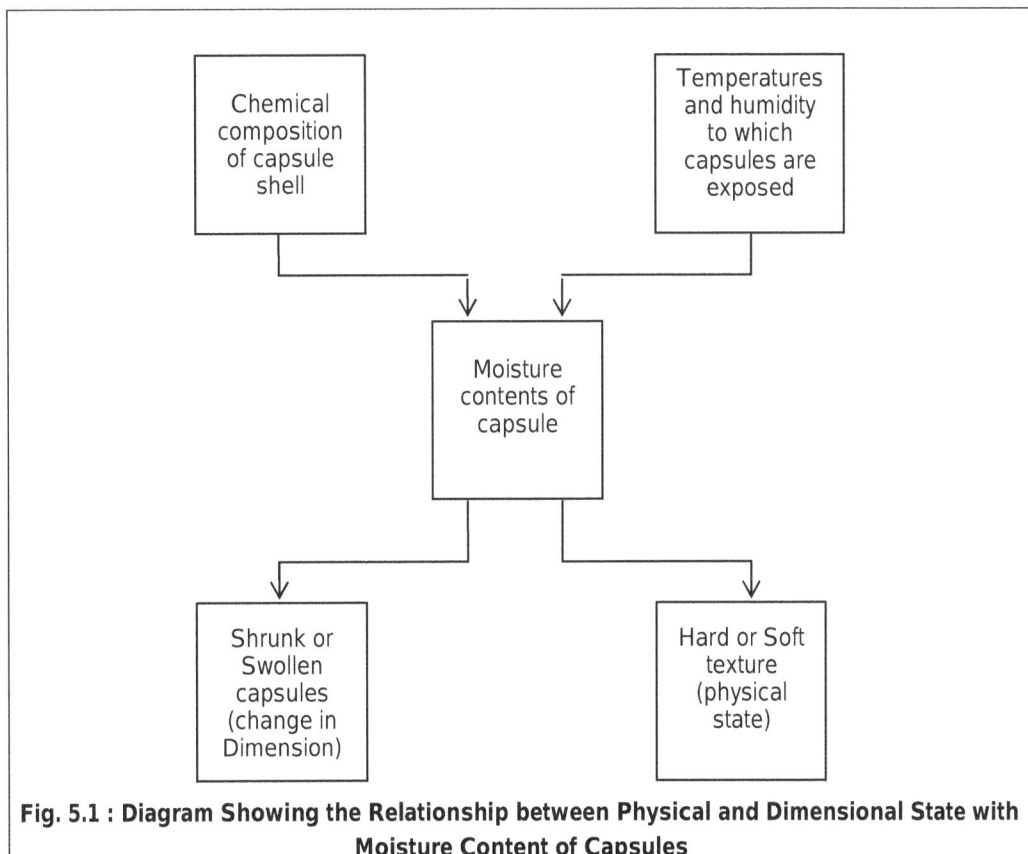

Fig. 5.1 : Diagram Showing the Relationship between Physical and Dimensional State with Moisture Content of Capsules

From the diagram, it can be seen that the strength (hardness and/or softness) of the soft capsule shell and its physical appearance (shrunk or swollen) are directly related to its moisture contents. The moisture of the capsule in turn depends upon :

(i) The composition of the shell along with other chemical ingredients used for making capsule shell.

(ii) The dry bulb temperature and the percentage relative humidity of the air surrounding the capsules.

(iii) The length of exposure of capsules to these conditions.

5.2 THE CHEMICAL COMPOSITON OF SHELL

The shell composition is mainly a mixture of plasticizer, blend of gelatins and water. The blend is composed of either only limed ossein bone gelatin or mixture of gelatins made from alkali processed bones, acid processed bones, pork and hides etc. Some additives, such as preservatives, opacifier, colourant, flavouring agents etc. are added to the shell composition, to achieve the desired effect.

The shell composition is required to be changed from product to product which is to be filled in capsules. It is also required to be changed from country to country (cold or tropical) where capsules are to be marketed. Normally, capsule manufacturer has his own formulas for shell compositions, which are based on practical experience.

5.3 RELATIONSHIP OF MOISTURE CONTENT OF CAPSULE WITH THE CONDITION OF AIR SURROUNDING IT AND THE CHEMICAL COMPOSITION OF CAPSULE

The moisture content of a capsule mainly depends upon the condition of the air surrounding it and its chemical composition. The condition of air is specified by its dry bulb temperature and the percentage relative humidity. The dry bulb temperature remaining constant, as the percentage relative humidity of the surrounding air increases, the moisture content of the capsule shell increases leading to some loss of strength and slight increase in shape. Further increase in relative humidity causes further rise in moisture content and eventually capsule shell loses the strength, flexibility and shape. The capsule swells and ultimately becomes difficult to handle.

Similarly, as the percentage relative humidity of the surrounding air decreases, the moisture content of the capsule decreases, resulting into shrinkage of capsule shell. With further reduction in relative humidity, the moisture content of capsule is further reduced, the capsule shell gets further shrunk and becomes very hard and brittle.

When capsules undergo number of such cycles, they lose their gloss and look dull.

These changes in the moisture content of capsules, occurring due to changes in the surrounding atmosphere conditions, are due to phenomenon of vapour pressure differential between the two entities i.e. gelatin shell and the atmosphere.

When a soft shell capsule is brought into contact with a stream of air whose direction, velocity, temperature and humidity are maintained constant and exposure is sufficiently long for equilibrium to be reached, the solid will reach a definite moisture content that will be unchanged by further exposure under the same conditions. This is known as 'equilibrium moisture content of the (soft shells) capsule' under the specified conditions.

It is important to note that the equilibrium moisture content of capsule also changes from composition to composition of the shell (i.e. ratio of gelatin to plasticizer).

The difference between the initial moisture content of the soft gel capsule which is kept for drying under a given set of drying conditions, and the equilibrium moisture content attained by the soft capsule afterwards under these given conditions of drying is called the "Free Moisture".

The equilibrium moisture content is the limit to which the material can be dried under a specific set of conditions. Under these specific set of conditions, the moisture content above the equilibrium moisture content (free moisture) can be removed by the drying process and not the total moisture content of the soft gel capsule, kept for drying.

During drying process, free mositure leaves the capsule shell to the atmosphere by evaporation. Simultaneously, water may transfer from shell into fill material temporarily, depending on the relative hydrophilic/hydrophobic nature of the fill material. As the drying proceeds, this interior water may partition back into the shell and pass ultimately into atmosphere before an equilibrium mositure is established in capsule shell.

During this process of moisture transfer, if the materials filled in shell are easily hydrolizable and readily oxidizable in nature, they can get affected by moisture much faster. Therefore the formulation filled in capsule needs thorough evaluation from the point of view of stability.

From the above discussion, one can see that to hold the moisture contents of soft capsules under control, the atmospheric conditions around the capsules need to be controlled. This is essential and important.

5.4 RECOMMENDED ATMOSPHERIC CONDITIONS FOR TRANSPORTATION AND STORAGE

To avoid damage to the capsules, the packed drums or boxes of soft gelatin capsules must be transported in an air-conditioned van where temperature and humidity of air are controlled. Same is applicable when capsules are transported by ship or rail. The recommended storage conditions for packed capsules are temperature range of 15°C to 25°C and relative humidity not more than 45%. Extremely high or low temperature or relative humidity should be avoided.

■■■

6.

DISINTEGRATION, DISSOLUTION, BIOAVAILABILITY AND NEW DEVELOPMENTS IN SOFT CAPSULE TECHNOLOGY

6.1 DISINTEGRATION

The disintegration of soft gelatin capsule is a problem. This is known in the capsule industry. The problem gets particularly enhanced when drugs containing reactive groups such as aldehyde groups are encapsulated. In recent years, this problem is resolved successfully by using "Succinylated pig skin gelatin". But the use of such modified gelatin is not yet approved for filling the allopathic drugs in soft capsules. However such gelatin is used in some countries to manufacture soft capsules for health and nutritional products.

When soft capsules are manufactured, initially they do not pose the problem of disintegration. But with the passage of time, the disintegration time goes beyond the time limits prescribed in pharmacopoeia. Indian pharmacopoeia (I.P.) 1996, gives the time limit for disintegration of soft capsules as less than 30 minutes.

6.2 DISSOLUTION

Dissolution tests are routinely carried out for testing hard (filled) capsules, soft capsules and tablets. Their results are plotted as concentration versus time. Values for $t_{50\%}$, $t_{90\%}$ and the percentage drug dissolved in 30 min are used as guidelines. The value for $t_{50\%}$ is the length of time required for 50% of the drug to go into solution. A value for $t_{90\%}$ as 30 min. is often considered satisfactory. In USP/NF, 75% of the drug is expected to dissolve in 45 min.

The work carried out in 1973 on dissolution by Homi and Associates indicated that the degree of agitation, the pH of the dissolution medium and the presence or absence of pepsin in the medium are important to the dissolution of the soft gelatin capsules.

The results of dissolution of soft capsules obtained by rotating bottle method (**Ref.** : NF XII, second supplement 1967) do not match with the results obtained by using U.S.P. apparatus. This was shown by Withey and Mainville by studying thirteen brands of commercial chlormophenicol.

Two objectives in the development of in-vitro dissolution tests are to show (1) that the release of the drug from the capsule is as close as possible to 100% and (2) that the rate of the drug release is uniform batch to batch and is the same as the release rate from those batches proven to be bioavailable and clinically effective. Since 1970 onwards US/NF have provided procedures for dissolution testing. They determine compliance with the limits on dissolution as specified in the individual monograph for tablet/capsule. The USPXX/NFXV, supplement 3, gave the details of two apparatus to be used for determining dissolution rates. These two apparatus are known as (1) Basket and (2) Paddle.

It is important that dissolution test (in-vitro test) must be correlated with bioavailability tests (in-vivo test); unless this is established, the dissolution test will have very little significance.

6.3 BIOAVAILABILITY

The bioavailability data of the drugs is collected by clinical trials. In clinical trials of some drugs, it was observed that they give better bioavailability in soft gelatin capsules than in the other dosage forms. The examples are given below :
1. (a) Name of the drug : Indoxole
   (b) Drug Dosage forms : Soft gelatin capsule (S.G.C.), Hard gelatin capsule (H.G.C.). Aqueous suspensions.
   (c) Results : Serum levels of the drug were maximum in case of S.G.C. than H.G.C.
   (d) Reported : Wagner and Co-workers.
2. (a) Name of the drug : Acetaminophen.
   (b) Dosage forms : S.G.C., suppository
   (c) Results : Urinary recovery of drug 4 to 8 times more with S.G.C. than fatty type suppository.
3. (a) Drug : Temazepam
   (b) Dosage form : S.G.C. and H.G.C.
   (c) Results : Onset of sleep was faster with S.G.C. than H.G.C.
4. (a) Drug : Digoxin
   (b) Dosage form : S.G.C, tablet, solution
   (c) Results : Best results with S.G.C. than the solution.
   (d) Reported : Ebert, Astorri and Co-workers.
5. (a) Drug : Papaverine hydrochloride
   (b) Dosage form : S.G.C., solution, sustained release H.G.C.
   (c) Results : S.G.C. gave high blood level and higher degree of vasodilation than others.
6. (a) Drug : Diazepam
   (b) Dosage form : S.G.C. tablets
   (c) Results : Faster drug absorption in case of S.G.C. than in tablets.

From the results, one can say that certain drugs give better bioavailability in soft gelatin capsules than the other dosage forms. Therefore, doctors prefer to use such drugs available in soft gelatin capsule than other dosage forms.

Other than the drugs mentioned above, there are many other drugs which are having better bioavailability in soft gelatin capsules. Few of them are flufenamic acid, prednisone, theophylline, triamcinolone, propranolol, phenytoin steroids etc.

6.4 NEW DEVELOPMENTS IN SOFT CAPSULE TECHNOLOGY

New developments in the area of soft capsule technology are taking place in finding out the new applications for soft gel. The second area of development is in the area of finding out the alternative raw materials to gelatin.

6.5 NEW APPLICATIONS

(a) **Enteric coating of soft gel capsules :** There are certain drugs which are required to be released only in intestine and not in stomach i.e. not in acidic stomach fluid. Therefore, capsule containing such drugs should not disintegrate in stomach. The gelatin shell of capsule very easily disintegrates in acidic fluid of the stomach. In order to provide protection for capsules from acid disintegration in the stomach, soft gelatin capsule can be enteric coated.

(b) **Sustained Release :** Sustained release products are mainly marketed either in hard capsule or in tablet dosage forms. The efforts are being made to make sustained release products in soft gelatin capsules. F.D.A. (U.S.A.) has approved the drug Theophylline S.R. 300 mg as sustained release product in soft gelatin capsule. This has opened a new avenue for soft gelatin capsule to manufacture sustained release drugs.

(c) **Chewable soft gel capsules (chewable gelatin shell) :** This technology has a variety of applications, including children's analgesics and vitamins, as well as cough-cold preparations.

(d) **Reduction of ulcerogenic potential of drugs :** Orally administered drugs, particularly if used chronically, can be irritating to the stomach. The dosage form of such drugs can affect gastric tolerance. One such drug dexamethasone which was causing such problem was studied on rats. Several liquid formulations, tablet formulations and soft-capsule formulations were administered to rats and both ulcerogenic and bioavailability were determined. It was observed that the soft capsule and liquid formulations had a reduced ulcerogenic potential than tablets. This work was carried out by Caldwell and co-workers.

6.6 ALTERNATIVE RAW MATERIALS TO GELATIN

The unique physicochemical properties, namely oxygen impermeability, the combination of film forming capability and thermoreversible sol. ⇌ gel formation capability favoured GELATIN for use in the soft capsule production, especially in the rotary die process.

Inspite of all the advantages, gelatin has several drawbacks; they are as follows :

(i)   Cross linking when in contact with aldehydes.

(ii) Solubility problems with certain fill materials.

(iii) Maillard reaction

(iv) Soft shell getting easily affected by high temperature and moisture.

To overcome these drawbacks, industry is looking for an alternative to gelatin, which will be cheaper, edible natural or edible synthetic polymers to make soft capsules. The work is on in this direction.

Today two natural and one synthetic polymers in combination with other chemicals are identified and they are patented. They are described below.

(i)   Iota carrageenan (12 - 24% w/w of drug shell) in combination with modified starch, hydroxylpropyl starch (30 – 60% w/w of dry shell) as a gelatin substitute.
      Ref. : WO, 0103677, Draper et. al 1999.

(ii) Potato starch (45 – 80% w/w) with specific molecular weight distribution and amylopectin content, together with conventional plasticizer such as glycerol (> 12% w/w), a glidant and disintegrant.
      Ref. : WO 0137817 (Menard et. al 1999).

(iii) PVA films composed of 70-75% (w/w) PVA, 10 to 15% (w/w) glycerol and 5-10% (w/w) starch. The capsule from this film is less sensitive to moisture than gelatin film with plasticizer. Efforts are being made to produce independently on a separate machine, a film of the above composition and then to put these film rolls on the soft capsule machine for manufacturing the soft capsules.
      Ref. : WO 9,735,537 (Brown 1996)

Before the capsules of new polymers are marketed by capsule makers, they have to get the approval to use these raw-material from the F.D.A. (of the respective countries) It will be a long process.

PART II

HARD GELATINE CAPSULE TECHNOLOGY

1.
HISTORICAL DEVELOPMENT OF TWO-PIECE EMPTY HARD GELATIN CAPSULE

1.1 INTRODUCTION

Two piece empty hard gelatin capsule has a history of more than 150 years. It was invented by PARISIAN PHARMACIST MR. C. LEBHUY. He was granted a patent on 20th Oct 1846 (French Patent 4435). It was stated in the patent that the capsules were made by dipping process. The dipping moulds used were silver plated metal cylinders about 4 to 5 cms long. For producing cap (lid) and body (container) the dipping moulds of different diameters were used. The diameters of the moulds were such that after the cap and body shells were produced, they would join smoothly to form a capsule. The capsules were made by dipping the moulds into decoction of starch or tapioca, the consistency of a bouillie, which was sweetened with little sugar and with 'fish silver'. In the subsequent patent he had taken on the composition of solution for dipping the moulds, the use of gelatin was included.

1.2 DEVELOPMENT OF CAPSULE TECHNOLOGY

The development of capsule technology had taken place mainly in the areas of

(i) Dipping moulds
(ii) Chemical composition of solution used for dipping
(iii) Air conditioning
(iv) Capsule making machines

1.2.1 Dipping Moulds

Dipping moulds of various materials were made to produce capsules. They were wood, iron rods, plated iron moulds, lead, brass, plastic and stainless steel. Finally the industry is now using the dipping moulds made from special free cutting stainless steel rods or from stainless steel (material) which can be heat treated after the moulds are made from them. The hardened moulds are used to minimize their wear during use (i.e. during stripping of dried capsule shells from the dipping moulds).

1.2.2 Chemical Composition of Solution used for Dipping

Various edible polymers were tried as a main component of the composition. They were starch, carrageen, gelatin, HPMC and Pullulan. HPMC polymer is made from cellulose and pullulan polymer is made by fermentation process from starch. The capsule made from HPMC and pullulan polymers are called vegetarian capsules as these polymers are of vegetable origin. This is a recent development.

Many other chemicals were added in small quantities into the polymer solution to get capsules which would be stable, look good, attractive and perform well on all types of capsule filling and packing machines. In early days substances like gums, sugars etc were added to improve the elasticity and strength. But they are not being used now. Presently additives in use are :

(i) Preservatives.
(ii) Plasticizers.
(iii) Edible colours and pigments.
(iv) Process performance aids.

(This part is given in details in the chapter number three.)

For capsules which are made from HPMC and pullulan, gelling agents like gellan gum, carrageenan etc. are added. Without them these capsules are difficult to manufacture.

1.2.3 Air Conditioning (A.C.)

In olden days, the production of capsules was a non-continuous operation. For continuous production of capsules it is essential to have air of specific constant temperature and humidity in the production areas. It is difficult to have such specific conditions in any production area all the time, all the year round as changes in temperature and humidity do naturally take place timewise i.e. daytime and nighttime as also seasonwise. Therefore in those days, the capsules were produced only when the weather conditions in the production areas were favourable. To overcome this problem, air-conditioning the production areas was the only solution.

M/s Eli Lilly and Co. of U.S.A., was the first capsule manufacturing company, who installed 'air-conditioning' system in the year 1912 for the production of capsule and thereafter they started producing capsules continuously 24 hours a day, all the year round.

1.2.4 Capsule Making Machines

Upto 1913, capsules were produced on semi-automatic capsule making machines. Cutting and joining operations were manually done. The efforts were on to develop the fully automatic machine for manufacture of capsules from the year 1900 onwards.

1.2.4.1 Stacker Machine

The first fully automatic machine was developed by Mr. B.W. Scott of M/s Arthur Colton and Co. (Detroit, U.S.A.) in the year 1913 for M/s Eli Lilly and Co. of U.S.A. (Ref. U.S. Patent No. 1,07,459). This machine was called "STACKER" machine. The production rate on this machine was 8000 capsules per hour. It became easy for M/s Eli Lilly and Co. to make capsules 24 hours a day and all the year on this machine because of their successful implementation of A.C. system for capsule making.

In the starting it was possible on this machine to make only single coloured capsule as there was only one single dipping tank to dip cap and body pin bars together. After few years, the machine was modified to accommodate two dipping tanks, one for dipping body pin bars and the other one for dipping cap pin bars. To make this possible, the machine was modified by adding the devices to separate the cap and body pin bars for dipping operation.

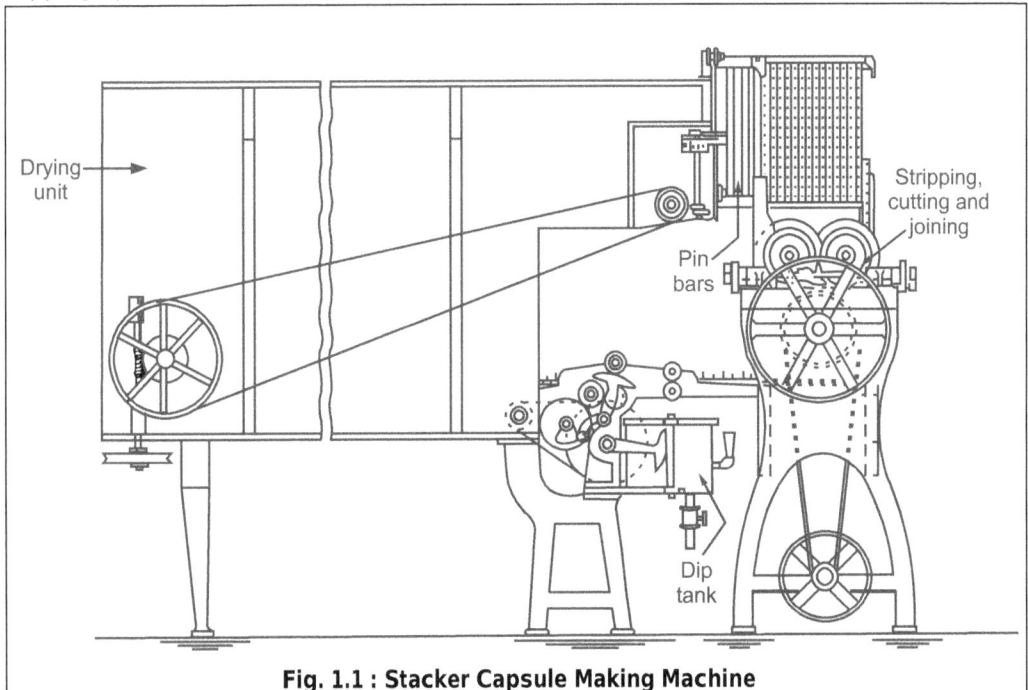

Fig. 1.1 : Stacker Capsule Making Machine

Another interesting part of this machine was that, pin bars were held stationary in the inverted position and dip tanks were raised upto them. The automatic capsule making machine made it possible to make capsules untouched by hands. This was important from the point of view of making capsule ideally suitable for pharmaceutical use.

1.2.4.2 Colton Machine

In 1931, Mr. Arthur Colton got a patent for his newly developed high output capsule making machine, (U.S. patent No. 1,787,777). This machine was called COLTON 750 machine. It had pairs of 750 bars as against 175 pairs of bars in STACKER machine. The machine was approximately 40' long, having 6' width and 5' height. It had a capacity to produce 30,000 capsules per hour. This machine was divided into two parts through which cap and body bars passed separately but synchronously. It was provided with two dipping tanks for dipping separately cap and body pin bars. Therefore it was possible to produce bi-coloured capsules right from the beginning without any difficulty. Mr. Colton was producing capsules on several of such machines with minimum man power. It was said that production of four machines was managed by one person at a time. Finally he sold all these machines to M/s Parke, Davis and Co. Detorit, U.S.A.

Around 1940/45, M/s Eli Lilly & Co. got two Colton machines and they started capsule production on them. Till then M/s Eli Lilly were producing capsules on STACKER machines.

The quality of capsules produced on fully automatic capsule making machines was far superior to the capsules made on semi-automatic capsule making machines. The net result of this was that the operations of semi-automatic machines were closed down and the capsule market became monopoly of two American companies namely M/s Eli Lilly and Co. and M/s Parke, Davis and Co. of U.S.A. who were operating fully automatic machines for production of capsules. This situation remained for quite a long period. Both these companies modified their machines and improved the process for higher output and better product. It is said that both these companies are producing empty capsules around 1,00,000 per hour per machine and the capsules perform well on automatic capsule filling machines whose production rate is more than 1,80,000 capsules per hour. Both these companies have expanded their activities and started producing empty capsules in different countries in the world. Around 1991/92, the capsule division of M/s Eli Lilly and Co. changed hands. It was sold to M/s Shionogi of Japan. M/s Shionogi have their capsule manufacturing operations at three different locations in the world, viz. Japan, Europe and U.S.A.

In 1963, the name of the capsule division of Parke, Davis and Co. was changed to CAPSUGEL. Few years back, the management of M/s Capsugel was taken over by M/s Pfizer, U.S.A.

Fig. 1.2 : First Colton Machine

In U.S.A. and Canada, few pharma companies entered in the field of manufacturing of capsules. They were S.K. and F. (now known as S.K. and B), Roche, R.P. Scherer (U.S.A) and R.P Scherer (Canada). All these companies were in this field for a short period of time.

There are countries in the eastern part of the world who entered in the field of manufacturing of capsules from 1960 onwards. They are Japan, Korea, Singapore, India, China and others. In some of the countries as mentioned above M/s Capsugel (Ex M/s Parke, Davis and Co.) is already producing capsules; but other than M/s Capsugel, other manufactures are also engaged in this activity.

As this book is written in India, a short review of development of capsule technology in India is given below.

1.3 DEVELOPMENT OF CAPSULE TECHNOLOGY IN INDIA

In India, Mr. C.P. Deodhar, a biochemist, initiated the work in the year 1954 to make empty hard gelatin capsule and he succeeded in producing the first hard gelatin capsule by using plastic dipping moulds in the year 1956. He developed the first semi-automatic machine with the help of one engineering company and started commercial production of capsules on that semi-automatic machine in the year 1958 in Mumbai (Bombay). This activity was started under the name of C and S laboratries whose name was subsequently changed to Pharmaceutical Capsule Laboratories. This company under the management of H.M. Mehta and Co. imported two fully automatic Colton 750 capsule making machines from U.S.A. in the year 1963 and started production of capsules on them in the year 1964.

M/s Gelikap in Baroda and M/s Associated capsule in Mumbai brought the machines and technology of making capsules from Italy in the year 1963 and 1964 respectively.

Around 1974, M/s Associated Capsules manufactured indigenously the fully automatic capsule making machine to make empty capsules in India. This machine was similar to the machine made by M/s Arthur Colton (Colton 750). Associated Capsule made lot of developments in the capsule making machine, in the process technology and slowly expanded their capsule making machine manufacturing capacity from one machine in 1974 to around 50 machines (indigenously manufactured) in the year 1995. Today they are the leading capsule manufacturer in India and second larger producers of capsules in the world. This company not only makes the capsules, but also makes capsule filling, sealing, polishing, sorting, (empty and filled), weighing and blister packing machines of international standards. Their capsules and machines are being exported and they are well received in the international markets.

1970 onwards, besides Associated Capsules, many other companies were producing capsules on semi-automatic and automatic machines. Exact reasons were not known, but around 91-92 there was a heavy recession in the capsule market in India and it continued for 2 to 3 years, as a result of which by 1995, all the semi-automatic capsule makers had to close down their manufacturing activity. Even the few manufactures who were producing capsules on fully automatic capsule making machines were forced to close down.

As it stands today, besides Associated Capsule Group there are other companies who are making automatic capsule making machines, dipping moulds, capsule filling and packing machines etc. in the country. There are 8 to 10 capsule manufactures of empty capsules, other than Associated capsules, producing capsules on fully automatic machines. The number of machines run by these manufactures are ranging from one to twenty machines. It is a matter of pride that India is now self sufficient in all the spheres of gelatin capsule manufacturing activity including the raw materials required.

It is said that India produces over 50 billions of capsules a year.

This figure was indicated in the year 2006.

1.4 HPMC AND PULLULAN CAPSULES

HPMC (Hydroxypropyl Methylcellulose) and PULLULAN capsules are also known as veg. capsules.

Many neutraceutical products are filled in HPMC capsules. Other than Shionogi and Capsugel companies, there are few other companies who manufacture these capsules in the world by dipping process.

Around 1997-98, Associated Capsules started experiments to make capsules from HPMC. Now, the quality of these capsules has reached the international standards and the company is now exporting these capsules also all over the world.

There is another company in India named Natural capsule, who also manufacture HPMC capsules. They named their product as 'Natural Capsule'.

■■■

2.

IDENTIFICATION ATTRIBUTES OF TWO-PIECE EMPTY HARD GELATIN CAPSULE

2.1 DESCRIPTION OF EMPTY HARD GELATIN CAPSULE

The two piece, telescopic, empty hard gelatin capsule is normally called as HARD GELATIN CAPSULE. It is a precision engineered dosage form consisting of two elongated, cylindrical, pliable gelatin shells. Both the shells are closed at one end in the shape of hemispherical, smoothly contoured dome and are open at the other end. They are slightly tapered outwardly towards their open ends. Among the two shells, the one which is bigger in diameter but shorter in length is called 'CAP' and the other which is smaller in diameter but longer in length is called "BODY". The inner diameter of cap at its dome base is kept slightly less than the outer diameter of body at its cut end. Due to outwards taper towards cut end, the inner diameter of cap at its cut end gets slightly bigger than the outer diameter of the body at its cut end, thus facilitating smooth entry of the body into the cap at the time of joining. When joined together (telescoped), the open end of 'body' fits perfectly at the dome base of 'cap' to form the empty gelatin capsule.

The hard gelatin capsule is basically a leak-proof container. After filling the medicament in the capsule, the contents are preserved intact till the capsule is consumed by the final user. Once consumed, the capsule shell disintegrates and dissolves in stomach within fifteen minutes, releasing all its contents in the stomach.

2.2 IMPORTANT FEATURES OF HARD GELATIN CAPSULE

Capsule is easy to swallow. It masks the unpleasant taste and/or odour of a drug. Gelatin capsule is easy to handle and because of its elastic nature, it is resistant to normal cause of breakage. Its elegant form and appearance present a good customer appeal. Its distinguishing features such as size, shape, colour and printability provide easy identification to a drug. The formulation of a drug in a capsule is normally easy. The capsule provides a good stability and protection to the drug filled in it, because the capsule wall is less permeable to oxygen and carbon dioxide and also to light when capsule is opaque. Disintegration time of capsule remains unaffected over a long period of time.

The two incompatible drugs can be administered in hard capsules. Powders, granules, pellets, microcapsules, tablets, small capsules, pastes and liquids can be filled alone or in combination in hard gelatin capsule. Hard capsule is much less susceptible to temperature and humidity than soft gelatin capsule.

2.3 IDENTIFICATION ATTRIBUTES OF CAPSULE

The qualifying or distinctive features of a capsule are called identification attributes. The hard empty gelatin capsule is identified by

(i)   Size (capacity)
(ii) Type (plain, locking, pre-clock and supro)
(iii) Shape
(iv) Embossed matter
(v)   Colour scheme and colour hue (of coloured capsule)
(vi) Printed matter, its pattern (on printed capsule) and
(vii) Form of printing (on capsule)
(viii) Colour of printing ink or inks
(ix) Flavour.

2.3.1 Size (Capacity)

In early days, capsules were made by dipping process on semi automatic hand operated mechanisms. Over a passage of time, increased mechanization of the manufacturing process led to mass scale production of capsules. Initially small scale capsule makers offered capsules as per the volumetric capacities demanded by capsule users. With the introduction of automatic capsule making machines, it became uneconomical to produce capsules with a varying range of volume capacities. Finally the range narrowed down to 8 sizes namely '000 to 5'. These eight sizes are now accepted internationally as 'STANDARD CAPSULE SIZES'. The United State Federal Standard, capsules No. 285-A, dated Oct 19, 1976, mentioned the above eight standard sizes.

The standard capsule sizes are given in Fig. 2.1.

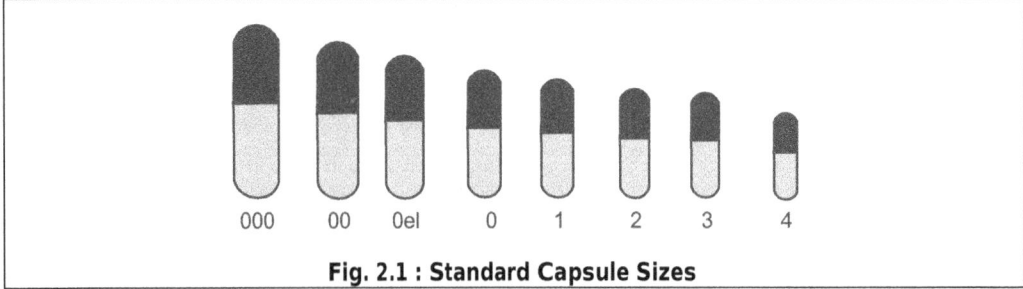

Fig. 2.1 : Standard Capsule Sizes

M/s Capsugel (Ex. Parke Davis) introduced coni-snap supro capsules, after Tylenol poisoning incident. Because of its novel design, the capsule was described as TAMPER EVIDENT. In these capsules the cap length is kept long enough to completely envelop the cylindrical portion of body, so that no body portion is left available to grip the body for opening the capsule. Thus, any tampering with filled and closed capsules becomes evident.

Coni-snap supro capsules are available in five special sizes namely A, B, C, D and E. Their volumetric capacities correspond to the capacities of conventional sizes 0, 1, 2, 3 and 4 respectively. These are shown in Fig. 2.2.

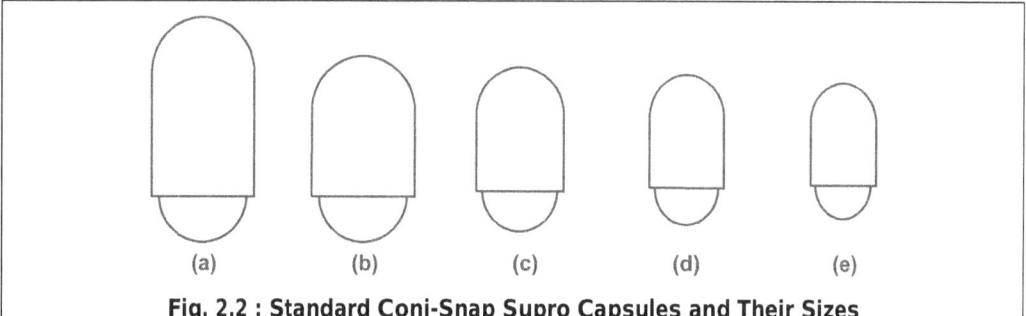

Fig. 2.2 : Standard Coni-Snap Supro Capsules and Their Sizes

Table 2.1 : Volumetric Capacity of Different Sizes of Capsule

Standard Capsule Size	Coni-Snap Supro Capsule Size	Volume in C.C.
000	-	1.37
00	-	0.95
*'O'EL	-	0.74
0	A	0.67
1	B	0.48
2	C	0.37
3	D	0.27
4	E	0.20
5	-	0.12

*Size 'O'EL means size 'O' capsule of extra length. This size has little extra volumetric capacity than size 'O' capsule. This size ('O'EL) is manufactured by all big capsule manufacturers in the world.

Capsules '000' to 5 sizes are used for human consumption. M/s Capsugel (Ex. Parke Davis & Co.) and M/s Shionogi (Ex. Eli Lilly and Co.) have developed size No. 9 tiny capsules for carrying out experiments on small laboratory animals like rats etc.

M/s Arthur Colton and Co. of U.S.A. first introduced MACRO capsules for veterinary use. They were made in following sizes.

Table 2.2 : Volumetric Capacity of Veterinary Capsules

Size	Capacity in ounces
7	1.5
10	1
11	0.5
12	0.25
12 ½	Not mentioned (special)
13	0.10

Arthur Colton and Co. ceased to produce these capsules many years ago. Veterinary capsules are manufactured in India by M/s Custom Capsules Pvt. Ltd and are marketed by M/s Torpac Inc. U.S.A. The capsules manufactured by M/s Custom Capsules have locking features.

There are few other veterinary capsule manufacturers in the world other than Custom Capsules.

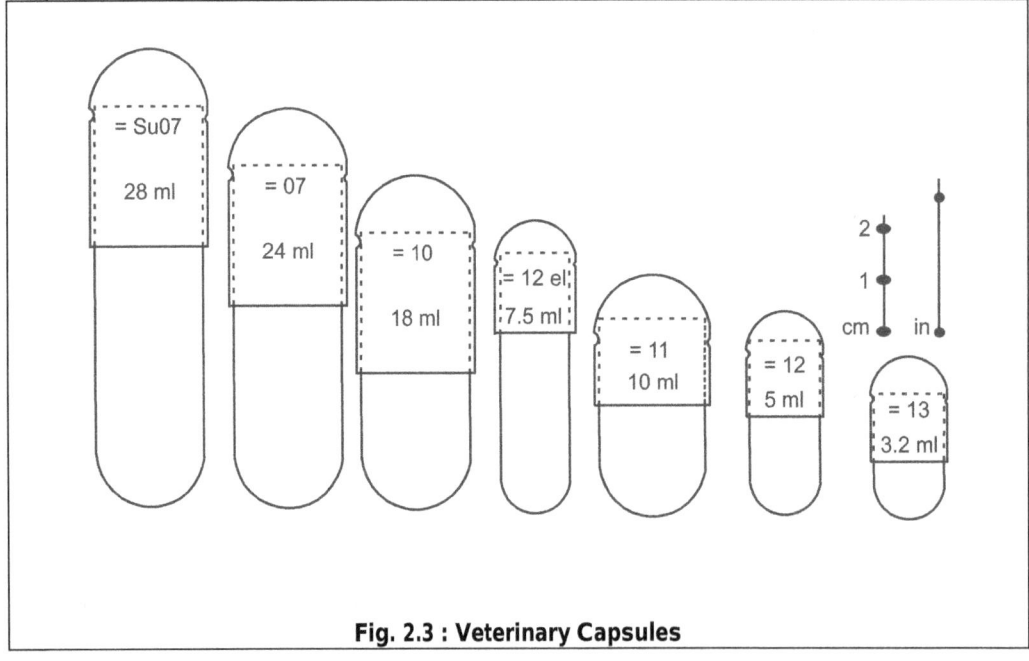

Fig. 2.3 : Veterinary Capsules

Table 2.3 : Sizes of Capsules Manufactured by M/s Customs Capsules Pvt. Ltd.

Size	Approx. capacity in ml
*6	109.0
07	24.0
10	18.0
11	10.0
12 el	7.5
12	5.0
13	3.2
Su07	28
*3180	54

* Capsules 6 and 3180 are not shown in the figure because their sizes are too big. (Table from Torpac of 18 Nov. 2006)

2.3.2 Type (Configuration)

Different types of capsules are manufactured. They are :

1. Plain capsules
2. Locking type and special features
3. Prelock capsules
4. Tamper evident.

2.3.2 (1) Plain Capsules

In early days, two piece hard gelatin capsules were manufactured without any dents, grooves, segmented grooves either on cap or on body or on both. It was plain in appearance. Therefore, the dipping moulds on which plain capsules were made, were also plain in appearance.

Various problems were experienced with plain capsules having different fits (loose fit, tight fit and rebound fit). Plain capsules were supposed to be produced with good or proper fits, but due to various reasons, along with good fit capsules, some very small percentage of unwanted fit capsules were getting produced, and they gave lot of problems during filling, after filling the drug powders and also in transportation.

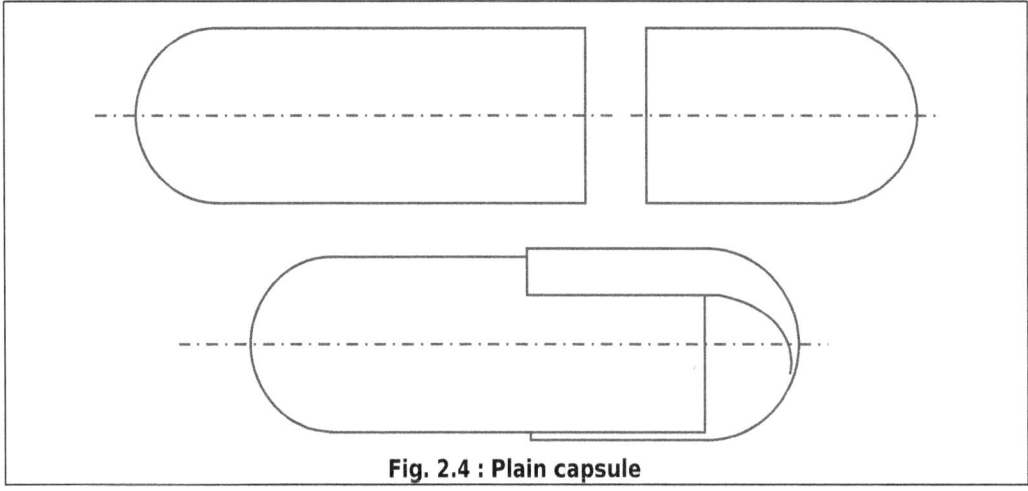

Fig. 2.4 : Plain capsule

The capsule manufactures overcame these problems by introducing different features on capsules through various configurations incorporated in the design of plain capsule moulds (dipping moulds) from time to time on priority basis. With these innovations they developed different types of capsules described below.

2.3.2 (2) Locking Capsules

After filling any type of powder, granules, tablets etc. and closing, the capsule should not open up on sorting, polishing and packing machines, as well as in final pack on account of handling, mechanical movements or vibrations. This need was satisfied with the introduction of 'locking' capsules after filling.

The basic idea in the design of 'locking capsule' was to get the filled body firmly held by the cap in the filled and closed state. This was achieved by introducing an annular groove, near or below the dome base of the cap. The diameter of the groove was less than the outer diameter of the body at the cut end. Because of this, filled body was held firmly by the cap in the joined state. It is important to note that locking capsules have two different joined lengths, i.e. joined length of unlocked capsule and joined length of the same capsule in the locked state.

In empty state, the body of a locking capsule is joined only upto the locking feature on the cap so that it is lightly held by the cap and its separation on filling machine by vacuum becomes easy. Since the joining of the body is not done into the locking feature on the cap or beyond such locking feature, *the joined length of locking capsule in empty state is longer than the joined length of filled capsule.* Though the joined length of a locking capsule is longer in empty state, its joined length in filled and closed state is equivalent to the standard joined length of a plain capsule.

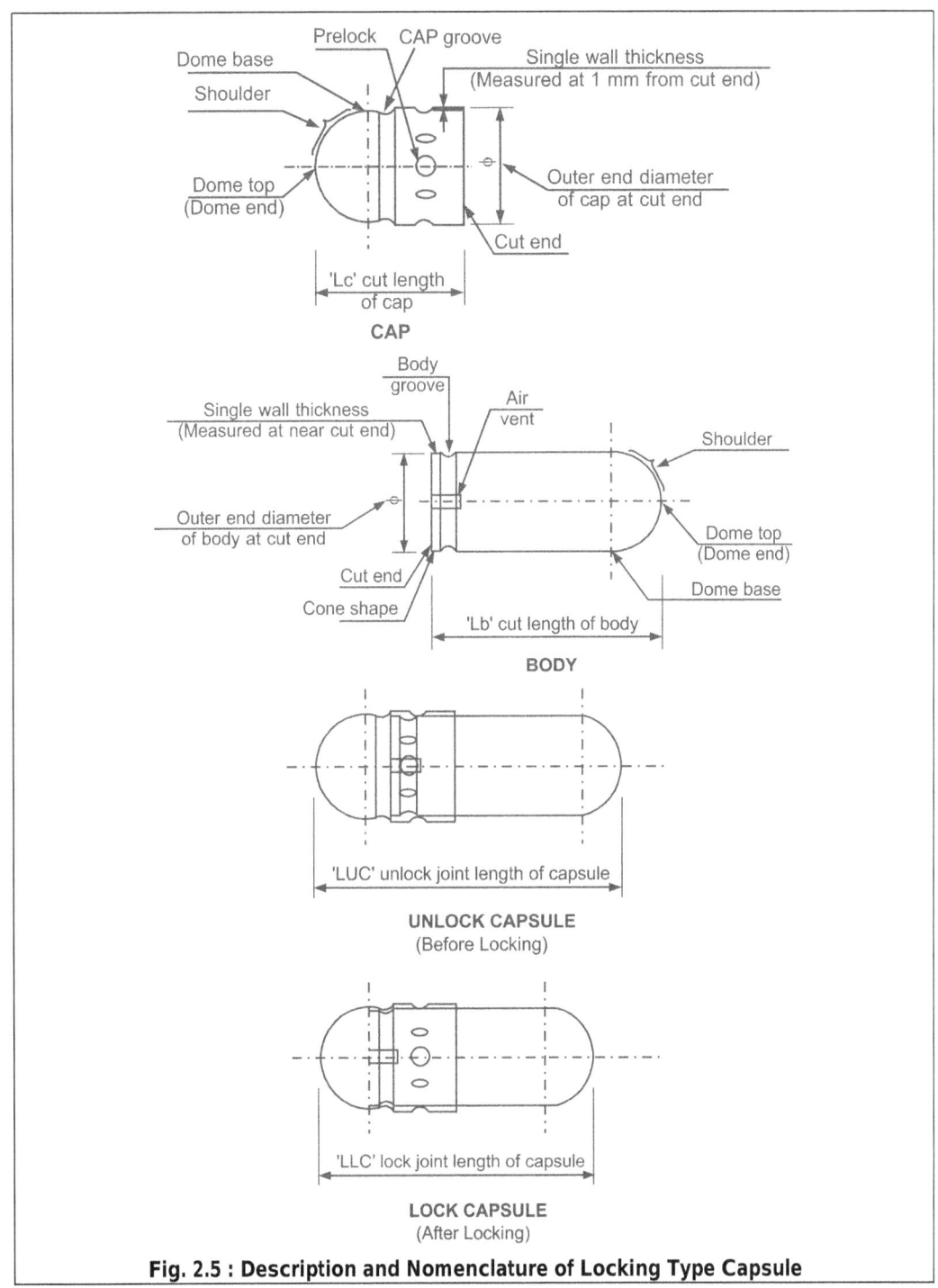

Fig. 2.5 : Description and Nomenclature of Locking Type Capsule

By keeping the same principle of locking, all the manufactures of capsules have now introduced locking type capsules with different configurations and marketed their lock capsules under different brand names.

The idea of locking capsule was first conceived by R.P. HOBBS in 1894. (U.S. patent No. 525,845 Sept. 11, 1894). In his patent he described this capsule as "when joined, there will be a "LOCK FIT" between the cap and the body of the capsule which will prevent the cap from rebounding during joining without a considerable pull on it and which will render the capsule, air and fluid tight". The essential feature of this concept consisted in contracting the diameter of the cap below its dome base. In closed state, the contracting condition of the cap locked the body with the cap.

1. LOK CAPS (Product of Eli Lilly and Co.)

Eli Lilly and Co. U.S.A. were the first to introduce locking capsules in the market around 1965. They developed wedging lock design which would make the capsule "Separation resistant" in the filled and closed condition. These capsules were marketed under the trade name of 'LOK CAPS'. The inventors of these capsules were Van B.H. Hostetler and Ivy Logsdon.

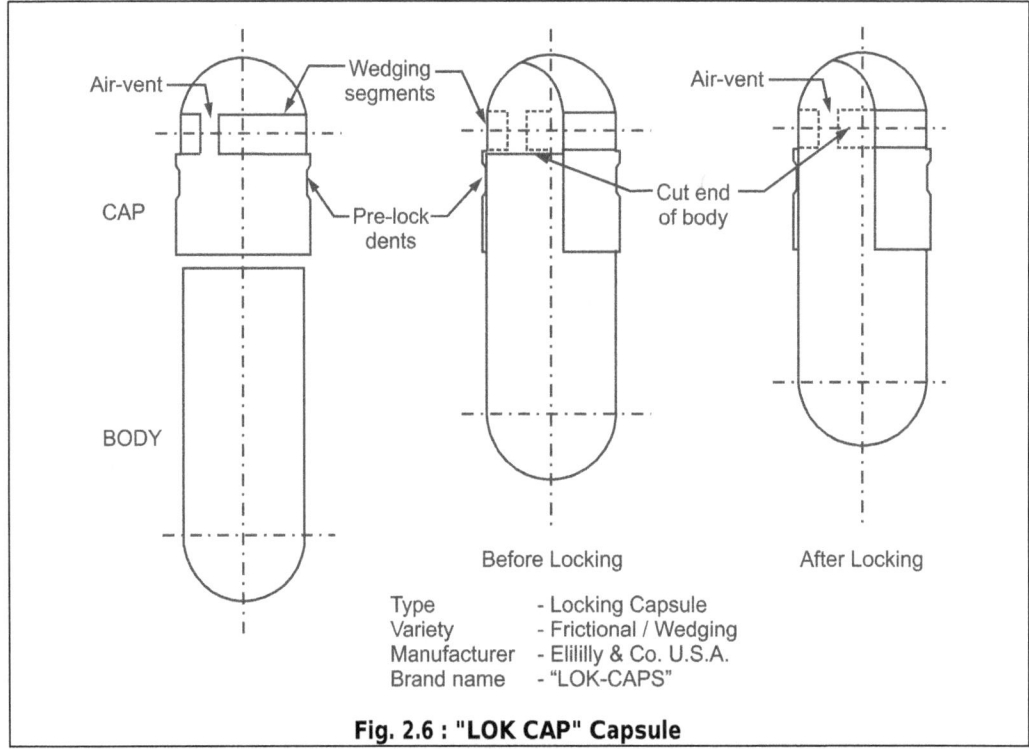

Fig. 2.6 : "LOK CAP" Capsule

In the lok-caps design, the cap has three built-in equidistant wedging segments (together covering 300° of circumference of cap at dome base). The wedges horizontally contract the inside diameter of cap portion, partly above and partly below its dome base. The segmented wedges project inwardly in the dome portion of the cap. The gaps in between the wedge portion on the circumference (covering 20° each) are provided for acting as vents for the air to escape at the time of joining the capsule fully after filling. The body part of the capsule is the same as that in the plain capsule.

During joining of 'LOK CAPS', the cut end of body gets compressed horizontally by the wedging segments on the cap when the body is fully telescoped upto the dome base of cap and a little beyond it.

Subsequently, two small dents were introduced on the cylindrical portion of the cap at opposite ends, little below the locking segments, to hold the cap and body together in empty state as well as to avoid the premature locking of empty capsules in transit. These dents are termed as PRE LOCK dents, along with the wedging locks continued to be called as LOK-CAPS.

2. POSILOK (Product of Eli Lilly and Co.)

Posilok capsule is a modification of LOK-CAPS. Here, a three segmented non-continuous groove is located on the lower portion of the wedge already present on the lok-caps cap. The groove is interrupted in the region of alternate gaps created inbetween two wedges. The gap provides vents to the air to escape during the closure of the filled capsule. In addition to the segmented groove, there is a continuous matching groove on the body little below its cut end. Therefore when fully joined together, the cap and the body are held more firmly by engaging the segmented groove on cap with the matching continuous groove on the body. The gap inbetween the segmented groove and the wedges still act as vents during the closure of the filled capsule.

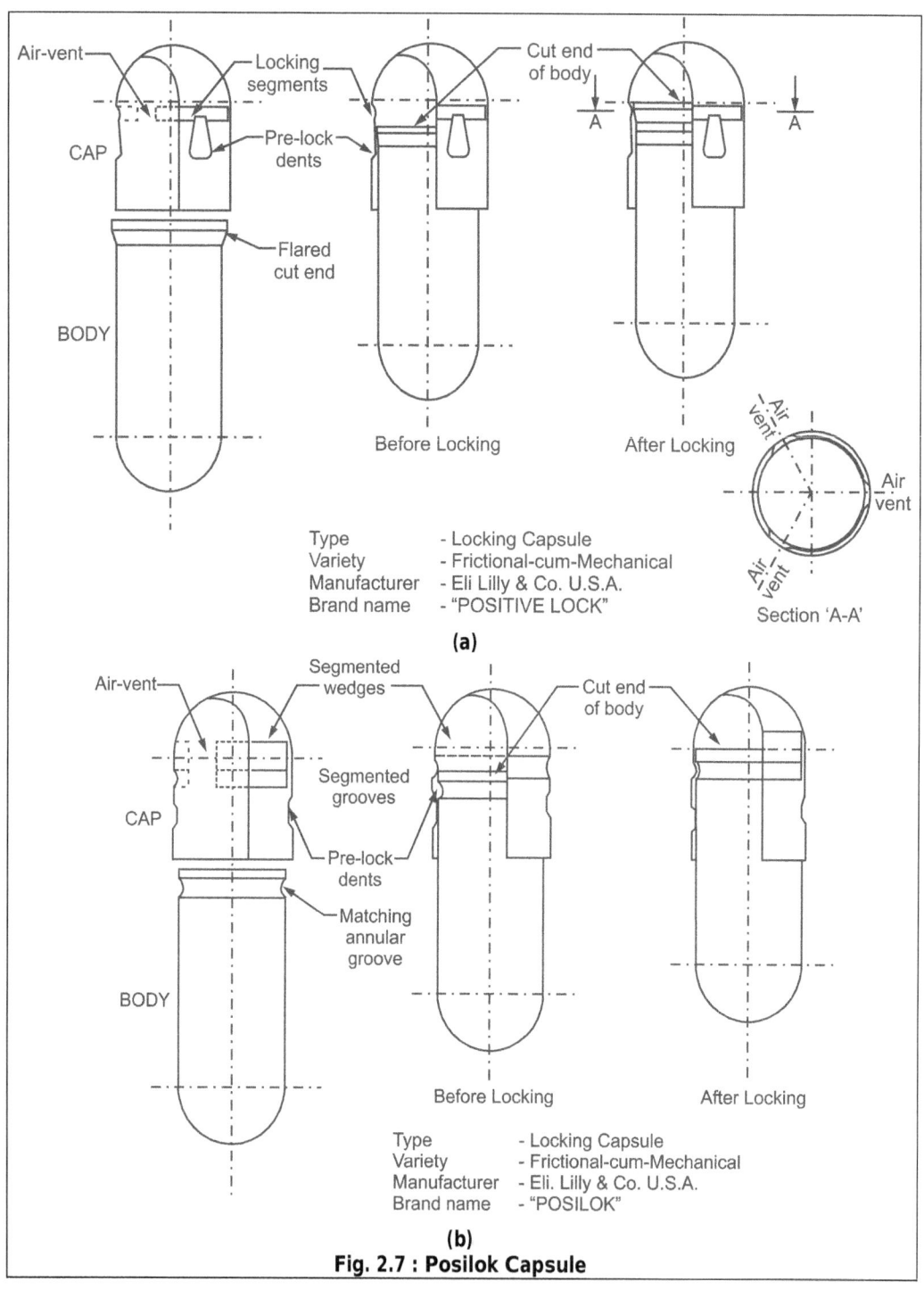

Fig. 2.7 : Posilok Capsule

Posilok capsule has pre-lock features on cap to resist separation or prevent premature locking of capsules during handling in empty state. At the same time, it can be separated easily by vacuum prior to filling on high speed capsule filling machine.

In Posilok capsule, the recommended joined length is controlled accurately because of the fixed locations of matching locking grooves on the cap and the body.

3. SNAP-FIT Capsules (Product of M/s Capsugel)

In the configuration of snap-fit capsule, there is an annular groove on the cap below its dome base and a body part which contains a matching groove little below its cut end. In snap-fit capsule, the recommended joined length is controlled accurately because of the fixed locations of matching grooves on the cap and the body.

Along with the annular groove on the cap, they introduced two (prelock) prefit dents on opposite points. Prelock dents resist separation during handling of capsules in empty state. (In snap-fit capsules, the prefit dents are engaged with the body groove, in empty state.)

During the process of joining, when the body is being telescoped into the cap from a partially closed position to a fully closed position, at a certain point below the groove on the cap, the cut end of the body is frictionally engaged with the inner surface of the cap around the circumference and continues to do so till the annular groove on the cap gets firmly engaged with the matching grove on the body. If the telescoping action is carried out slowly, due to taper on cap and body the air in the cylindrical portion of the cap gets sufficient time to make way for the incoming body. But on high speed capsule filling machine, the closure of filled capsule is achieved at a much faster rate, so that there is no sufficient time available for the inside air to escape. Therefore air gets compressed inside the cap dome. In such capsules the cap and the body slide away from one another, to equalize the pressure or at times the cap and body come apart with force and powder comes out of from the filled body spoiling the other filled capsules. This is called as POPPING phenomenon.

Type - Locking Capsule
Variety - Mechanical
Manufacturer - Parke-Davis U.S.A.
Brand name - "SNAP-FIT"

(a)

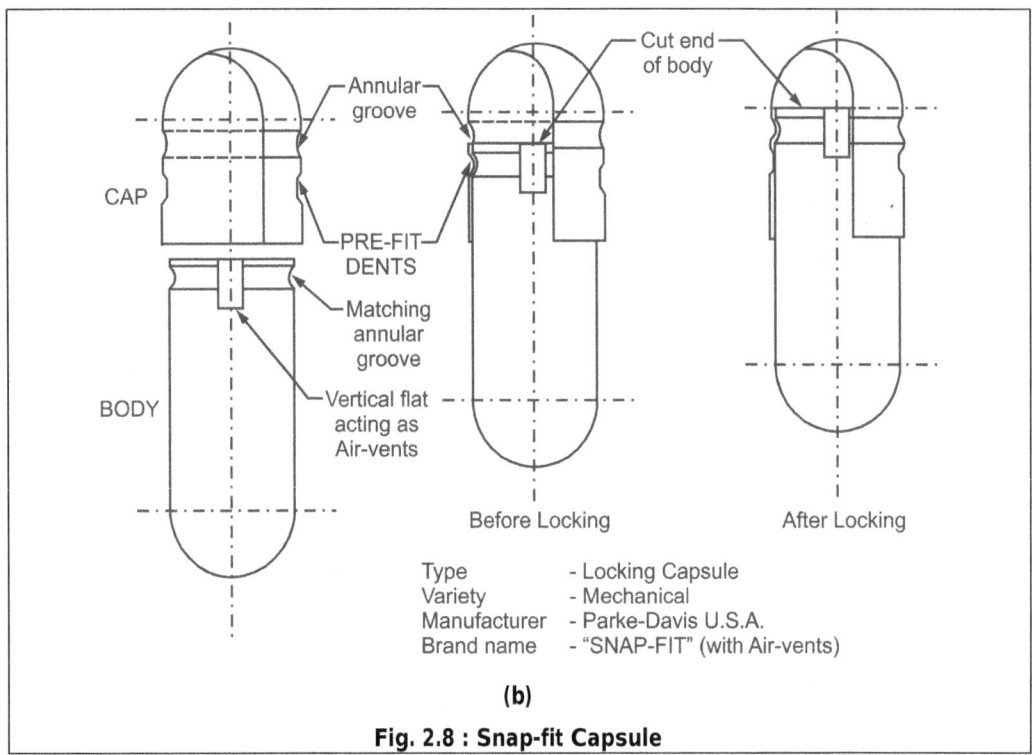

(b)
Fig. 2.8 : Snap-fit Capsule

To overcome the problem of popping of capsule on high speed capsule filling machine, two elongated vertical flats of approximately one fourth length of the cylindrical portion of the body starting from two opposite points at the cut end of body are provided to act as air vents.

Popping of capsules is not seen with LOK CAPS and POSILOCK capsules as the air vent is provided in the design of the cap.

The snap-fit capsules are available in the market, without air vents as well as with air vents.

4. CONI-SNAP CAPSULES (Product of M/s Capsugel)

During rejoining of filled bodies into the caps on capsule filling machine, occasionally few capsules used to get telescoped and or dented. Such damaged capsules used to get mixed up with good filled and joined capsules. It was essential to sort out the damaged capsules prior to further operations.

In 1979, Parke, Davis & Co. (M/s capsugel) modified the body design to minimize the trouble of denting and telescoping of capsules during filling and called the new design as 'CONI-SNAP' capsule.

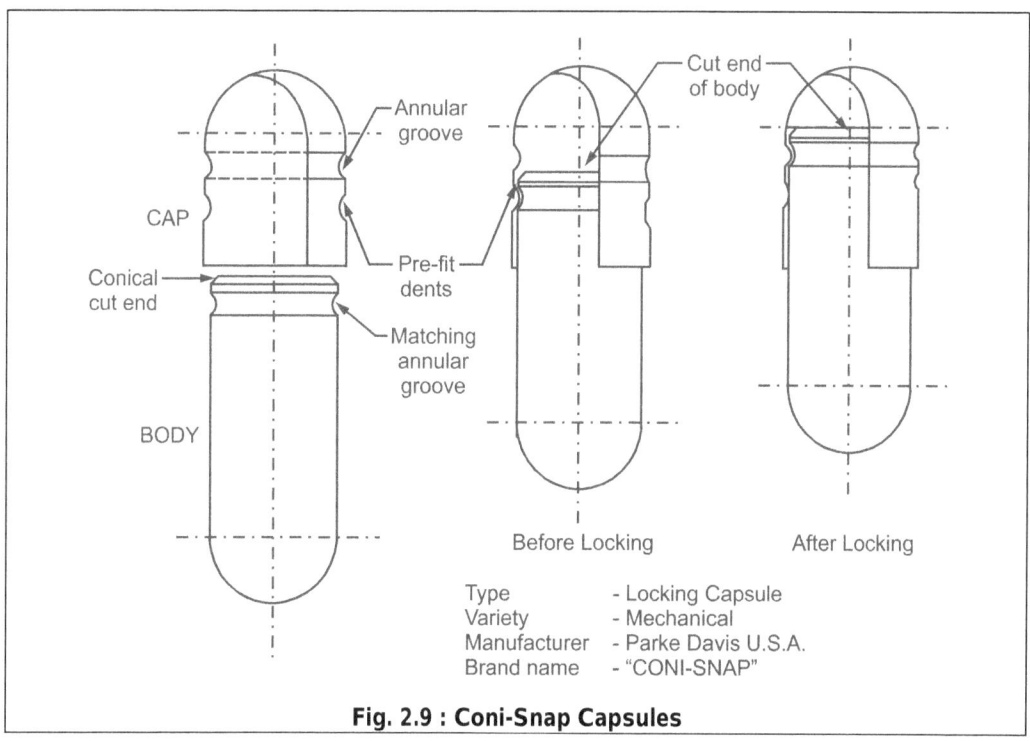

Fig. 2.9 : Coni-Snap Capsules

Coni-snap capsule had one additional feature than the snap-fit capsule. In coni-snap capsule, the additional feature was that the cut end of the body was slightly bent inwards in smooth conical fashion, so that the chance of telescoping or denting was minimized at the time of entry of the body into the cap (in the joining of empty capsule and in the rejoining of the filled capsule).

5. CONI-SNAP SUPRO CAPSULE (Product of M/s Capsugel)

In 1982, the famous TYLENOL (Mc Nell Johnson and Johnson Co. U.S.A.) poisoning case highlighted the possibility of tampering with the contents of a filled and locked capsule. Therefore the capsule makers had to provide a capsule design which would make the tampering with capsule contents visibly evident.

Thus, in 1983 M/s capsugel came up with a modified version of coni-snap capsule which was claimed to be 'TAMPER EVIDENT'. This capsule had all the features of 'CONI-SNAP' but it had a major change in diameters and lengths of the cap and the body. The length of the body was so kept that the cap almost entirely enveloped the body. After locking the filled capsule fully, only rounded end of the body remained available for gripping. This small round portion of the body end was not at all sufficient for gripping the body to separate the filled and closed capsule. Due to lack of body surface sufficient to grip the body for pulling the body apart from the cap, it became practically impossible to open the filled closed capsule without deforming or damaging it.

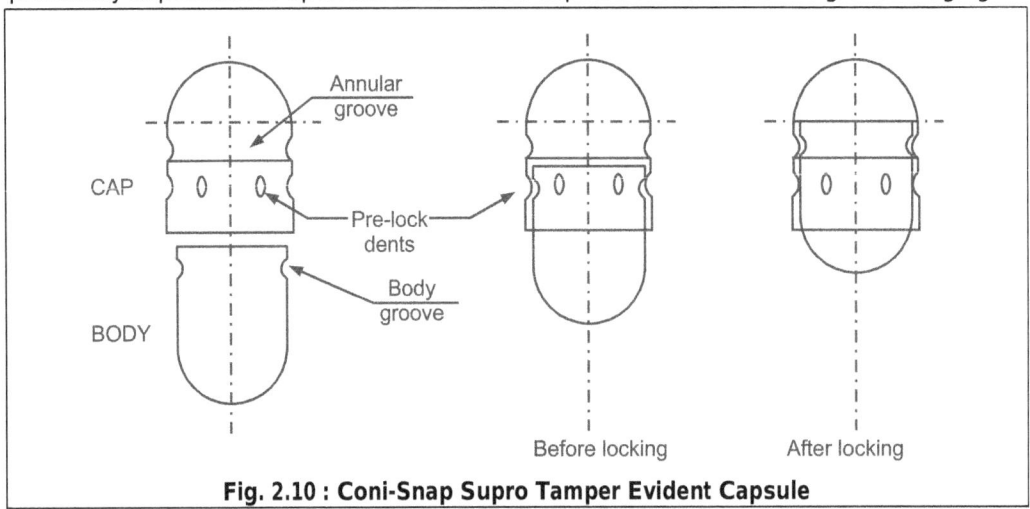

Fig. 2.10 : Coni-Snap Supro Tamper Evident Capsule

The coni-snap supro capsules are available in five different sizes viz. A, B, C, D, and E. Their volume capacities correspond to those of conventional sizes 0, 1, 2, 3 and 4 respectively.

In sizes A and B, the diameters of cap and body are kept as those of conventional size '00'. In sizes C, D and E, the diameters correspond to those of size '0', '1' and '2' respectively. In all sizes of coni-snap supro capsules the lengths of caps and bodies differ from those conventional sizes, still the volume capacities of corresponding conventional sizes are maintained.

Since the new capsule sizes have been introduced, the parts in printing, filling and packing machines, which are connected with capsule length and diameter have to be changed. Therefore these capsules cannot be used on existing printing, filling and packing machines used for regular locking type capsules.

6. LOX-IT (Product of GCL of Canada)

After seeing the advantages of locking type of capsules, around 1971, Bela Lorincz patented locking capsule designed for Scherer GCL Co. Canada, who marketed it under the brand name of LOX-IT. Instead of narrow annular groove, there was a broad contracted band below the dome base of cap. The body had no configuration on it. This provided a wider area of functional engagement between cap and body in closed condition. The capsule of this design also suffered from the problem of escape of air during the process of closure.

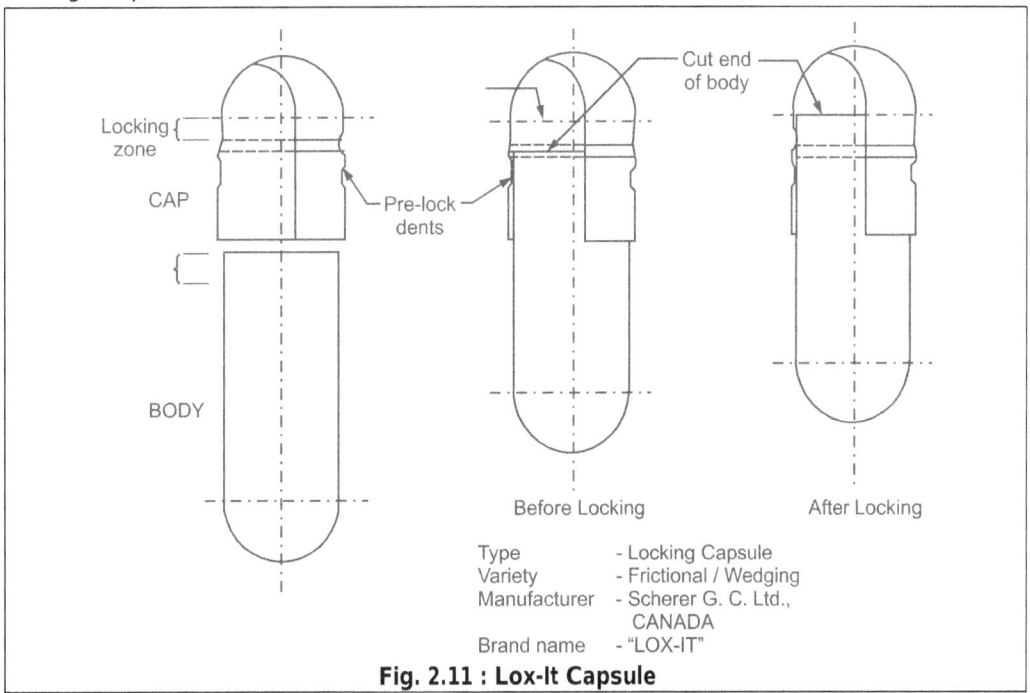

Fig. 2.11 : Lox-It Capsule

7. STAR-LOCK CAPSULE (Product of R.P. Scherer and Corporation)

Mr. Scherer patented a new design of locking capsule for R.P. Scherer Corporation U.S.A. in 1977. For providing vents for the air to escape during the closure of filled capsules, he introduced a segmented groove on the cap below its dome base. The ring of the annular groove was divided into equidistant segments, with the result that there were equidistant gaps in the inward projecting ridge on the cap below the dome base. These gaps were designed to act as vents for the air to escape during the closure of filled capsule. Therefore there was no necessity to provide vertical flats on body. Here also the body had no configuration on it. R.P. Scherer, U.S.A., marketed the capsule of this new design under the brand name of STAR LOCK. It had eight equidistant segments in the form of groove on the cap below its dome base.

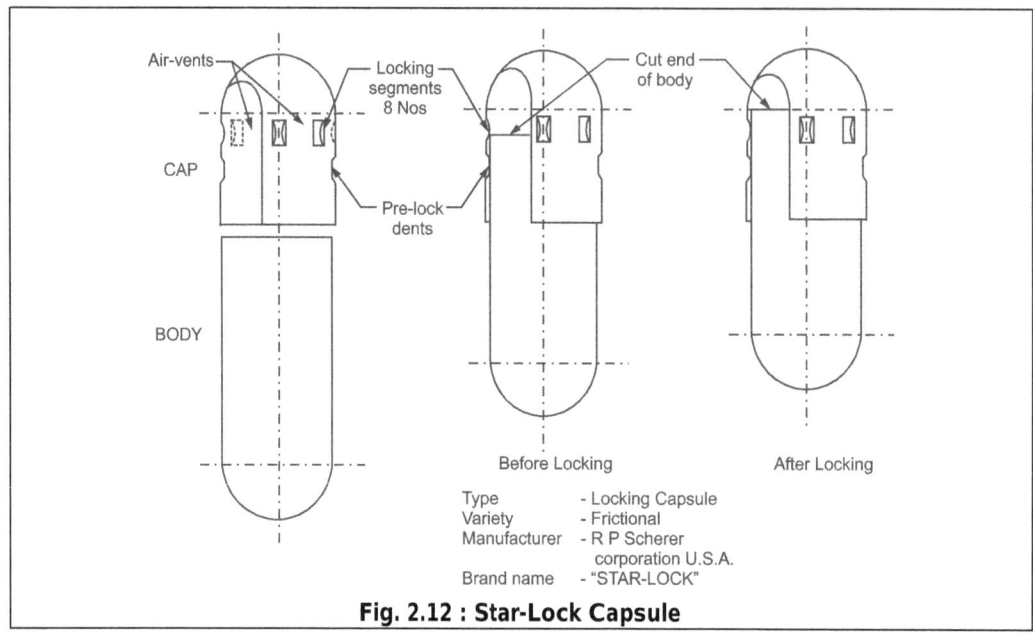

Fig. 2.12 : **Star-Lock Capsule**

8. EMBO CAP (Product of Su-Heung Capsule Co.)

M/s Su-Heung Capsule Manufacturing Co. of Korea, has come out with a design which prevents the capsule from getting locked or semi-locked during printing of empty capsules. This avoids the non-separation problem on capsule filling machine during opening operation by vacuum. In this design, capsule has four small notches at the dome base of cap. Between the two adjoining notches, the distance is 90°. The locking features are on similar lines as designed by other capsule manufacturing companies.

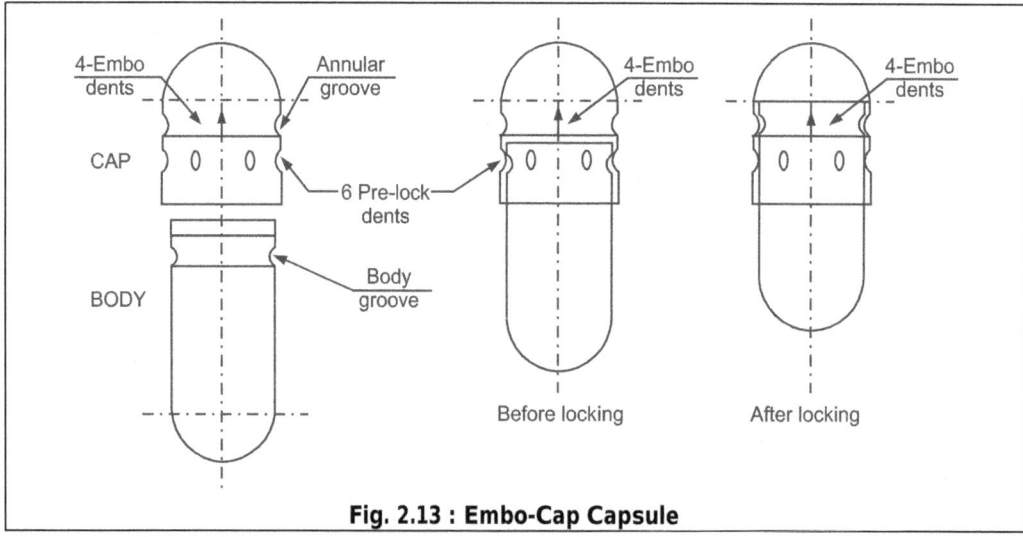

Fig. 2.13 : **Embo-Cap Capsule**

Empty capsule manufacturers all over the world are now making capsules with locking features. Only few empty capsule manufacturers manufacture PLAIN capsules against the order.

9. LOCK-FIT Capsules (Product of Ex. Pharmaceutical Capsule Laboratories)

Locking capsules were introduced in India around 1976. Ms. Pharmaceutical Capsules Laboratories (Mumbai) had procured dipping moulds having locking features for size No. 2 capsules from M/s Cherry Burrell Corporation of U.S.A. and they were the first to start manufacture of locking type empty capsules in India. These capsules had annular ring below the dome base of cap and no features on body. M/s Pharmaceutical Capsules Lab. named these capsules as LOCK FIT capsules.

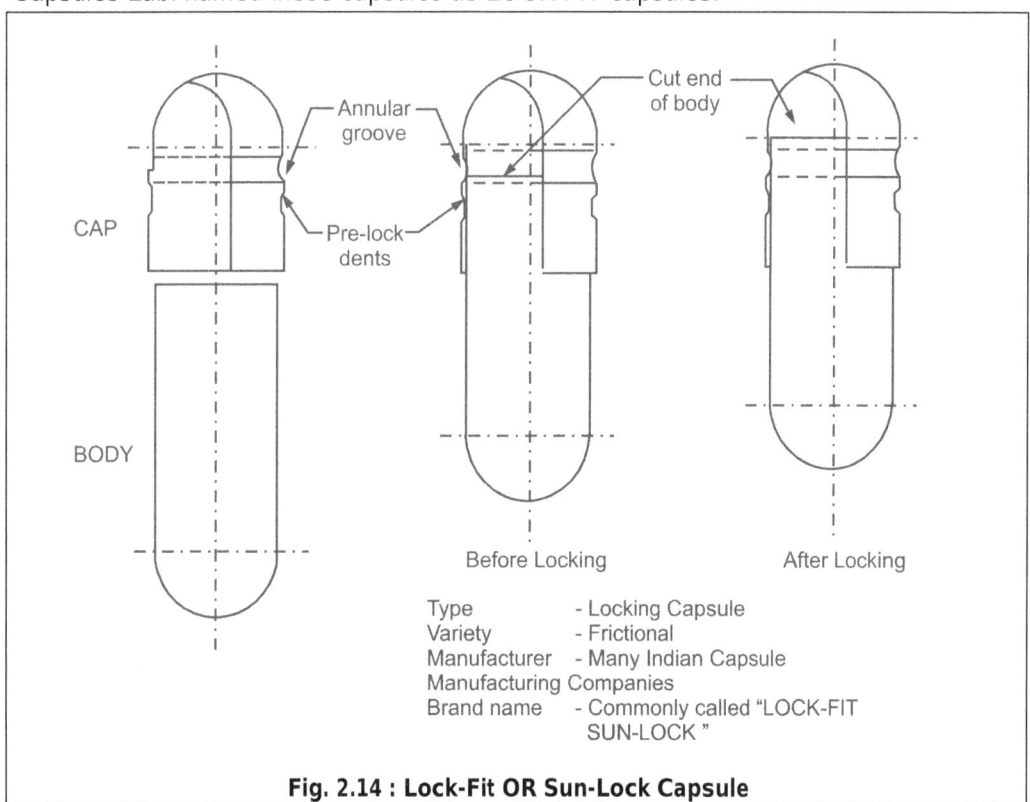

Fig. 2.14 : Lock-Fit OR Sun-Lock Capsule

10. SUN-LOC Capsule (Product of Sunil Synchem)

M/s Sunil Synchem at Alwar in Rajasthan introduced locking capsule under the brand name of 'SUN-LOC' capsule. The locking capsules produced by Pharmaceutical Capsule Laboratories (Mumbai) and by Sunil Synchem had the same design of locking features (Fig. 2.14).

11. EZEE FIT AND NEW SEAL LOCK Capsules (Product of Associated Capsule)

M/s Associated Capsules (Mumbai) had introduced locking capsules having 4 segmented grooves on cap below the dome base and no features on body. Over a period of time, Associated Capsule (Mumbai) made many changes in their lock design and now they have two types of locking capsules under the brand name of EZEE-FIT and 'NEW SEAL LOCK' capsules.

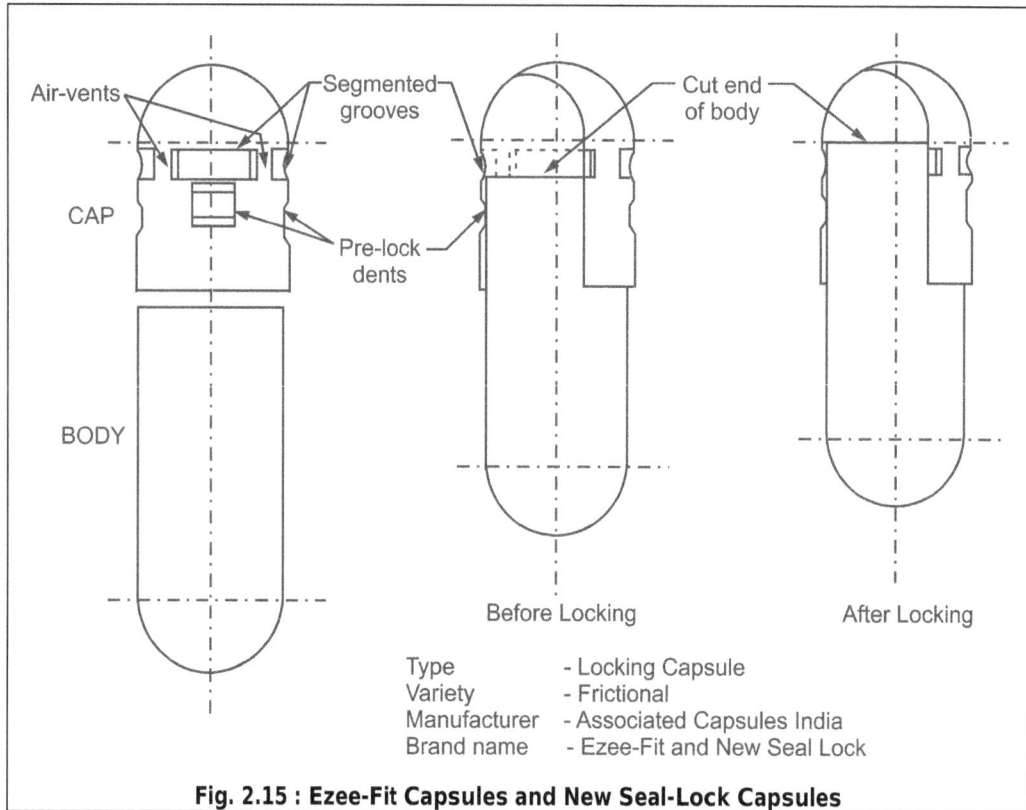

Fig. 2.15 : Ezee-Fit Capsules and New Seal-Lock Capsules

The locking features of both these capsules are on similar lines with that of other capsule manufacturers, keeping the basic principle same i.e. to hold the cut end of filled body with the annular groove near the dome base of cap.

2.3.2 (3) Pre-Lock Capsule

In plain capsule, the cut end of body was held by dome base of cap by slight wedging action. Therefore the slight shifting of body from dome base of cap by any vibrations or mechanical handling would result into loose fit capsule.

It was a well identified need of capsule fillers to have empty capsules which would not open up in handling, as well as in the hoppers of printing and filling machines due to vibrations on account of mechanical movements. At the same time, the capsule should separate into cap and body on capsule filling machine when vacuum (of 10" to 12" Hg column) was applied for separation, prior to filling of powder into the body. This need was satisfied by introducing PRE-LOCK features on cap of the locking capsule and later on cap of the plain capsule. Parke, Davis and Co. (Capsugel) named the pre-lock dents in their design as "PRE-FIT" dents and Eli Lilly and Co. (Shionogi) in their design as "PRE-LOCK" dents.

The concept of PRE-FIT feature on snap-fit capsules was patented by R.J. Graham and R.E. Mottin for Parke Davis and Co., U.S.A. in around 1970. The idea of introducing PRE-FIT features on plain capsules was patented by these same inventors for Parke, Davis and Co. in around 1972. Capsules incorporating both the above concepts were marketed by Parke, Davis and Co. in 1970 and 1972 respectively.

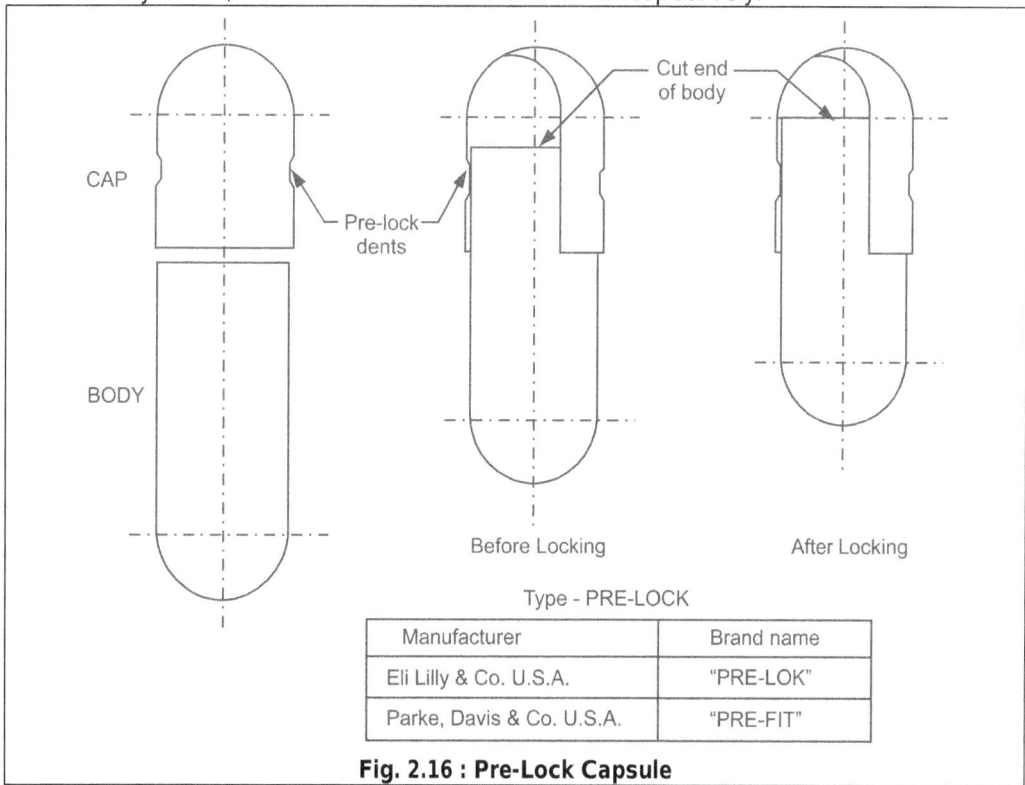

Type - PRE-LOCK

Manufacturer	Brand name
Eli Lilly & Co. U.S.A.	"PRE-LOK"
Parke, Davis & Co. U.S.A.	"PRE-FIT"

Fig. 2.16 : Pre-Lock Capsule

In pre-lock capsule two pre-lock dents on opposite points on cap were present between dome base and cut end of cap. They hold the body of capsule fairly tight in empty state. Therefore, in pre-lock capsule the possibility of formation of loose cap and body as well as capsule with two caps became practically impossible.

In the recent design of PRE-LOCK capsule of some capsule manufacturers, the number of dents has increased from 2 to anywhere upto 9. It is being done, to keep the roundness of body and cap more firm to avoid telescoping and denting during joining.

At present, all the locking type of capsules have PRE-LOCK features on their caps.

By introducing pre-lock features on locking capsules, as well as on plain capsules, major problems faced by capsule fillers were minimized.

2.3.2 (4) Tamper Evident Capsule (Coni-Snap Supro Capsules)

Coni-Snap Supro Capsules are claimed to be Tamper Evident Capsule as discussed earlier.

2.3.3 Shape

Empty hard gelatin capsule can be of different shapes. A particular shape may be exclusively reserved by a particular pharmaceutical user for protecting the image of his products. Special dipping moulds are required for manufacturing capsules of special shapes, because the requirement is specific. The requirement has also to be large enough to need an exclusive shape. The different shapes of hard capsules as well as soft capsules are described under the heading "Shapes of capsules" in United States Federal Standard, capsules No. 285-A dated Oct 19, 1976. They are :

1. Shape 'a' - Conventional
2. Shape 'b' - Bullet like
3. Shape 'c' - Elliptical (oval)
4. Shape 'd' - Oblong
5. Shape 'e' - Round
6. Shape 'f' - Tapered ends
7. Shape 'g' - Special as specified

From the above shapes a, b, f and g relate to hard capsules, whereas the remaining shapes relate to soft capsules. The shapes of hard capsules are detailed as under.

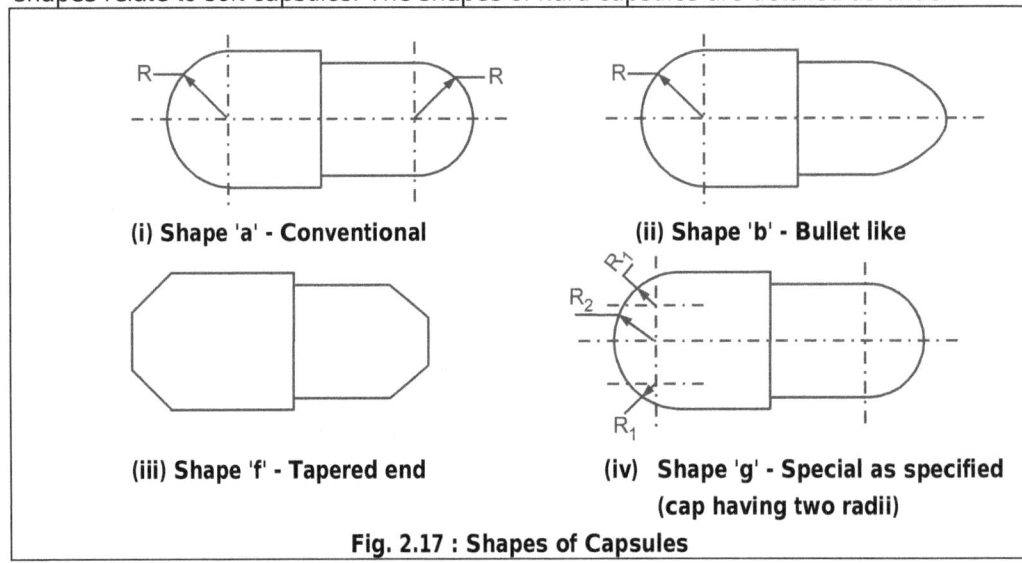

(i) Shape 'a' - Conventional
(ii) Shape 'b' - Bullet like
(iii) Shape 'f' - Tapered end
(iv) Shape 'g' - Special as specified (cap having two radii)

Fig. 2.17 : Shapes of Capsules

Shape 'a' (Conventional) : This capsule looks like elongated cylinder, being hemispherical on both ends.

Shape 'b' (Bullet like) : This capsule really looks like a bullet. The cap has standard conventional look and the closed end of the body is shaped like the end of bullet. This capsule is registered as "PARA BOLOIDAL CAPSULE" by Eli Lilly and Co. (U.S.A.) who have marketed all their special pharmaceutical products in the bullet shaped capsules.

Shape 'f' (Tapered end) : In this capsule, the elongated cylindrical portion has tapering ends. Capsules with this shape are marketed by S. K. and F (U.S.A) for their own products.

Shape 'g' (Special as specified) : It is possible to make capsules with different shapes other than those described above. These special shapes are preferred by some pharmaceutical users for product identification. Item 'g' in the schedule is incorporated for covering these special shaped capsules introduced by pharmaceutical users. In this type 'double radii cap' capsule made by 'Eli Lilly & Co.' can be included. 'Doble radii cap' capsule has flat cap end and hemispherical body end.

2.3.4 Embossed Matter

Non-coated tablets are normally identified by engraved letters present on them. These letters are raised on the punches. When the powder is pressed by the punch to form tablet, letters on the punch appear on the tablet in the form of an indented impression. Similarly, embossed capsule can be produced by making dipping moulds with suitably raised letters or emblems on the dome top. Such moulds will produce capsules with permanent identification mark in the form of desired letters or emblems and would provide exclusive identification for pharmaceutical user and /or his products.

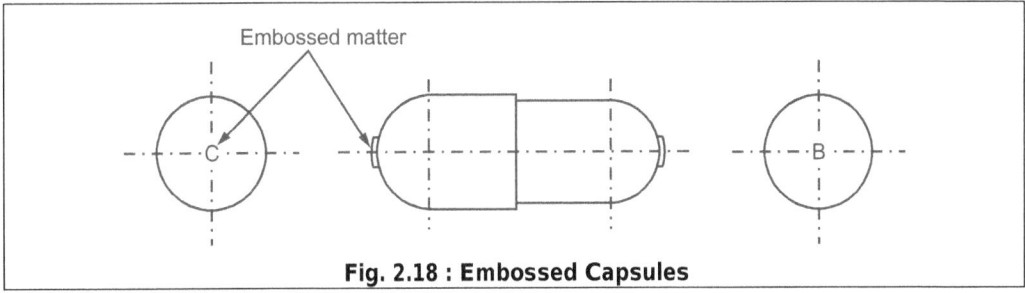

Fig. 2.18 : Embossed Capsules

Abbot Laboratories had one preparation in plain transparent capsules, where letter 'A' was embossed on the body of the capsule.

The desired letters or emblems in raised form are normally put at the dome of the cap and/or body mould to facilitate stripping of the capsule shells from the dipping moulds. Eli Lilly Industries (U.K.) have patented various conceptual designs for embossed cap and body moulds.

2.3.5 Colour Scheme and Colour HUE (of coloured capsules)

Around 1911 coloured capsules were manufactured by using harmless food colours. Later F.D.A. approved opacifying agent (titanium dioxide) was used to manufacture opaque white and coloured opaque capsules.

U.S. Federal Standard Capsules 285-A, dated Oct. 19, 1976 classified the coloured capsules under the heading 'Transparency of capsules' as below.

Grade A Opaque

Grade B Clear

Grade C Combination

Grade D Special

Description of all the grades is given in the document.

Grade 'A' : Opaque capsules are those which protect contents from light rays.

Grade 'B' : Clear capsules are those in which the contained material may be seen through the capsules. Such capsules may be coloured or uncoloured.

Grade 'C' : Combination capsules are those in which the shell of capsules are of different grades of transparency i.e. one shell clear (coloured or uncoloured) and the other shell opaque. Grade 'C' capsules shall be in accordance with manufacturer's commercial practice, which is not specified in the present document.

Grade 'D' : Special capsules shall be of the grade specified in the procurement document.

All capsules from plain transparent to coloured capsules can be classified under the four grades as stated above. But the capsule manufacturers have adopted a different practice of classifying capsules. These categories are :

(a)   Plain transparent.

(b)   Coloured transparent

(c)   Opaque white

(d)   Opaque coloured

(e)   Combination or bi-coloured

(a) Plain Transparent : Plain Transparent capsule is transparent in look. Therefore the drug in this capsule can be seen from outside. This capsule is made from the gelatin solution to which no edible water soluble colour or opacifying agent is added. When the drug manufacturer wants the medicament, especially beads or pellets, in the capsule to be clearly seen from outside, he preferably uses plain transparent capsule. After the coloured and bi-coloured capsules were introduced, the demand for plain transparent capsule was reduced substantially. But with the recent introduction of nutraceutical products in HARD CAPSULES, the demand for plain transparent capsule has gone up. It is because, the manufacturers of nutraceutical products prefer to use capsules without any colour and opacifying agent.

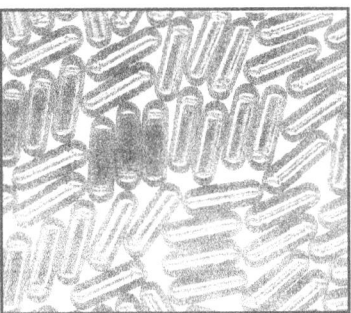

Fig. 2.19 : Plain Transparent Capsules

(b) Coloured Transparent : The cap and body of this capsule has same colour. This capsule is transparent, yet coloured. It looks more attractive than plain transparent capsule. With advent of coloured transparent capsule, the use of plain transparent capsule was considerably reduced. These capsules are available in variety of colours and shades which are normally obtained from combination of three basic colours viz. Red, Blue and Yellow. Only Red, Blue and Yellow F.D.A. approved colours for human consumption are used. Some colours are very susceptible to heat, light, oxidizing and reducing agents alone or jointly and it results into discolouration of the colour of the capsules. Some times, an ingredient of the medicament contained in the capsule affects the colour of the capsule resulting in its discolouration. A pharmaceutical user has therefore to ensure against all the above possibilities, before selecting a particular coloured capsule for his product.

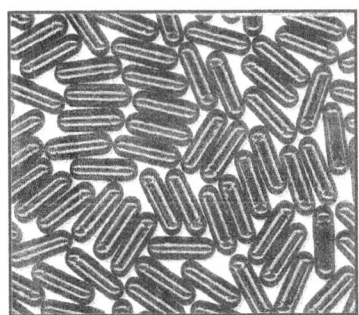

Fig. 2.20 : Coloured Transparent Capsules

(c) Opaque White : Cap and body of this capsule are both opaque white. Therefore, the capsule is not transparent. Hence, the medicament contained in it cannot be seen from outside. Being opaque, this capsule helps to protect its contents from external light. An opacifying agent viz. Titanium dioxide (I.P./B.P./NF grade) is used for making the capsule opaque. Titanium dioxide is safe for human consumption. It is chemically inert. Therefore, there is no chance of chemical interaction between the medicament filled in the capsule and the titanium dioxide present in the capsule shell.

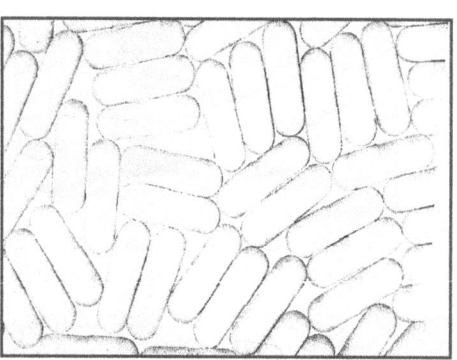

Fig. 2.21 : White Opaque Capsules

(d) Colured Opaque : The cap and body of this capsule have same opaque colour. This capsule being opaque, the medicament filled in it cannot be seen from outside. Its opacity helps to protect its medicinal contents from external light. Being coloured, this capsule looks more attractive. These capsules are available in variety of colours.

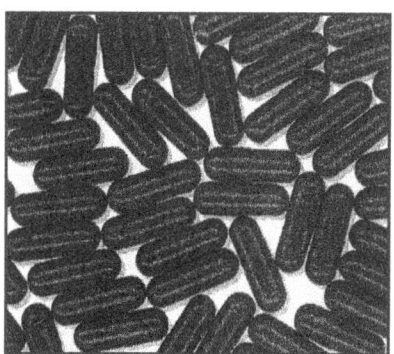

Fig. 2.22 : Opaque Coloured Capsules

The following pigments and edible colours approved by F.D.A. for internal use are used in production of these capsules.
- (i) Titanium dioxide (White pigment) – F.D.A. approved
- (ii) Three basic colours :
  Red, Blue, Yellow synthetic and/or natural colours – approved by F.D.A.
- (iii) Synthetic iron oxides :
  Yellow, Red and Black – approved by F.D.A.

(e) Combination or Bi-Coloured Capsules : The cap and body of this capsule are of different colours and/or shades. The cap may be plain transparent, coloured transparent, (or any shade of that colour), opaque white or coloured opaque, or shade of that colour) whereas the body may be plain transparent or coloured transparent (or any shade of that colour), opaque white or coloured opaque (or any shade of that colour). Being more attractive, this variety of capsule gets customer preference over all other capsule varieties.

A combination of plain transparent or coloured transparent cap and opaque white or opaque coloured body is generally disliked because of aesthetic reasons. Therefore such combination is normally not used.

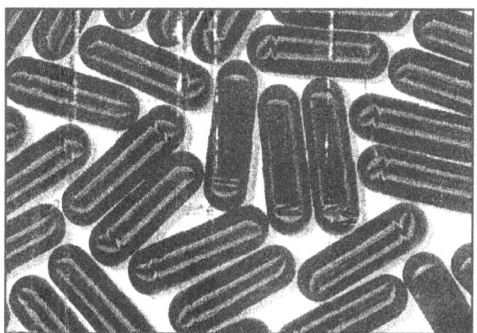
(a) Bi-coloured Transparent Capsules

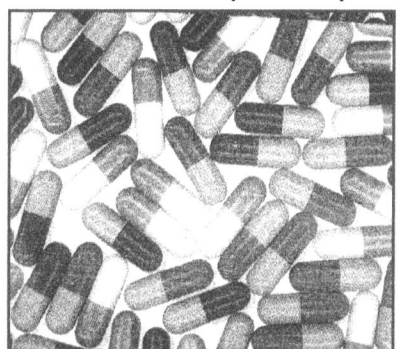
(b) Opaque Bi-coloured Capsules
Fig. 2.23

Pearly Appearance / Metallic Appearance Capsule

This variety of capsule is not included in U.S. Federal Std. Capsules 285-A, 1976.

This was a new variety of capsule developed by Parke, Davis and Co. (Japan). Pearly appearance capsule was manufactured by using natural pearl essence (derived from fish scale).

Metallic appearance capsules were made by adding small quantity of approved synthetic colorants along with natural pearl essence. These capsules were not approved for human consumption.

Recently Associated Capsules (India) have introduced these capsules by using certain chemicals which are approved for human consumption.

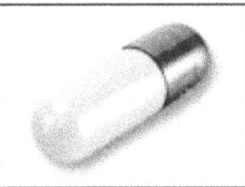

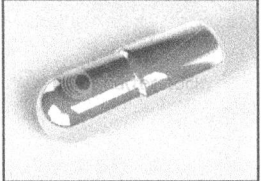

Fig. 2.24 : Pearly or Metallic Appearance Capsule

To sum up, coloured capsules
(i) have aesthetic appeal.
(ii) help in product identification.
(iii) help in dosage strength identification.
(iv) can have psychological effect on a patient.

2.3.6 Printed Capsules

Coloured capsules helped the pharmaceutical community to establish the identity of their products. With the introduction of printing on capsules, this identity could become more specific. Printing on capsules helped not only capsule makers and pharmaceutical users (pharma companies), it benefited doctors and patients too. The latter two could feel assured about the genuineness of the drug used.

Normally printed matter on capsule conveys the following information.
(i) Logo or emblem of the pharmaceutical company.
(ii) Brand name of the product.
(iii) Product code number of the pharmaceutical company.
(iv) Name of the pharmaceutical company.
(v) Dosage specification.

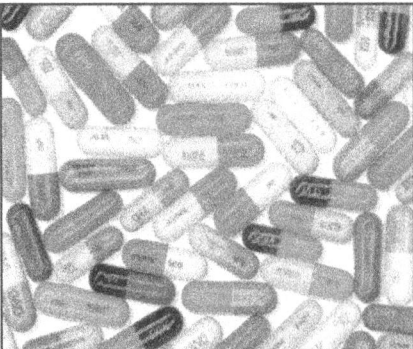

Fig. 2.25 : Linearly Printed Capsules

Initially, only single side linear printing (longitudinal or axial printing) was introduced. That time, it was not possible to accommodate all the above message for printing on capsule. With the introduction of double side printing, it became possible to accommodate more matter for printing on capsule. With the advent of radial printing (spin printing) much more additional matter could also be printed. In radial printing the most of the surfaces of cap and body (excluding their domes) became available for printing. With the introduction of orientation mechanism of capsule in printing machines, it became possible to have specific messages printed on caps and bodies. With the further advancement in radial printing, it is now possible to have full 360° printing around the circumferences of cap and body with specific messages printed on caps and bodies respectively with different coloured inks.

2.3.7 Form of Printing

Due to all these developments in capsule printing, it is now possible to get the capsules printed in various forms. They are listed below.

(i) Single side linear printing on non-oriented capsule.
(ii) Double side linear printing on non-oriented capsule (on opposite sides).
(iii) Radial printing on non-oriented capsules.
(iv) Linear and radial printing on non-oriented capsule.
(v) Single side linear printing on oriented capsule.
(vi) Double side linear printing on oriented capsule (on opposite sides)
(vii) Radial printing on oriented capsule.
(viii) Linear and radial printing on oriented capsule.
(ix) 360° printing around the circumference of cap and body (oriented and non- oriented.)

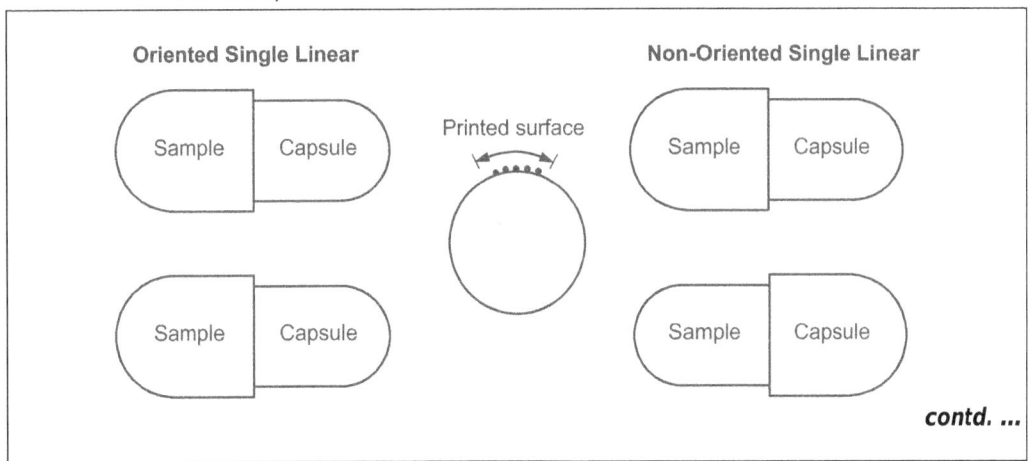

contd. ...

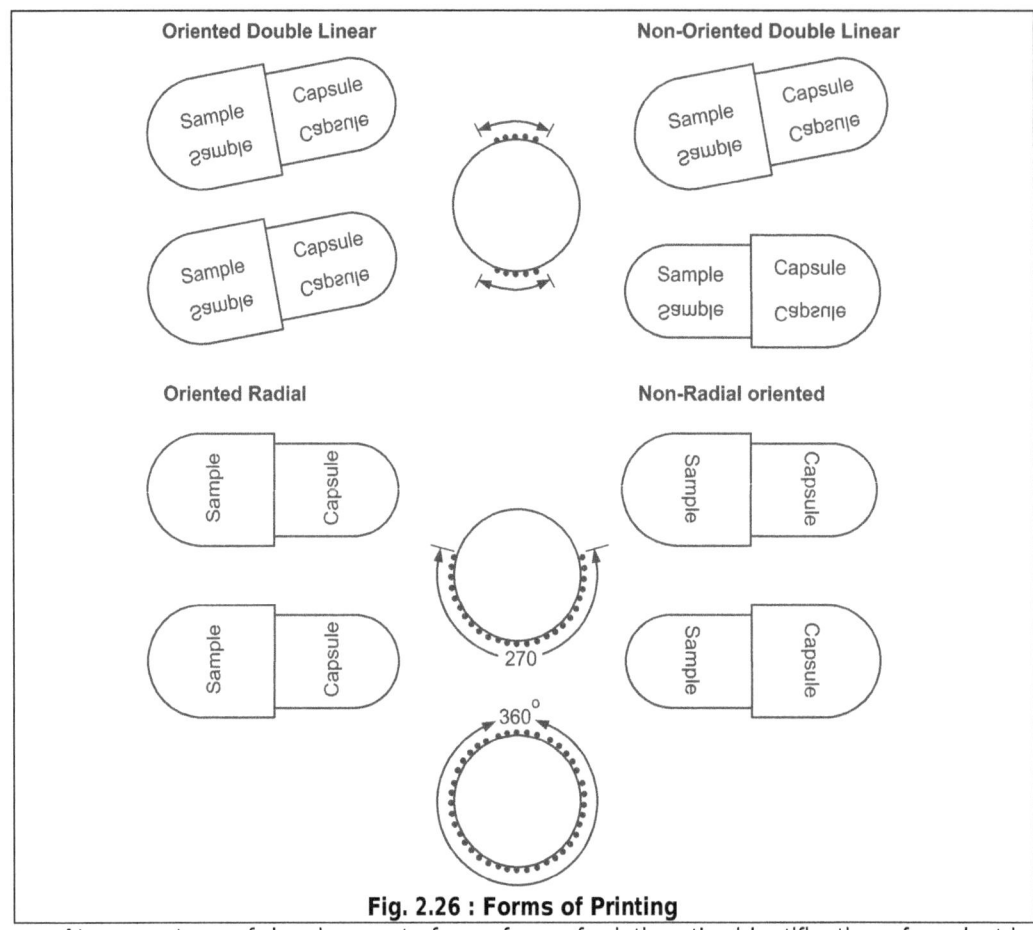

Fig. 2.26 : Forms of Printing

At every stage of development of new from of printing, the identification of product in capsule became more and more specific, thereby becoming difficult for others to copy. Therefore normal trend now is that pharmaceutical companies try to select that form of printing which is difficult for others to copy. (Please refer the chapter on printing of capsule).

2.3.8 Colour of Printing Ink

This is described in details under the heading of identification of soft gelatin capsule.

2.3.9 Flavour (Flavoured Hard Gelatin Capsules)

Normally hard gelatin capsules are not flavoured. If the formulation in soft gelatin capsule is made by adding flavouring agent in the soft shell composition, and if such formulation is converted into hard gelatin capsule, then the requests are made to make hard capsule by adding such flavouring agents in hard shell composition. The flavouring agents approved by F.D.A. are used for making only such capsules. Some times, flavouring agents are sprayed over filled capsules, to achieve the same effect.

∎∎∎

3. RAW MATERIALS USED IN THE MANUFACTURE OF TWO-PIECE EMPTY HARD GELATIN CAPSULES

The list of raw materials used for making two piece empty hard gelatin capsule can be categorized into four groups. They are :

1. Gelatin
2. Preservatives
3. Other ingredients
4. Colouring agents

The materials in each group are detailed below.

1. Gelatin :

Gelatin is the main raw material for making hard gelatin capsules. Gelatin was significantly selected for making capsules because of its following properties.

(a) It is safe for human consumption.

(b) Its solution has the thermo-reversible property of sol ⇌ gel transformation.

(c) The film formed from molten gelatin solution

    (i)   has an agreeable (neutral) taste and odour.

    (ii)   when dried, becomes elastic and has sufficient mechanical strength.

    (iii) when dried, and comes in contact with water it becomes slippery (because of this property, the capsule becomes easy to swallow).

    (iv) solubilizes easily in stomach medium at body temperature ($37°C \pm 2°C$).

Gelatin is a natural polymer. Gelatin is derived from fibrous protein collagen. Collagen is present in animal skins and bones. Therefore, it is also said that gelatin is derived from animal bones, skin and hide. During manufacturing steps of gelatin, the 1st step is to get collagen by chemical process in such a form that it can be extracted in hot water where the collagen first gets converted into gelatin which is soluble in hot water (collagen is not soluble in hot water). This is the base line of how the gelatin is made.

U.S.P. defines "Gelatin is a product obtained by the partial hydrolysis of collagen derived from skin, white connective tissues and bones of animals". It is a fibrous protein consisting of long amino acid chains associated together in a form of triple helix.

There are three types of gelatin which are usually used in the manufacture of hard as well as soft capsules, namely

Type A - Acid processed pig skin gelatin.
Type A - Acid processed hide gelatin.
Type A - Acid processed bone gelatin.
Type B - Alkaline processed bone gelatin.
Type B - Alkaline processed hide gelatin.

For type A – Acid processed pig skin gelatin, the basic raw material required is pig skin hide. For type A and B – Acid and alkaline processed bone gelatin, the basic raw material required is animal bones. By treating animal bones with dilute hydrochloric acid, ossein is obtained. Ossein, thus obtained is further processed to get collagen and then gelatin. The detailed flow diagram for manufacturing gelatin is given in Chapter No. 2 of Soft Gelatin Capsule Technology viz. Shell Composition and Manufacturing of Gelatin. In each type, gelatin is manufactured by extracting the collagens for 4 to 5 times under different sets of temperature conditions. Each extract after drying, gives gelatins of different specifications. The required grades of gelatins are obtained by suitably blending the gelatins obtained from different extracts. Schematically it is represented below.

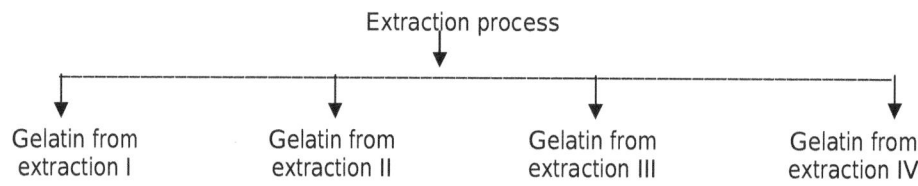

The gelatins from above extractions are suitably blended to get the grades of gelatin suitable to manufacture.

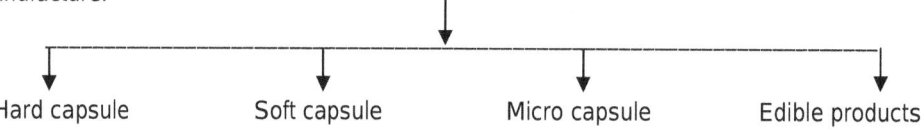

The source of raw materials (collagen) and the type of manufacturing process influence the physical and chemical properties of the derived gelatin. Each capsule manufacturer finds from experience a suitable blend ratio of three types of gelatin i.e. pig skin, and acid and alkali processed bone gelatine to give him capsules of good flexibility, strength and overall good quality.

There are certain known properties of type A and type B gelatins. Type B gelatin (limed bone gelatin) has the highest inherent strength but is slower in drying than Type A pig skin gelatin. Porkskin (Type A) gelatin is prone to brittleness, but it is faster in drying. It is very interesting to note that, Type A gelatin when blended with Type B gelatin imparts flexibility to the capsule.

The specifications typical of type A and type B gelatins used in the manufacture of hard gelatin capsules are given below.

Table 3.1 : Typical Specifications for Hard Capsule Gelatin

	Test	Limed bone Type 'B' gelatin	Acid bone Type 'A' gelatin	Acid Pig skin Type 'A' gelatin
1.	A.O. AC bloom 'g'* 6.2/3% w/w gelatin solution in water at 10°C for 17 hours.	235 – 260	245 – 270	260 – 285
2.	Viscosity 6.67% $\left(\frac{w}{w}\right)$ at 60°C mPaS corrected to 11.5% moisture.	4.3 – 4.7	3.3 – 3.7	4.3 – 4.7
3.	Viscosity 12.5% $\left(\frac{w}{w}\right)$ at 60°C mPaS corrected to 11.5% moisture.	18.5 – 20.5	12.5 – 14.5	18.5 – 20.5
4.	% viscosity drop in 18 hours at 60°C max.	20	20	20
5.	Moisture % (max.)	13.0	13.0	13.0
6.	Ash % (max.)	1.0	1.0	1.0
7.	pH, 1% solution.	5.5 – 6	5.5 – 6	5.2 – 5.8
8.	iso – ionic pH.	4.7 to 5.3	6.0 – 8.0	7.0 – 9.0
9.	Particle size % passing 4U.S. mesh. % passing 40 U.S. mesh (max.)	100 5	100 5	100 5
10.	Sulphur dioxide PPM (max.)	40	40	40
11.	Heavy Metals PPM (max.)	50	50	50
12.	Arsenic PPM (max.)	0.8	0.8	0.8
13.	Hydrogen Peroxide	Absent	Absent	Absent

contd. ...

14.	Nitrate PPM (max.)	300	300	300
15.	Nitrite PPM (max.) Microbiological standards	30	30	30
16.	Total count orgs per gram (max.)	500	500	500
17.	Salmonellae in 10 g	Absent	Absent	Absent
18.	Coliforms in 10 g	Absent	Absent	Absent
19.	*E. coli* in 10 g	Absent	Absent	Absent
20.	Thermophiles	Absent	Absent	Absent
21.	Bactericides and Bacteriostats	Absent	Absent	Absent

The specification of gelatin is so derived that capsule manufactured from such gelatin will meet the functional requirements of capsule manufacturing process and the capsule itself.

If the tests given under the gelatin specifications are examined, one would understand the significance of these tests. For example :

1. To make capsule safe for human consumption, supplied gelatin has to pass, (a) the microbiological, (b) arsenic and heavy metal tests. These tests are directly related to safety of human beings.
2. For identifying type A and type B gelatin, iso-ionic pH is important.
3. The stock solution made for dipping has to have the same viscosity all the time. Therefore it is essential to get every time the gelatin batches having the same basic viscosity values. That is why specification of viscosity of gelatins and the measurements of them is important.
4. Bloom strength specification and its measurement are important, as the mechanical strength and flexibility of gelatin film is dependent on the bloom strength value.

In short, every test mentioned in the specification has a role to play in the manufacturing of capsule.

In the year 1986, a new problem cropped up in using ossein gelatin in the manufacturing of hard gelatin capsule, as a case of Bovine Spongiform Encephalopathy (BSE) was identified for the first time in U.K. BSE is a fatal disease of cattle believed to be related to CREUTZ – JAKOB disease in human beings. Therefore to keep away such a disease, the general feeling was to avoid the use of edible products particularly made from gelatin of cattle bones.

This BSE problem, how far it was related to the gelatin manufactured from cattle bones was thoroughly investigated by the University of Goettingen (Germany) and gelatin manufacturers in Europe. During investigations one important thing came forward viz. Bovine Bones are non-infectious with respect to the BSE agent. However a potential BSE risk arises from the possibility of contamination with infected specified risk material (SRM) such as skull, spinal cord, vertebrae etc. If such specified risk materials (SRM) are removed from the bone raw materials, gelatin manufactured from such raw materials would be safe for human consumption as it would then be almost free from TRANSMISSIBLE SPONGIFORM ENCEPHALOPOTHIA (TSE).

It was also observed that the gelatin produced would be further safe, if the bone gelatin is manufactured from bones (which are already free from SRM) as per the process guidelines given by CPMP/CVMP (2001). The gelatin thus produced would be almost totally free from BSE risk, as the remnant TSE, if any, in bone raw materials would get destroyed during processing.

The BSE risk free gelatin produced by taking all the care as stated above, is now available for production of gelatin capsules.

It is important to note that the gelatin produced from pig skin and hide has no such potential of BSE risk and it is therefore safe for human consumption.

Important shortforms used :

BSE - Bovine spongiform encephalopathy
TSE - Transmissible spongiform encephalopathy
SRM - (Infected) specified risk materials
CPMP - Committee for proprietary medicinal products
CVMP - Committee for veterinary medicinal products

2. Preservatives :

The moisture content of gelatin powder (raw material) and empty gelatin capsule being low, it is difficult for bacteria to grow on them. Bacteria needs sufficient moisture in gelatin for their growth. In other words, gelatin is an excellent media for bacteria and fungus to grow on it, provided it has enough moisture. Such a moisture is available in gelatin when it is in the solution form. The capsules are manufactured by dipping the stainless steel dipping moulds in gelatin solution. Since gelatin solution is an excellent media for bacteria to grow, bacterial contamination in dipping solution is unavoidable.

As the capsules are required to be produced with very low bacterial count, and free from pathogenic organisms, the gelatin solution used for making capsules, should be free from such bacterial contaminations. To overcome this problem, preservatives are used in the gelatin solution and the capsules are made from preservative added gelatin solution.

Normally, preservatives are added during preparation of gelatin solution. A few of them are bactericidal, but majority are bacteriostatic. As empty capsules are to be used for filling drugs, the preservatives which are used have to be approved by Food and Drug Authorities (of the respective country). Similarly the capsule makers would not like to use preservatives which affect the capsules adversely.

Table 3.2 : Preservatives Used in Gelatin Solution for Making Capsules

Sr. No.	Name of preservative	Concentration of preservatives used	Problems faced
1.	Beta napthol	Low concentration	Capsules turning brown after keeping
2.	SO_2 in the form of sodium sulfite or sodium metabisulfite	Less than 1000 ppm of SO_2 in capsule	Coloured capsules produced from indigo carmine, amaranth, Sunset Yellow FCF- getting faded.
3.	Acetic acid	Used in very low concentration	Capsules give smell of acetic acid
4.	Mixture of methylparaben and propylparaben in ratio of 4:1 respectively	Not more than 0.2% of the weight of dry gelatin blend	Still in use (with the approval from the customer)

Now-a-days many capsule users do not want any preservative in capsules. However many developing countries still allow the use of preservatives in capsules. Looking to the trend, sooner or later no capsule user will be allowed to use preservatives in capsules. Looking to the demand for preservative free capsules, capsule manufacturers have solved this problem on war footing. They have found out all the possibilities of bacterial contaminations and each possibility was studied and the corrective action taken. Few of them are detailed below :

All the raw materials were tested for microbial contaminations and it was found that the contamination was of a high degree from the point of view of manufacturing preservative free capsules. Each manufacturer of capsule had set up his own new bacterial standards for raw materials used for making capsules. The standards specified were "they would totally be free from pathogenic organisms having very low viable count".

The microbial standards given for gelatin in old I.P. was 10,000 organisms per gram. In 1996, the I.P. standard was revised and the count was brought to 1000 org/gr; but capsule manufacturers, have revised (for their own use) the standard for gelatin as 500 count/gram and pathogenic organisms as absent.

The capsule manufacturing operations were modified in such a way that there would not be any chance for bacteria to grow on the materials under processing.

It was observed that microbial count of coloured solution goes high within 24 hours, inspite of making the solution in water free from bacteria. The growth was avoided by keeping the coloured solution all the time at 60°C till it was consumed. Like this, many other precautions were taken.

By adopting the good manufacturing practices in capsule manufacturing operations, the bacterial count of capsule was kept under control. As it stands today, without the use of preservatives, capsules are being made with microbial count less than 500 org./gr and they are free from pathogenic organisms.

It is also important to note that the preservative free capsules are not sterilized by the mixture of ethylene oxide and Freon gas (They are mixed in the ratio of 1:8 respectively).

3. Other Ingredients

Other ingredients are added to the gelatin solution in order to improve :
(i) The uniform casting of gelatin film on lubricated stainless steel dipping moulds.
(ii) The plasticity of dried gelatin film.
(iii) The flow of empty gelatin capsules through feeding tubes (of filling machine) which is required for high speed capsule filling machines.

Sodium Lauryl sulfate (SLS pharma grade) is added in small quantities in the gelatin solution to reduce its surface tension. The low surface tension gelatin solution wets uniformly on the surface of the lubricated dipping mould. The lubricant applied on the mould otherwise does not allow to wet the pin surface fully with the gelatin solution when it is dipped in it. Addition of SLS has overcome this problem. After drying, uniform film is obtained which is free from weak or thin areas. Capsules produced with weak areas can give rise to leakage of powder after filling.

Glycerine, Propylene glycol, PVP etc. are added in small quantities to allow the capsules to remain flexible, (plasticity) and dimensionally stable during long storage.

M/s Shionogi (Japan) are manufacturing capsules with addition of PEG 4000 in their capsules composition to keep capsules dimensionally stable and flexible even at low moisture content of capsule. This product is marketed by this company as special grade of capsules to fill hygroscopic powders.

It is interesting to note that there are few empty capsule manufacturers who claim that they do not add any plasticizer in their capsule composition.

The surface friction of empty capsules has to be low, for better flow of capsules through the feeding tubes and bushes of high speed capsule filling machines. This is required in order to get the rated output on filling machines.

The flow problem is sorted out in a couple of different ways.

(a) The fine suspension of silicon dioxide (pharma grade) made in water is added in small quantities into gelatin solution. The capsules made from such composition flow properly into the feeding tubes and get easily into the filling bushes of high speed filling machines.

(b) Small amounts of materials like sodium lauryl sulfate or edible waxes like carnauba wax, in powder form are sprinkled over the empty capsules and they are rotated in a drum for uniform application of powder on the surface of the capsules. Such externally lubricated capsules also flow properly.

(c) The static charge gets generated onto the capsules due to friction, which affects the flow of capsules. Some capsule manufacturing companies add edible antistatic agents in gelatin solution from which capsules are made. It is said that such capsules have good flow.

4. Colouring Agents :

Following is the list of edible colours which are reported to be used in the colouration of capsules. They are grouped into three categories :

(i) Water soluble dyes.
(ii) Pigments
(iii) Natural colourants.

Table 3.3 : Water Soluble Dyes (Pharmaceutical Colourants)

Common name	C.I. number	E.U. number	U.S.A. name	Chemical class
Reds :				
Allura Red	16035	E 129	F.D.& C. Red No. 40	AZO
Amaranth	16185	E 123	–	AZO
Azorubine	14720	E 122	–	AZO
Ponceau 4R	16255	E 124	–	AZO
Erythrosine	45430	E 127	F.D. & C. Red No. 3	Xanthene
Phoxine B	45410	–	D & C Red No. 28	Xanthene
Orange :				
Sunset yellow	15985	E 110	F.D. & C. Yellow No. 6	AZO
Yellows :				
Tartrazine	19140	E 102	F.D. & C. Yellow No. 5	AZO
Quinoline yellow	47005	E 104	F.D. & C. Yellow No. 10	Quino-pthalene
Blues :				
Indigo carmine	73105	E 132	F.D. & C. Blue No. 2	Indigoid
Brilliant Blue	42090	E 133	F.D. & C. Blue No. 1	Triphenylmethane
Patent Blue V	42051	E 131	–	Triphenylmethane

(Pharmaceutical Certifiable Colours)

Table 3.4 : Pigments (Pharmaceutical Grade)

Name	C. I. number	E.U. number	Formula
Titanium Dioxide	77891	E - 171	TiO_2
Black Iron Oxide	77499	E - 172	$FeO\ Fe_2O_3$ (synthetic)
Red Iron Oxide	77491	E - 172	Fe_2O_3 (synthetic)
Yellow Iron Oxide	77492	E - 172	$FeO\ (OH)_n\ H_2O$ (synethetic)

(Pharmaceutical pigments are not certified)

Table 3.5 : Natural Colourants (Pharmaceutical Grade)

Name	C. I. number	E.U. number	Hue
β Carotene	40800	E - 160 a	Orange
Canthaxanthin	40850	E - 1619	Orange
Chlorophyll	75810	E - 140, E - 141	Green
Cochineal	75740	E - 120	Red

(Natural Colorants are not certified)

C.I. No.   –   Colour Index Number

E.U. No.   –   European Union Number

F D & C   –   Food, Drug and Cosmetics

FDA   –   Food and Drug Administration

There are three bodies who give the information on the specifications for dyes used in pharmaceuticals.

(i) European Union (EU),

(ii) The American Food and Drug Administration (FDA), and

(iii) Food and Agriculture Organization of the United Nations and World Health Organization (WHO/FAO).

All the capsule manufacturers use colours which are approved for human consumption. This is for human safety.

For making the coloured transparent capsules, approved colours are dissolved in water and colour solution is added into gelatin solution in required quantities to get desired coloured capsules.

For making opaque white capsules, Titanium dioxide dispersion made in water is added to the gelatin solution in desired quantity. In short, to make coloured or opaque white, or coloured opaque capsule, colour solution or pigment suspension is required to be added to the gelatin solution.

As far as possible, natural colours (pharma grade) are not used for making coloured capsules, as the colour of the capsules get faded very fast due to sunlight.

■■■

4.

MANUFACTURE OF TWO-PIECE EMPTY HARD GELATIN CAPSULE

4.1 INTRODUCTION

Majority of capsule manufacturers, manufacturing the capsules on automatic capsule making machines are using "COLTON TYPE" machines. The given rated capacity of capsule production on 'COLTON NO. 750' machine was 6,72,000 capsules of size no. '0' in 24 hours.

Progressively capsule manufacturing companies modified their machines to get higher production of capsules. It is said that the modified machines have rated capacity of production of more than 2 million capsules per machine in 24 hours. The efforts are on to increase the output to 3 million capsules per machine in 24 hours.

Broadly speaking the manufacturing of capsules is done as under.

A stock solution of gelatin is prepared in stainless steel melter mixer. A part of it is processed for making cap shells and other part is processed for making body shells. The processing of each part is being done by adding the process additives and colourants to make the solution ready for dipping. Processed gelatin solutions are transferred into respective cap and body dip (tanks) pans fixed on the capsule making machine.

Cap and body shells are made by dipping prelubricated cap and body dipping moulds (pins) into the gelatin solution of cap and body dipping pans respectively. The gelatin films thus formed on the surface of cap and body dipping moulds are set by blowing the cold air on them. Thereafter they are dried in cap and body drying hoods by the air whose temperature and humidity are precise and controlled. Thus, dried shells are stripped (removed) from the moulds, cut to proper size and joined together in the joiner blocks of the machine to form capsules.

4.2 MANUFACTURE OF HARD GELATIN CAPSULES

The flow diagram of manufacturing of Hard Gelatin Capsule is given below :

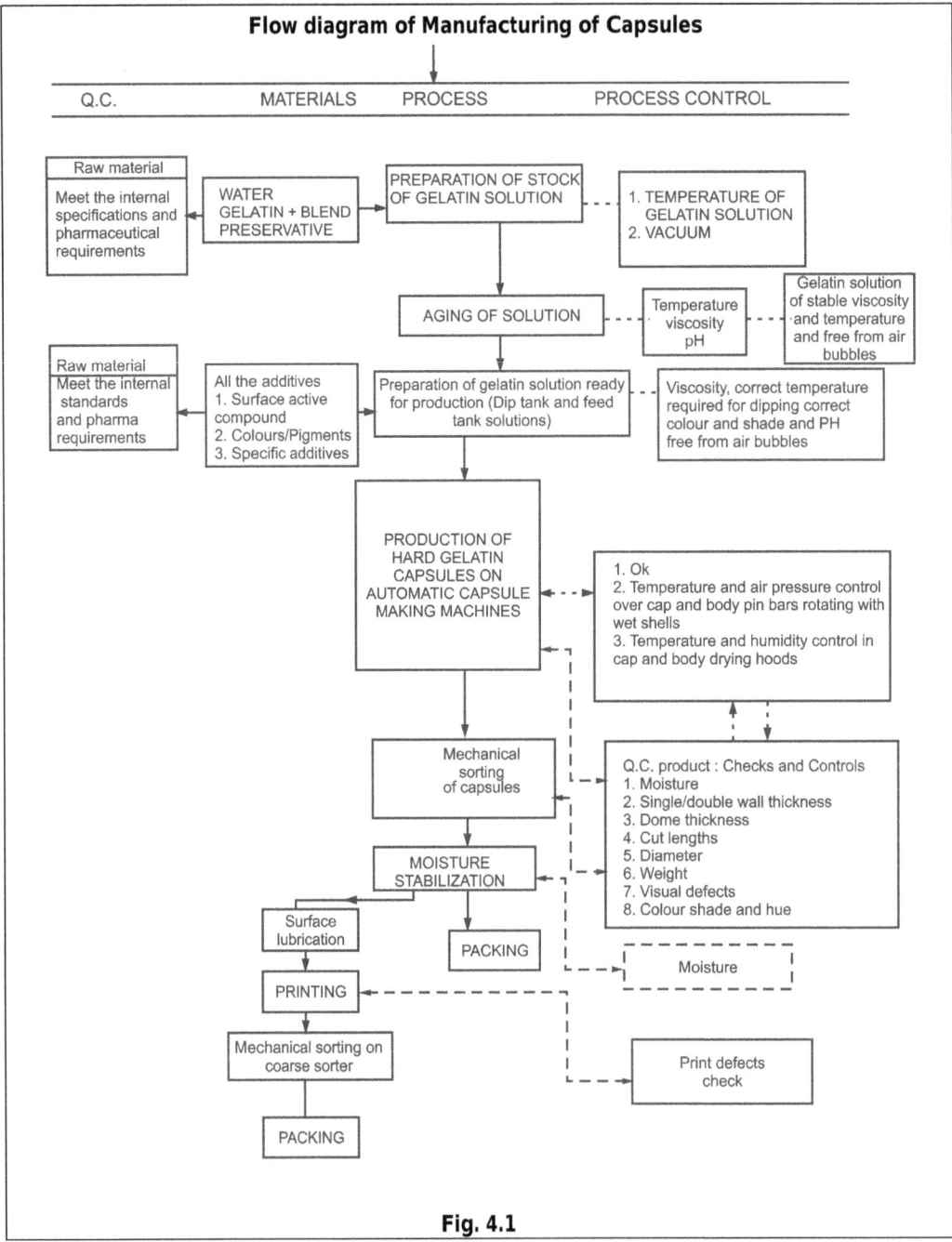

Fig. 4.1

Each manufacturing step shown in the flow diagram is given in detail as under :

4.3 PREPARATION OF STOCK GELATIN SOLUTION

Gelatins of required specifications are normally procured from more than one supplier. The required quantity of gelatin for making the stock solution is obtained by blending the gelatins procured from different suppliers. While blending the gelatin (granules or powders) the main objective is to get optimum production and best quality of capsules. Therefore, each manufacturer maintains a proprietary blend.

Deionised and microbial free hot water is used for making the gelatin solution. Normally, temperature of the hot water used is of 60°C (140°F). Some manufacturers maintain the hot water temperature at 80°C. This is being kept to reduce the bacterial load of gelatin solution and to solubilise the gelatin properly.

If the preservatives are to be used, they are added at the time of making the solution.

Normally, the time cycle for making the gelatin solution is of $3^1/_2$ to 4 hours. At the end of this cycle, clear transparent gelatin solution is obtained.

The jacketed stainless steel tank, fitted with stirrer (for mixing), known as 'MELTER MIXER', of desired capacity is used for making the gelatin solution. The melter mixer is designed to stand for high vacuum. The jacket is made to heat the tank with the help of heating media within the jacket. Heating system is fitted with temperature controller to heat and control the temperature of the heating media. Through this system the temperature of the gelatin solution in the melter mixer is controlled.

Deionised, microbial free hot water of required quantity is added into the melter mixer. The gelatin blend of required quantity (pre-weighted) is added into the hot water. The added mass is kept being stirred with the help of stirrer. The mass is kept at required temperature with the help of jacketed heating system. The required temperature is maintained till the time solution is inside the tank. During stirring and melting, vacuum is applied to the tank to remove the entrapped air from the gelatin solution. If the air bubbles are not removed and the solution is used without removing the air bubbles, for dipping, they will appear on the gelatin shells in the form of air bubbles. It is important to note that particle size of gelatin granules is closely related to bubble problem. If the particle size of gelatin granules is very fine and if it is used in solution making, it gives lot of air-bubbles in the gelatin solution. After the solution is ready, it is taken into another stainless steel tank called 'aging tank' for cooling.

4.4 AGING OF GELATIN SOLUTION

The gelatin solution is made at higher temperature (60°C) in melter mixer. This temperature is much higher than the temperature of the gelatin solution, used for (45°C to 50°C) dipping. At higher temperature, the degradation rate of gelatin solution is high; therefore, the rate of loss of viscosity is also high. Such gelatin solution is not suitable for making capsules. The rate of loss of viscosity of gelatin solution is much less in the temperature zone where the dipping is carried out. In this temperature zone, the viscosity of gelatin solution remains fairly stable. This state of solution is good for dipping operation.

The process of cooling down the temperature of gelatin solution removed from the melter mixer is carried out in jacketed stainless steel tank. The tank is fitted with temperature controlled heating arrangement. This is required to control the temperature of the gelatin solution, in the tank. This tank is also called as 'aging tank'.

In this tank, the temperature of the gelatin solution is brought down to the temperature slightly above the dipping temperature (50 to 55°C). At this temperature the viscosity is fairly stable.

During the process of cooling, two things take place :

(i) Fine bubbles still present in the gelatin solution (produced due to handling) come upon the surface of gelatin solution. Therefore, the solution below the surface, which is to be used for making capsules, is practically free from air bubbles.

(ii) The temperature of the gelatin solution gets uniform throughout and it attends the required temperature.

4.5 PREPARATION OF GELATIN SOLUTION FOR DIPPING AND FEEDING

The hard gelatin capsule making machine has two dip tanks, one for dipping cap dipping moulds and another for dipping body dipping moulds. They are fitted in the dipping section of the machine.

Each dip tank is attached with one feed tank, (also known as make up tank) to feed the gelatin solution which is consumed during dipping.

All these tanks have water jackets, and are fitted with independent heaters and temperature controllers to control the gelatin solution present in them. For starting a new batch of capsule, aged transparent gelatin solution is taken into cap and body feed tanks respectively. Cap and body solutions are coloured according to the customers requirements, by adding colour solutions, pigment suspensions etc. Surface active agent sodium lauryl sulfate (SLS) and other production aids are added as per the requirements. After addition of all these, the viscosities of the gelatin solutions, in the respective feed tanks for cap and body are adjusted as required for dipping by adding deionised hot water. It is important to note that the requirement of viscosity of gelatin solution for dipping, depends on size of capsule cap and body of that size and speed of machine. Thus prepared solutions in the feed tanks are fed into the dip tanks. The next feed tanks are made with lower viscosity, than the first one. This is required to compensate the water loss in the dip tank due to evaporation. Instead of adding the evaporated water directly into the dip tanks, it is added through feeding solutions.

4.6 PRODUCTION OF EMPTY HARD GELATIN CAPSULE ON FULLY AUTOMATIC 'COLTON' TYPE HARD GELATIN CAPSULE MAKING MACHINE

For understanding the manufacturing process of capsule on fully automatic machine, it is essential, first to know about (i) Dipping moulds or pins, (ii) pin bars and (iii) machines. They are described below :

4.6.1 Dipping Moulds or Pins (Basic Design)

For manufacturing every size of capsule, two different dipping moulds are required, one for cap and another for body. These moulds are made from stainless steel rods and their dimensions are very precisely controlled. The moulds are so designed that cap and body shells formed on them have a hemisphericle shape at their closed ends and cylindrical portion tapering towards the open end. The taper of the mould is of the order of 0.1 mm to 0.3 mm/cm in length. The dimensions on the moulds are so designed and their tolerances are so selected that, outer diameter at the cut end of body shell formed on the body mould is slightly more than the inside diameter at the dome base of corresponding cap shell. The cap and body shells made on such pins hold them together when joined.

The locking type of dipping moulds are made by putting the locking features on them.

4.6.2 Pin Bars

The stainless steel (SS) bar on which cap pins are fixed, is called CAP PIN BAR. The stainless steel bar on which body pins are fixed, is called BODY PIN BAR. On each bar 30 pins are fixed with uniform pitch. On "COLTON 750" machine, 750 pin bars of cap and 750 pin bars of body are used.

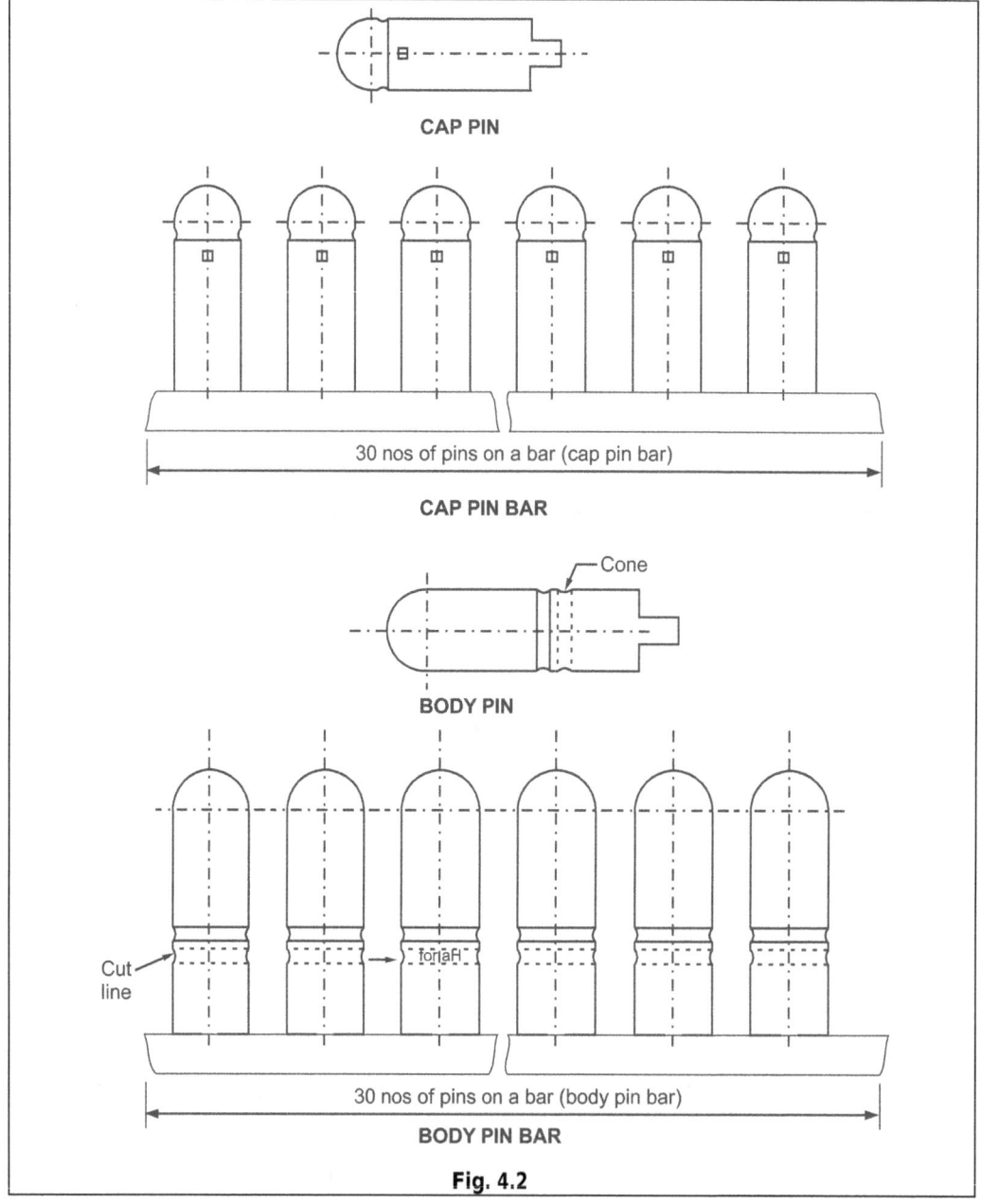

Fig. 4.2

4.6.3 Colton Type Capsule Manufacturing Machine

Fig. 4.3 : 750 Automatic Coltan Machine

'COLTON 750' machine is approximately 40' in length, 6' in width and 5' in height. The machine has two independent sections, one for holding and processing cap pin bars and second section for holding and processing body pin bars. Each section has 750 pin bars of cap and 750 pin bars of body respectively. Pin bars are cycled in the machine in approximately 45 minutes. Each section has independent mechanism for (1) Lubricating 30 pins at a time, (2) Dipping a set of 5 pin bars in gelatin solution in dipping bath, (3) Rotation of 5 pin bars, coated with gelatin solution for uniform distribution and turning the pins from facing downward position to upward position. The upward position is essential for blowing the air to set and dry the gelatin film on pins, (4) Moving the pins in the drying hoods with the group of 20 pin bars, (5) after drying, separating each bar and then pushing it into autohead for stripping, cutting and joining operations. When pin bars undergo all these operations, they complete one cycle.

It is important to note that cap and body pin bars undergo all the above operations, independently in their respective sections, but all these operations are done simultaneously in a synchronous way. The continuous running of machine is very important for the production of good quality of capsules. Therefore, the mechanisms used in the machine must be very reliable and sturdy.

4.6.4 The Manufacturing of Capsule is Subdivided into the Following Steps

1. Lubrication of dipping moulds.
2. Dipping of pins bars.
3. Distribution of gelatin film uniformly.
4. Setting of distributed film.
5. Drying.
6. Stripping, cutting and joining.
7. Coarse sorting.
8. Off the machine drying.
9. Electronically and/or visually sorting.
10. Final packing.

It is important to note that all operations of capsule manufacturing, right from beginning to final packing in boxes are carried out in a fully air-conditioned area. The finally packed capsules are also kept into air-conditioned godowns.

Flow Diagram of Operations Carried out on Capsule Making Machine :

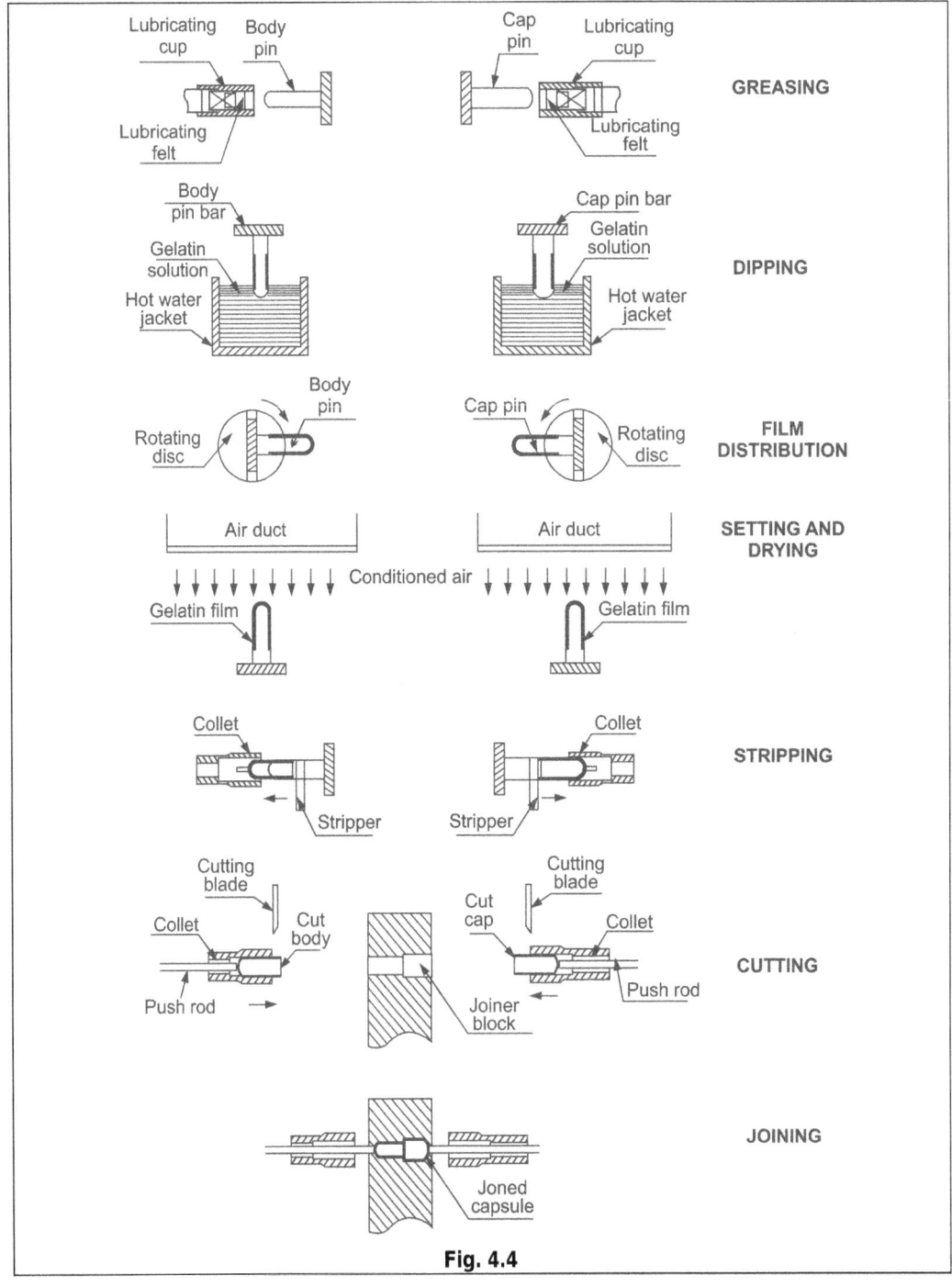

Fig. 4.4

The locations on the machine where the operations (Fig. 4.4) are carried out are shown in the Fig. 4.5.

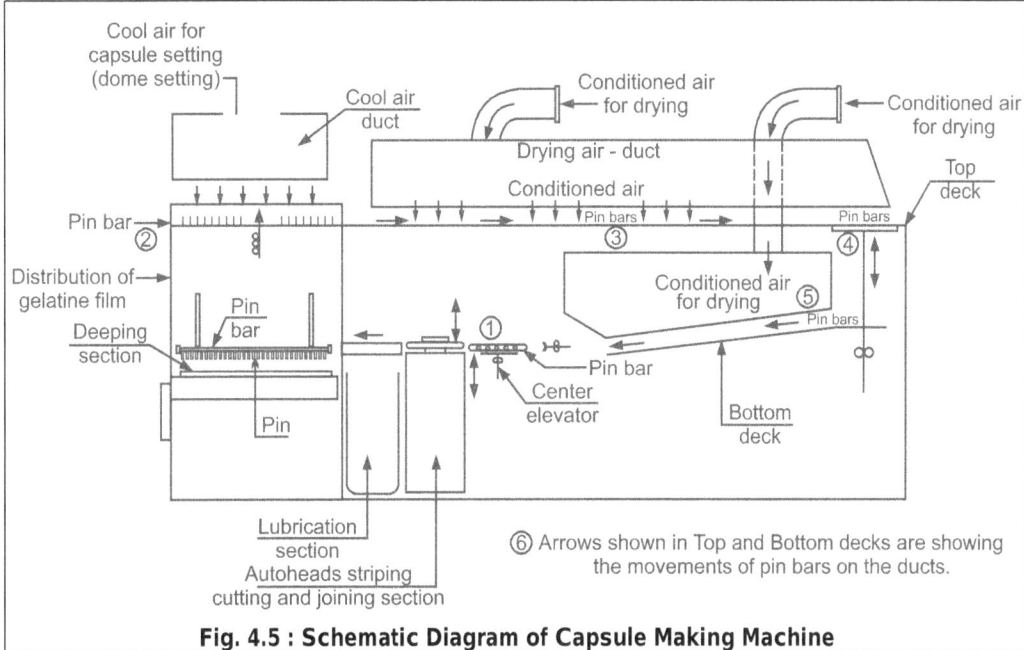

Fig. 4.5 : Schematic Diagram of Capsule Making Machine

4.6.4.1 Lubrication of Dipping Moulds

In the lubrication process, very small amount of lubricant is uniformly applied to the surface of the dipping mould with the help of lubricated felt. This operation is carried out with the help of rotating metallic or plastic cup containing lubricated felt. This metallic or plastic cup is called 'lubricating cup'.

The function of the lubricant is to prevent the gelatin film from adhering too strongly to the dipping mould. This helps the easy stripping of dried gelatin film from the mould surface during stripping operation. Each manufacturer uses his own lubricant formula. In old days the mixture of calcium soap dispersed in oil alongwith waxes was used as the lubricant.

In Colton machine, after stripping operation, bar is pushed into lubricating section of the machine. 30 dipping moulds are lubricated at a time by 30 rotating lubricating cups. After lubrication, bar is pushed forward into dipping section for dipping operation.

4.6.4.2 Dipping of Pin Bars

Dipping tank is rectangular in shape. It is made from stainless steel material. It is made up of two rectangular boxes fitted into one another. The top surfaces of both the boxes are open. The two boxes are fitted into one another in such a way that a sufficient gap is maintained between them. The outer surface of the outer tank is provided with water jacket fitted with heater and temperature controller. This is provided to control the temperature of the gelatin solution in the two boxes. The inner box is fitted with inbuilt gear pump. It rotates the gelatin solution by taking it from outer box to inner box. Thus, pumped gelatin solution goes back to outer box again by passing it over the edge of inner box. This process of circulating the gelatin in two boxes is ON all the time, during production. This arrangement is made in order to maintain the constant level of gelatin solution in the inner box. By this arrangement, when the dipping moulds are dipped in the gelatin solution in the inner box, the dip length of the film remains constant. When the dipping takes place, the level of the gelatin solution in the outer box goes down, but the level of gelatin solution in the inner box remains constant. The makeup solution is always added in the outer tank to make up the pick up loss.

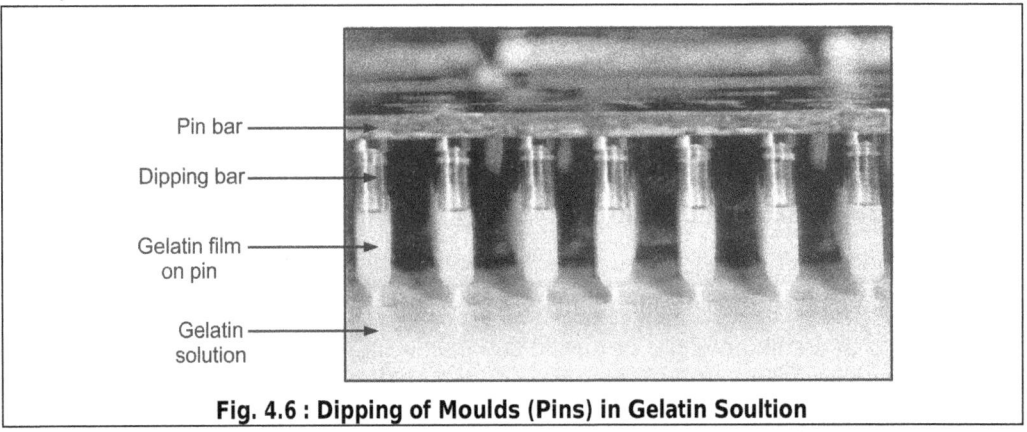

Fig. 4.6 : Dipping of Moulds (Pins) in Gelatin Soultion

Before starting the dipping operation, it is made sure that gelatin solutions in the dip tank and feed tank have correct viscosity and temperature as per the production norms and controls fitted on the tanks are functioning perfectly. Different capsule manufacturers have different production norms for viscosity and temperature values. Normally, the gelatin solution temperature range used for dipping operation is between 45°C to 55°C.

The viscosity of the gelatin solution in the dip tank is controlled with the help of Brookfield type Industrial Viscometer. If viscosity goes out of order, it gets automatically controlled by addition of water.

The pin bars are at room temperature before dipping. The sets of 5 pin bars (150 pins) are gently lowered into the gelatin solution in the cap and body dip tanks respectively. Then, they are slowly withdrawn. Gelatin solution is picked up on the dipping moulds due to gelation. The quantity picked up by the dipping moulds is governed by the viscosity of the solution, the temperature of the dipping moulds and the withdrawal rate of moulds.

4.6.4.3 Distribution of Picked Up Gelatin Film Uniformly on Pins and Setting of Film

Immediately after withdrawal, there is an accumulation of unset gelatin solution which runs down towards the dome of the mould. To spread this gelatin solution evenly over the surface of the dipping moulds, the set of pin bars are rotated around the horizontal axis for two and half times, in the rotating disc. (Two and half time rotation of pin bars is provided on COLTON 750 machines).

While rotating, the bars are moved to the top deck of the machine, and the direction of the moulds gets changed by 180°; thereby hemispherical domes of the dipping moulds get pointed in the upward direction. As the bars rotate, they pass through a stream of cool air which sets the film firmly on the moulds. Once the film is set firmly on the mould, it does not change its profile.

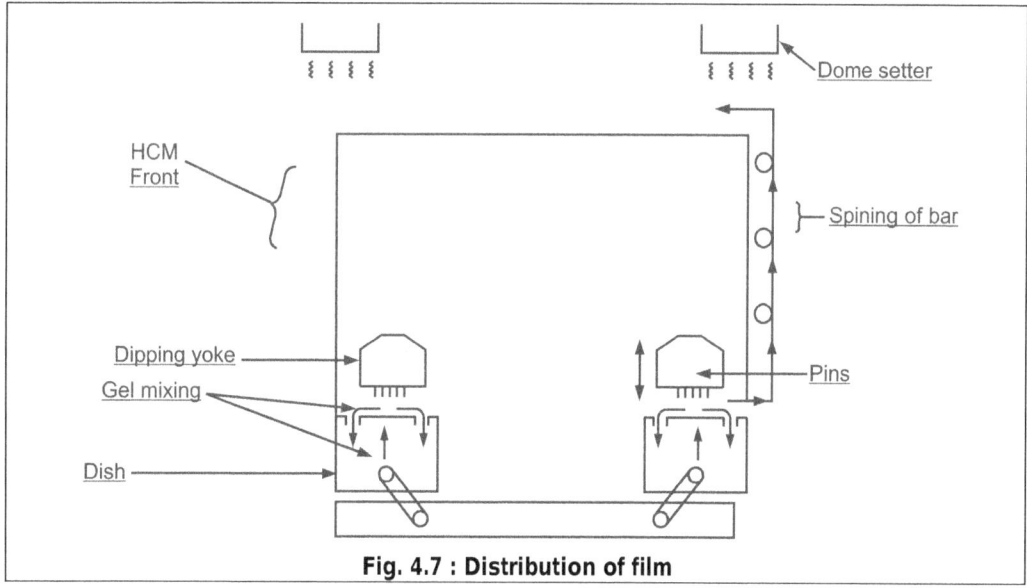

Fig. 4.7 : Distribution of film

4.6.4.4 Drying

Pin bars travel through 5 drying hoods. Three drying hoods are provided on the top deck and two hoods are provided on the bottom deck. When the pin bars travel through all the drying hoods, the wet film (capsule) on the dipping moulds get dried.

When the pin bars travel on top and bottom decks through drying hoods, a large volume of humidity and temperature controlled air is directly blown over the pins to dry the film. Direct blowing of air on the pin is achieved through perforations which are provided at the bottom plate of the drying hoods.

For capsule drying, the following guidelines are important :

1. Gelatin gel gets into solution state at high temperature. Therefore air of high temperature cannot be used for drying, especially in first hood.
2. If the drying rate is high, wrinkles are formed on dome during drying and shells get vertical split because of heavy shrinkage.
3. Viscosity norms of dipping are fixed on the basis of pin temperature. Therefore the air temperature of the last hood is kept at room temperature.

The viscosity values for dipping get changed if the pin temperature changes. Therefore in drying process, when the pin bars come out of final drying duct, they are at room temperature. The drying conditions are adjusted such that the drying rate is low to start with, slowly reaches a maximum at the rear of the machine and then slows down when it is approaching the front. When the capsules are stripped from the dipping moulds, the moisture content is approximately between 15-18%. At this moisture content, capsules have good strength to stand mechanical operations of stripping, cutting and joining. Similarly at this moisture content, shells are smoothly cut.

4.6.4.5 Striping, Cutting and Joining

Stripping, cutting and joining operations of capsule are carried out in the autohead sections of the capsule making machine. After the shells are dried on the moulds, one cap pin bar, and one body pin bar is independently, but simultaneously fed into cap and body auto head sections. Here the cap and body shells are removed from the pins with the help of metal jaws. The jaws are normally made from brass pieces. The jaw material is softer than the dipping moulds, to avoid the wearout. The jaws get closed and pulled back along the pins and in the process, transfer the shells into the collets. Once the shells are transferred in the collets, the shell length is reset for correct cut length. The collets hold the shells tightly and collets are rotated against sharpened and hardened knives and the excess portion of the shell gets removed. The excess cut portion is called trimming. The trimmings of cap and body are collected by vacuum arrangement into the drums. They are used immediately or kept aside for reuse. The cap and body cut shells are moved into joiner blocks from collets with the help of push rods. After this operation, cap collets move backward and cap push rods support the caps at their domes and hold the caps in steady position for joining. Thereafter bodies are pushed into the caps by the body push rods. Once the joining operation is over, cap push rods move back and allow the joined capsules to get pushed on the conveyor belt from the joiner blocks with the help of body push rods. From conveyor belt capsules get transferred to coarse sorter.

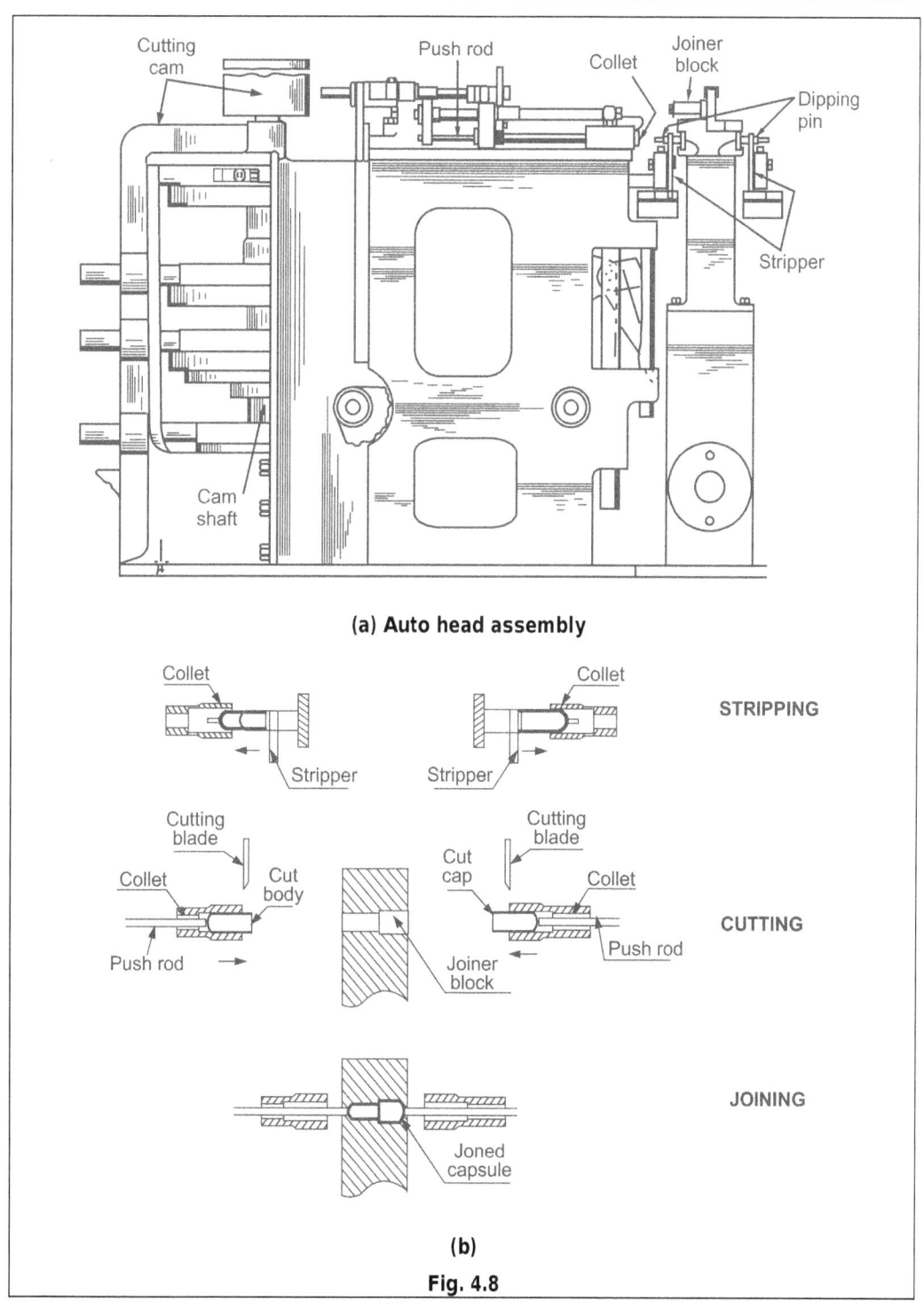

(a) Auto head assembly

(b)
Fig. 4.8

4.6.4.6 Coarse Sorter

Small percentage of damaged capsules do get produced during production. Therefore, such capsules need to be sorted out. In olden days, they were sorted out by human inspection on conveyor belt. Now, such capsules are sorted out on mechanical sorter, known as coarse sorter. On this machine, defective capsules like badly joined capsules, telescoped capsules, capsule with cap rough cuts, loose caps, loose bodies, double capsules, oval capsules, long and short capsules etc. get automatically sorted out. Therefore, all the capsules coming from capsule making machine are conveyed to the coarse sorter to sort the damaged capsules. The capsules coming out of coarse sorter are collected in special drums. These drums have perforated base at the bottom. Size of the perforation is such that capsules do not come out of it.

4.6.4.7 Off Machine Drying

It is essential to bring down the moisture content of capsules from 15–18% to 13–16%. It is because at this level of moisture of capsules, they are flexible; at the same time, they have good mechanical strength. Similarly the dimensions of capsules at this moisture content are most suitable for capsule filling machines. The moisture content of capsule is brought down to the required level in the following manner.

The capsules, as stated above, are collected from the coarse sorter into the drum having perforated bottom. Conditioned air is blown on the capsules from the bottom of the drum. This process brings the moisture of capsule from 15–18% to 13–16%. The drying of the capsules from 15-18% to 13-16% moisture, is not done on the machine; therefore, it is called "off machine drying".

4.6.4.8 Electronic/Manual Sorting

The defects of capsules which are not possible to sort out on coarse sorter, are manually and/or electronically sorted. Foreign capsule (different colour, size) can only be sorted by human eye or electronic eye. Difference in colour shade of capsule can only be sorted by human eye. By sorting the capsules in this way, defect free capsules are supplied to the customers.

4.6.4.9 Final Packing

The capsules free from all the defects are counted first and finally packed in high density, antistatic poly bag. This bag is put either into round drum or in rectangular cardboard box.

4.7 QUALITY CONTROL

20 to 25 years back, quality control department i.e. inspectors who check the quality parameters of capsules were responsible for the quality of capsules produced. This situation has changed.

Now, the operators who produce capsules on machine are responsible for quality of capsules. They also control the process parameters.

Quality Assurance Department cross checks the product and finally accepts or rejects the lot.

Normally, following parameters are checked on the computer screen and are controlled by the operators.

1. Viscosity and temperature of dipping and feeding solutions.
2. Dew point of air used for setting, drying.
3. Temperature and air pressure of air used for setting wet film.
4. Temperature and air pressure of air used in various drying ducts.

The product is checked at fixed intervals :

1. Weight of cap, body and capsules.
2. Single/double wall thickness at the cut end of cap and body.
3. Dome thickness of cap and body.
4. Shoulder thickness of cap and body.
5. Cut length of cap and body.
6. Unlocked joined length.
7. Diameter of cap and body at cut end.
8. Profile of cap and body.

The colour shade of cap and body is checked very frequently by pasting periodically the sample of the capsule from the running production on the control chart.

If the product is going out of specifications, the operator immediately tries to correct the process/machine and brings back the product in specification limits. The product which is produced out of specification limits is set aside and destroyed.

If the machine is stopped for correcting the process, the equilibrium condition of drying the capsule gets disturbed. The equilibrium condition is very important for production of good capsules. Therefore, as far as possible, all efforts are made to correct the process without stoppage of the machine. The product produced during the correction is set aside. "Set aside product" is evaluated and accept/reject decision is taken. It is said that this correction is more economical than stopping the machine and losing the production. If the machine needs to be corrected for mechanical correction, then the only choice is to stop the machine.

In short, good capsule manufacturing is not an easy task. One has to be vigilant throughout the production run.

■■■

5.

PRINTING OF EMPTY CAPSULES

5.1 INTRODUCTION

With the introduction of printing on capsules, the identity of the product became more specific. To make it further more specific, there was a need to print more information like name or emblem of the company, brand name of the product, product code number of the pharmaceutical company, dosage specifications etc.

With today's capsule printing technology, all these things stated above can be printed on capsule. This has resulted into creating more confidence about the genuineness of the drug in use. (Please refer Chapter 2 – printed matter, its pattern on printed capsules – page no. 2.26, Article 2.3.6).

5.2 HISTORY OF CAPSULE PRINTING

The printing of empty capsules started in U.S.A. It started in early 1950's and dramatically increased in 1960's. The idea of printing capsule came from printing of candy gum.

Initially experiments were done to print filled capsules; but they were not very successful as during printing of filled capsules, some capsules used to get broken, resulting into spillage of powder. Similarly, print quality used to be poor and printing equipment used to get damaged. Due to these problems, instead of printing on filled capsules, printing on empty capsules was started.

In U.S.A. there are three companies who are manufacturing capsule printing machines namely,

1. M/s. R. W. Hartnett Company.
   Philadelphia, U.S.A.
2. M/s Ackley Machine Corporation
   Moorstown N.J., U.S.A.
3. M/s Markem Corporation
   Keene N.H., U.S.A.

There are few empty capsule manufacturing companies who manufacture capsule printing machines for their own use. They have done modifications on their machines to get better print quality. The names of few such companies are :

1. M/s Associated Capsules (Pvt.) Ltd.
   ACG Worldwide – Mumbai India.
2. M/s Shionogi – Qualicaps – Japan.

The capsule printing machine manufacturers are producing different models to meet the requirements of single or double linear printing, radial printing on oriented or non-oriented capsules with single or bicoloured prints. The different models give different outputs.

5.3 HISTORY OF PRINTING OF CAPSULES IN INDIA

The printed capsules, printed with edible coloured ink were first started in India around 1960s. M/s Unichem laboratories desired to put 'CHLORAMPHENICOL' in the form of printed capsules only. The printing machines were not available in India at that time; therefore capsules were printed manually one by one by the lady operators with the help of rubber stamps bearing the letter "Unichem". The drug was filled in size 'o' Blue/Blue Colour capsules and the ink used was edible black colour ink, manufactured locally.

M/s Lepetit (Now Ranabaxy) in new Delhi brought printing machine from Italy to print filled capsules. It was a very low output printing machine (10,000 to 20,000 capsules printing per hour). Due to breakage of filled capsules during printing operation they could not operate this machine for a long time. The printing machine used by Ranabaxy was by M/s Fratelli Zanasi s.p.a. Bologna Italy.

M/s Deys Medical Stores, Kolkatta brought low output capsule printing machine from R.W. Hartnett – U.S.A.

M/s Pfizer – Dumex imported high output R.W. Hartnett machine from U.S.A. They used this machine till the time they started getting the supply of printed capsules from empty capsule manufacturing companies in India.

Today almost all the empty capsule manufacturing companies are supplying printed capsules to their customers. Associated Capsules (Pvt.) Ltd. – ACG Worldwide, Mumbai is one of the companies in India who has excellent facilities to print most complex type of printing on empty capsules.

In India, all types of printing on capsule is carried out. It may be linear or double linear, non-oriented or oriented. It may be radial non-oriented or oriented or 360° printing on full cylindrical surface of capsules. The figures of different types of printing are given in Chapter No. 2 on Identification attributes of capsules.

5.4 CAPSULE PRINTING PROCESS

The printing on capsule is carried out by "OFF SET" process. The schematic diagram of off-set process is given in Fig. 5.1. The message to be printed is engraved on highly polished metal roller or cylinder. This is also called rotogravure roller or cylinder. This revolves in the reservoir of printing ink. During revolving, the ink gets filled in the engraving. When the metal roller rotates further, it comes in contact with sharp edge known as "doctors blade". It only removes the ink from the surface of the metal roller or cylinder, but not the ink in the engraving. The ink impression in the engraving of rotogravure roller or cylinder gets transferred to the rubber roller when rubber roller comes in contact with the rotogravure roller or cylinder. Finally when capsules pass under rubber roller, the ink impression on the rubber roller gets transferred on to the surface of capsule; thus capsule gets printed.

All the capsule printing machines which are available are running on the same basic principle as described above.

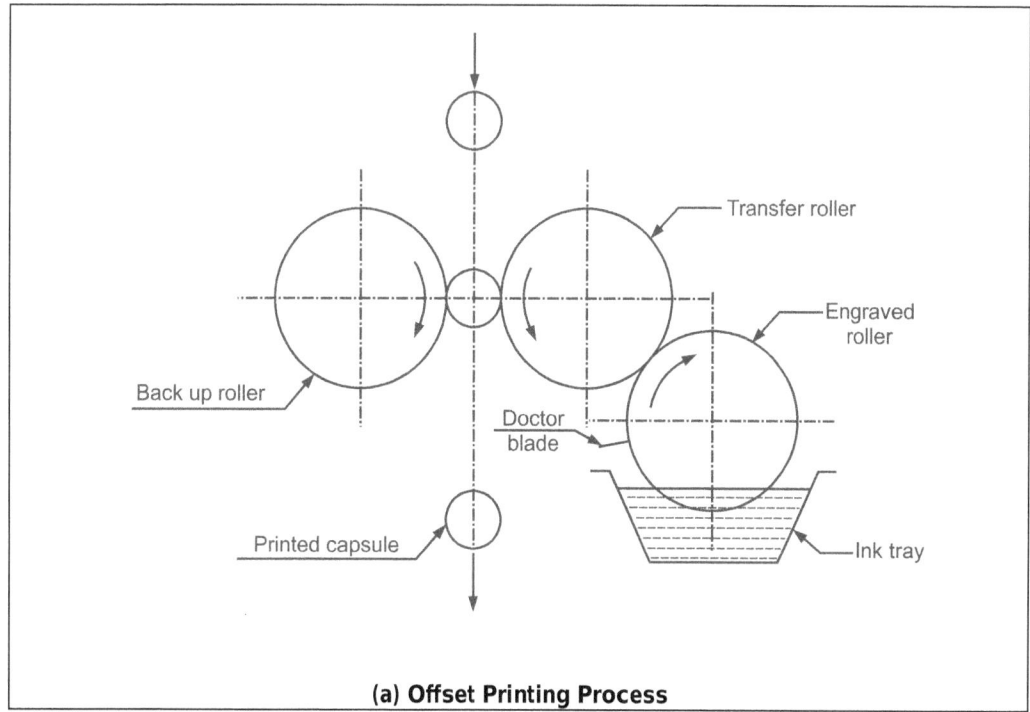

(a) Offset Printing Process

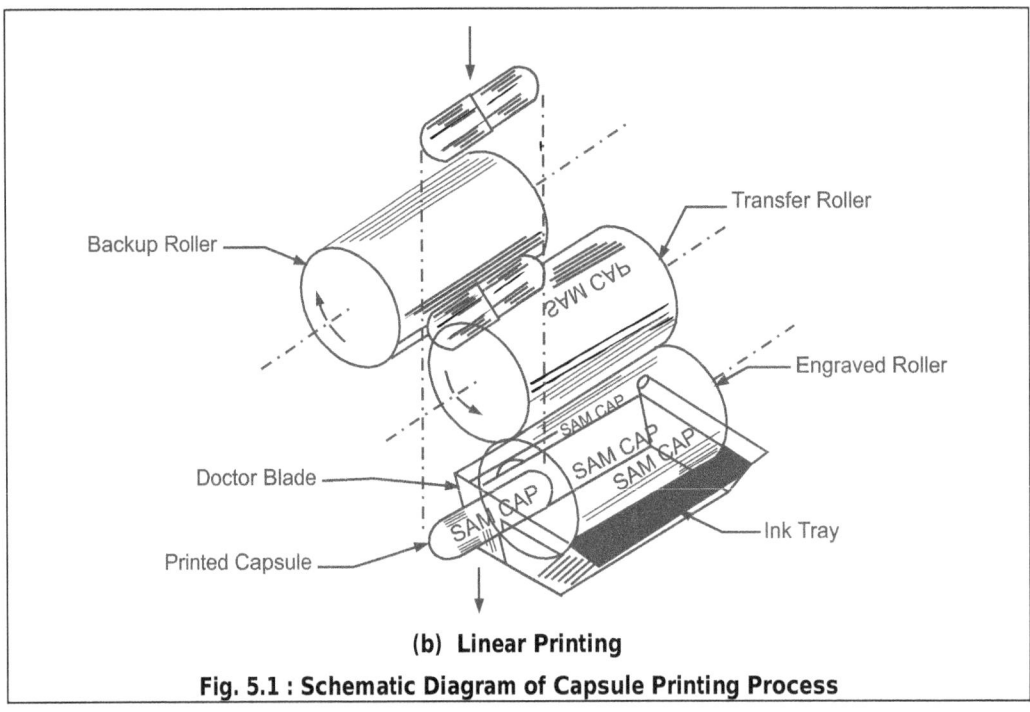

(b) Linear Printing

Fig. 5.1 : Schematic Diagram of Capsule Printing Process

5.5 CAPSULE PRINTING MACHINES

Different machines are available for carrying out different types of printing. They are shown in the following figures :

1. Markem Machines.

(a) Capsule Printing Machine, Markem

(b) Capsule Printing Machine, Markem Mark 11
Fig. 5.2

2. R.W. Hartnett Machine δ-model.

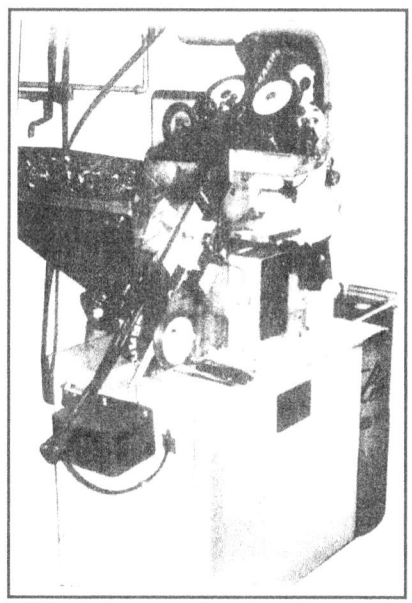

Fig. 5.3 : Capsule Printing Machine, Hartnett (Model DELTA)

3. 16 row R.W. Hartnett machine.

(a) 16 Row R.W. Hartnett Machine

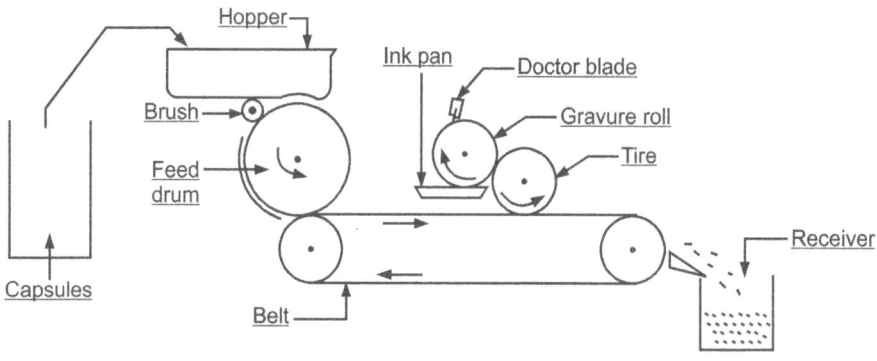

(b) Schematic Diagram of Printing Process

Fig. 5.4

4. High Output Ackley machine.

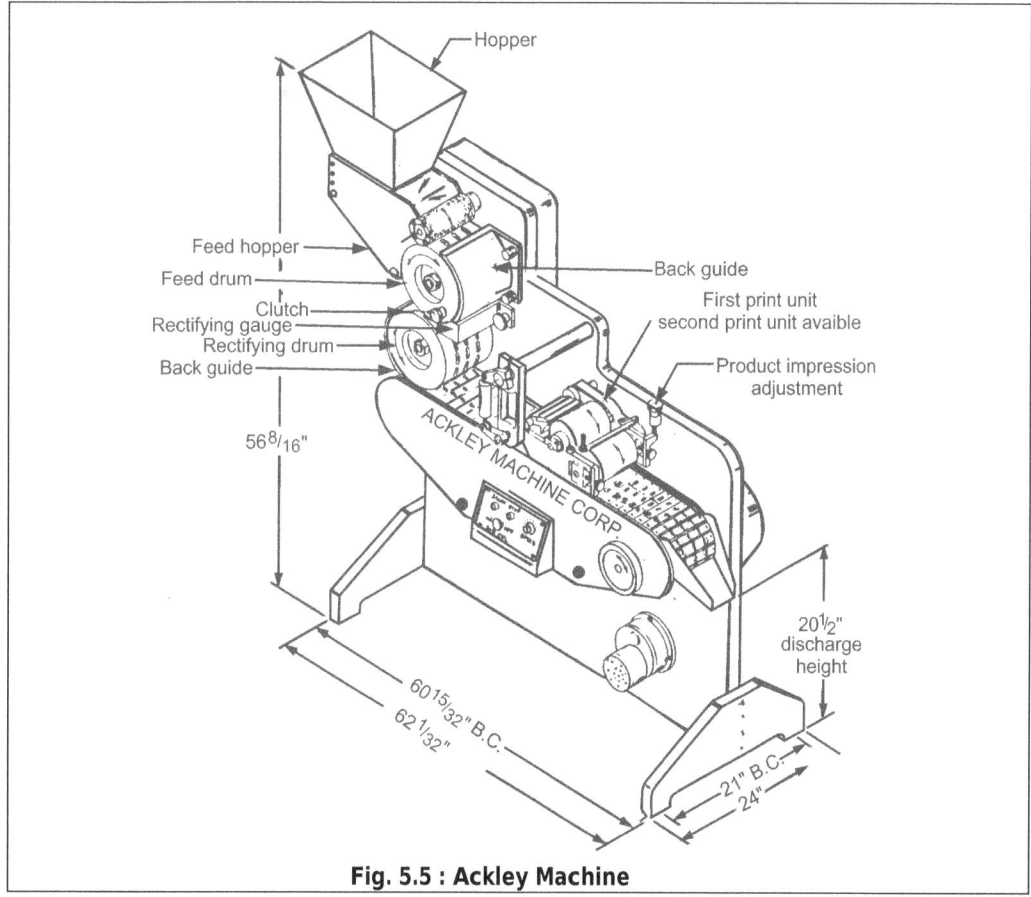

Fig. 5.5 : Ackley Machine

As the printing of empty capsule is carried out by empty capsule manufacturers, they normally provide the formate which gives the "Average printing coverage area in various types of printing". One such formate given by ACG worldwide – India is given below :

Table 5.1 : Logo Dimensions for Linear Printing

Capsule size	A	B	C	D
00	16.6	3.0	3.8	6.4
0	15.8	2.8	3.8	6.0
1	14.2	2.5	3.8	5.2
2	12.8	2.3	3.8	4.5
3	11.4	2.1	3.8	3.8
4	10.8	1.9	3.8	3.5
'0' EL	16.6	2.8	3.8	6.4

With the courtesy of ACG Worldwide, Mumbai.   **in millimetres**

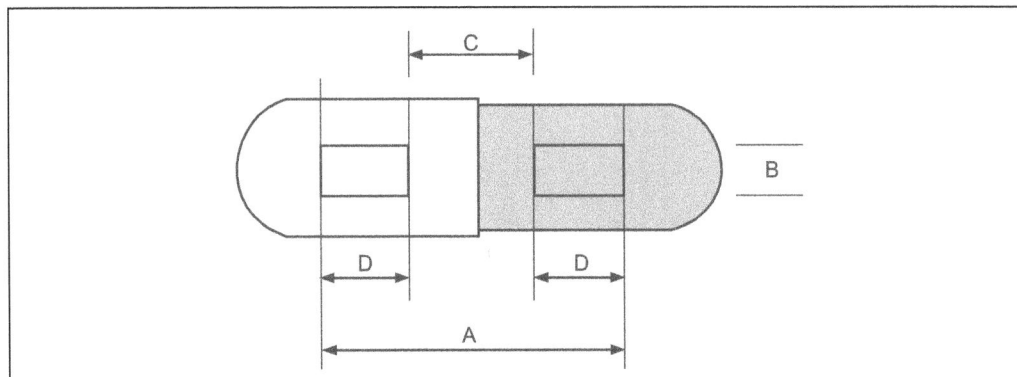

B - Connotes maximum height of the letters in mm
D - Represents recommended available space for linear printing

Fig. 5.6

Table 5.2 : Logo Dimensions for Radial Printing

Capsule size	A	B	C	D
00	15	19	4	5.5
0	14	18	4	5
1	12	16	4	4
2	10	14	4	3
3	9	13	4	2.5
4	8.2	12	3.8	2.2
'0' EL	15	18	4	5.5

With the courtesy of ACG Worldwide, Mumbai.   **in millimetres**

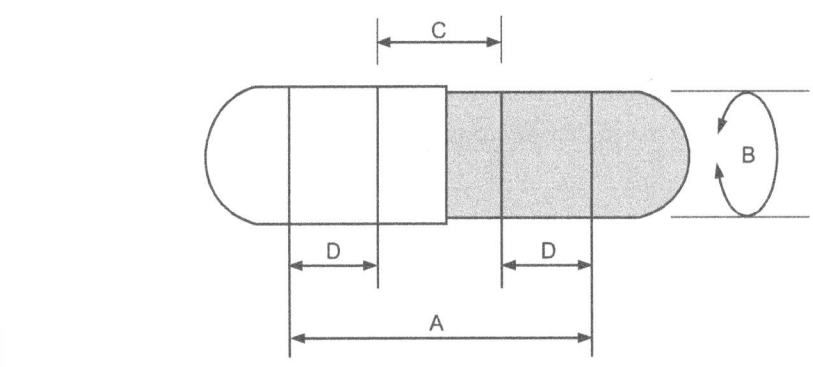

B - Connotes maximum peripheral length in mm.
D - Represents maximum height of the letters above the locking zone.

Fig. 5.7

Table 5.3 : Logo Dimensions for 360° Printing

Capsule size	A	Circumference (B)		C	D
		Cap (B2)	Body (B1)		
00	15	26.85	25.81	4	5.5
0	14	24.05	23.05	4	5
1	12	21.76	20.82	4	4
2	10	20	19.09	4	3
3	9	18.37	17.49	4	2.5
4	8.2	16.74	15.89	3.8	2.2
'0' EL	15	24.05	23.05	4	5.5

With the courtesy of ACG Worldwide, Mumbai.   **in millimetres**

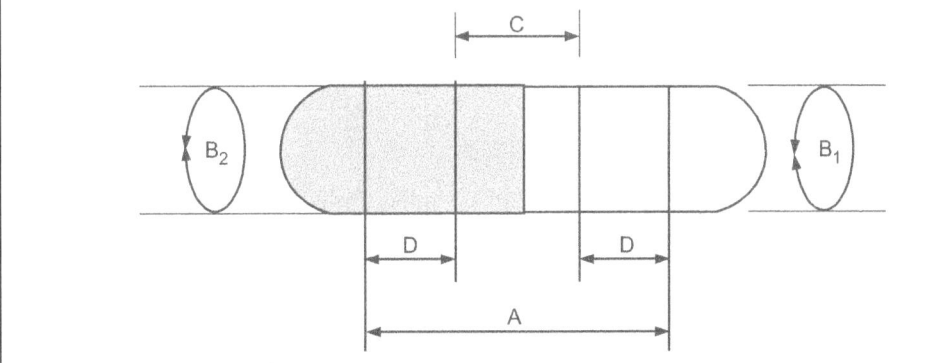

B_1 - Denotes maximum peripheral length of cap of capsule in mm.
B_2 - Denotes maximum peripheral length of body of capsule in mm.
D - Represents maximum height of print message above the locking zone C.

Fig. 5.8

5.6 PRINTING INK

One of the early makers of edible printing ink for printing empty capsules was M/s F.G. Oke Inc. U.S.A. M/s colorcon U.S.A. also manufacture edible printing inks in various colour shades. M/s. Markem U.S.A. also markets the edible printing inks along with their capsule printing machines.

Now-a-days good number of empty capsule manufacturing companies manufacture their own printing inks to reduce the printing cost.

Edible capsule printing ink is manufactured by dispersing the insoluble pigments or lake colours (edible grade) in shellac solution made in alcohol. Other ingredients of pharma grade are also added in ink to improve the quality of printing. Edible printing inks are also manufactured from water soluble edible polymers, but the quality of print is not good. Therefore, shellac base printing ink is mainly used by the capsule printers.

The components of shellac base printing ink are as follows :

1. Shellac
2. Surface active compound
3. Colourants
    (a) Pigments
    (b) Lake Colours
4. Suspending agent
5. Organic solvents

The general information about each component and its purpose is given below :

1. **Shellac :**

Shellac is a natural resinous material. It is used in food industry. It is safe for human consumption. 30 to 40% w/v shellac solution in ethyl alcohol rectified spirit denatured alcohol is normally used in printing ink.

Instead of using shellac, M/s colorcon co. is using esterified shellac for making ink. This is a patented process. The mechanical parts of the machine which come in contact with shellac base ink are difficult to wash. But with the introduction of esterified shellac base ink, this problem is almost eliminated.

2. **Surface Active Compounds :**

Dimethyl polysiloxane, Lecithin are used as surface active compounds to reduce the surface tension for good pick-up of ink by the engraving on the metal roller.

3. **Colourants :**

The following pigments and lake colours of pharma grades or food grade are used for making coloured inks :

(i) Titanium dioxide.

(ii) Synthetic iron oxides (food grade), yellow, red, brown and black.

(iii) Aluminium or calcium lake colours of food grade.

(iv) Synthetic edible (water soluble) colours (food grade) are also used sometimes.

4. Organic Solvents :

Ethyl alcohol is the best solvent to make shellac solution for manufacture of capsule printing inks. The use of pure ethyl alcohol in the industries is discouraged in many countries. Ehtyl alcohol is also very expensive because of Government Taxes.

To overcome this problem, industrial spirit is used for making shellac solution. Sometimes it is also used alongwith iso-butyl alcohol, butyl alcohol etc. For controlling the drying rate of inks in the printing process, combinations of different alcohols are used.

The solvents which are used are covered by a guidance based on harmonized regulation from ICH (International Conference on Harmonization) initiative (EMEA 1997 : USDHH 1997).[*]

This guidance recommends the acceptable amounts of residual solvents in pharmaceuticals in terms of patient safety.

As the solvents used in printing ink are volatile, hardly any residual solvents remain in the print of the printed capsule.

The printing inks which are used are edible and their composition comply with the pharmaceutical legislation prevailing in the country of use.

During printing, lot of alcohol vapours get generated in the printing area. These vapours are harmful to the operators who operate the printing machines. Lot of care is taken to minimize this problem, but the best solution is to use the water base ink, instead of solvent base ink. Efforts are on to make good water base inks to overcome this problem.

5.7 PRINT DEFECTS

Printing of empty capsule is a process. It is therefore natural to get some print defects in printed capsule. The efforts are on to improve the printing process so that print defects would be eliminated to the extent possible. The standards followed in the industry are given hereunder in 'Print Defects Categorization'.

Classification of Print Defects :

---

[*] Ref : EMEA (1997) ICH Topic Q3 C; Impurities residual solvents note for guidance on impurities : Residual solvents (CPMP / ICH / 283 / 95) London. European Agency for the evaluation of medical products, PP 18).

Critical defect	Missing print or complete absence of the logo.
Major defect	Defects resulting in illegibility of print or non-identification of printed logo.
Minor defect	Printing defects, which do not affect the legibility or identification of the printed logo but detract from the visual appearance of the capsules.

Categorization of Print Defects :

Critical defects	Major defects	Minor defects
Unprinted	Illegible print	Multiple print Broken letters Smudged print Off-register Ink spots/Ink lines Light/dark print.

Categorization and description of Print Defects :

Sr. No.	Visual Defects	Description
1.	(PRINT | LOGO)	**INDICATION OF FULL PRINTED CAPSULES WITHOUT DEFECT**
2.	(PRINT | LOGO) (|)	**MISSING PRINT** It is a capsule with complete absence of print matter **CRITICAL DEFECT**
3.	(PRINT | LOGO) (PRINT | LOGO)	**SMUDGED PRINT** Capsule with extensive smudging resulting in illegibility of print matter **MAJOR DEFECT** Capsule with smudging resulting in partial illegibility of print matter.

contd. ...

4.	MULTIPLE PRINT
	Capsule with print in multiple positions resulting in illegibility of the print.
	MINOR DEFECT
5.	**CUT PRINT**
	Capsules with interruption in print matter causing illegibility of print matter
	MAJOR DEFECT
	Capsule with partial interruption in print matter but print matter remains legible
	MINOR DEFECT
6.	**OFF REGISTER PRINT**
	Capsules with letters missing resulting in non-identification of print matter.
	MAJOR DEFECT
	Capsules where registration is offset but print matter remains intact
	MINOR DEFECT
7.	**INK SPOT**
	Capsules with ink spots greater than 4 mm diameter.
	MAJOR DEFECT
	Capsule with ink spots between 1 mm diameter to 4 mm diameter.
	MINOR DEFECT
8.	**INK LINE**
	Capsules with line through print matter. Legibility is not affected
	MINOR DEFECT

* With the courtesy of ACG Worldwide, Mumbai.

Assessment of Capsule Print Defects :

Visual and printing defects are evaluated based on sample size and acceptance number derived from the ISO 2859 Part I using single sampling plan.

The AQLs indicated could be verified on a composite random sample drawn from $\sqrt{k} + 1$ cartons in the shipment, where k = number of cartons in the shipment.

Corresponding AQL and AOQL values are also provided therein.

AQL : Acceptable Quality Limit.

AOQL : Average Outgoing Quality Limit.

Printing Defects :

	Sample size[*]	Acceptance number	Rejection number	AQL %	AOQL %
Critical	1250	0	1	0.01	0.029
Major	1250	2	3	0.065	0.110
Minor	1250	21	22	1.0	1.2

[*] To be selected from $(\sqrt{k} + 1)$ cartons where k = number of cartons in the lot.

6.

PHARMACOPOEIAL AND INDUSTRIAL STANDARDS OF EMPTY HARD GELATIN CAPSULES

6.1 INTRODUCTION

If the product's monograph is given in pharmacopoeia, and if the product is to be used in pharmaceutical preparations, it is then mandatory that the product should meet all the standards given in the respective pharmacopoeia.

There are very few pharmacopoeias in the world who have covered monographs on empty hard gelatin capsules. The known pharmacopoeias who have covered the monographs on empty hard gelatin capsules are :

1. Indian pharmacopoeia (I.P.)
2. Japanese pharmacopoeia (J.P.)
3. Chinese Pharmacopoeia (C.P.)

It is interesting to note that all the pharmacopoeias have tests for filled capsules.

6.2 PHARMACOPOEIAL STANDARDS

Indian pharmacopoeia had published the monograph on empty gelatin capsule in I.P. 1986. Addendum II page 91-92 published on 1st January, 1992. In that monograph, under the standards the following points were covered :

1. Visual examination
2. Dimensions
3. Uniformity of weight
4. Loss on drying
5. Disintegration
6. Microbial limits

After the monograph was published, the capsule manufacturers in India found it difficult to make the capsules as per the standards given in the monograph. To overcome this problem, the monograph was modified by joint discussions among the I.P. committee, manufacturers of empty capsules and capsule users.

The modified monograph was published in I.P. 1996. In that monograph, following points were covered under standards :

1. Identification
2. Average weight
3. Disintegration
4. Microbial limits
5. Loss on drying

The test of "odour" is not covered under "standards" but it is described in this monograph under "Description".

It reads as follows :

"Odour – Keep 100 capsule shells in a well closed bottle for 24 hours at a temperature between 30° and 40°C the shells do not develop any foreign odour".

The similar test is given in United States of America FED. STD. No. 285 A Oct. 19, 1976, under characteristics of capsule 6.2.6. It appears that the purpose of the test was to know whether capsules have undergone any decomposition or deterioration. If it has undergone any deterioration, then such capsules should not be used for filling any medicinal powders.

The standards specified in I.P. 1996 are elaborated below :

6.2.1 Identification

This test is important to confirm that capsules are made from gelatin. The gelatin solution gives precipitation with tannic acid solution as well as picric acid solution. The capsule is tested as per this test to confirm that it is made from gelatin.

6.2.2 Average Weight

The monograph very clearly states that capsule should be conditioned at temperature 25°C ± 2°C and relative humidity 50% ± 5% for not less than 12 hours before conducting the test for Average Weight. The target weight of size 0, 1, 2, 3 and 4 is specified. The requirements of target weights for other sizes of capsule are not specified. It is to be decided mutually between the manufacturers of Hard gelatin capsule shells and the users. The average weight of particular size is determined by weighing 100 capsules of that size. The average weight is to be within ± 10% of the specified target weight.

Table 6.1

Size	Specified Target Weight (mg)
0	96
1	76

2	63
3	50
4	40

6.2.3 Disintegration

As specified in I.P., "the capsule shells comply with disintegration test for tablets and capsules using the discs (Appendix 7.1). The capsules disintegrate within 15 minutes".

This test is of functional importance. It is given in Japanese Pharmacopoeia and also in Federal Standard No. 285 A (Oct. 19, 1976) U.S.A.

As per the Japanese Pharmacopoeia individually five capsules are tested. Each one is taken separately, placed in a 100 ml. conical flask, 50 ml. of water is added and the flask is shaken repeatedly. During this test, water is maintained at 37°C ± 2°C. All capsules must completely dissolve within 10 min. This resulting solution must be odourless and neutral or slightly acidic.

In Federal Standard No. 285 A, the test is given under "acid solubility". In the test, the capsule shell is to be immersed in 0.5 per cent by weight aqueous hydrochloric acid solution at 36°C to 38°C and allowed to remain at this temperature for 15 minutes. A sample of 20 capsule shells, has to be tested for compliance with this test.

When tested by this procedure, shell shall completely fall apart, dissolve or disintegrate within 15 minutes.

Alongwith this test, "water resistance" test is given in this monograph but the purpose of "water resistance" test is not very clear. It is stated that "unless otherwise specified, the capsule shell shall show no signs of disintegration when tested as follows : The capsule shall be immersed in purified water at 25°C ± 1°C for 15 minutes. A sample of 20 capsule shells be tested for compliance with this test".

6.2.4 Microbial Limits

Under I.P. 1996, the microbial limits are given as the total microbial count not more than 1000 per gram of capsule shell. One gram capsule shell is also free from Escherichia coli and Salmonellae (Test procedure is given in Appendix 9.4 I.P. 1996).

It is interesting to note that a capsule which is taken along with the drug inside the human body had no microbial specifications upto 1992.

6.2.5 Loss on Drying

The test is performed with one gram of capsule shells by drying them in an oven at 105°C for 4 hours. Loss on drying should be between 12% to 16%.

This test is very important. If the moisture of the capsule is below 12% (w/w), the capsule tends to become brittle and if the moisture of the capsule is above 16% (w/w), the capsule tends to become soft. Such capsules are not suitable for capsule filling machines.

Empty capsules meeting all the standards mentioned above are termed or called as "Empty Gelatin Capsule I.P". Such capsules can be safely used in pharmaceutical industry for filling pharmaceutical products.

6.3 INDUSTRIAL STANDARDS

Industrial standards, not specifically defined or documented anywhere, can be explained as quality requirements of the capsule by the Pharmaceutical Industry from the capsule manufacturer for the intended use of the capsule.

These requirements are specified as under :

1. Capsule should pass all the tests given in Indian pharmacopoeia.
2. It should meet all the additional microbial safety standards.
3. It should have efficacy as a container.

Besides, in a supply lot they should comply with following requirements.

1. Presence of all relevant identification attributes.
2. Maintaining the visual defects affecting accuracy and uniformity of dosage less than the values specified under AQL by empty capsule manufacturer and the control on individual weight of empty capsule for better evaluation of fill weight.
3. Smooth performance on various machines of capsule usage.
4. Aesthetic appeal.

6.3.1 Indian Pharmacopoeial Standards

Tests given in Indian pharmacopoeia are already covered adequately in the early part of this chapter.

6.3.2 Additional Microbial Standards

Pseudomonas aeruginosa, staphylococcus aureus microbes should be absent in capsules. Similarly yeast and fungi should be absent. These are not covered in I.P. Most of the capsule users do not want their presence in capsules.

6.3.3 Efficacy as a Container for Medicament

Capsule is a container for medicament. It is therefore expected to hold the medicament filled in it physically intact, till the time the filled capsule is consumed by the patient. The following defects (visual) are responsible to fail the capsule as a container of medicament.

(1) oil holes, (2) stripper holes, (3) split and (4) crack.

These defects are categorized as critical defects.

6.3.4 Presence of All Relevant Identification Attributes

In a capsule lot supplied to a pharmaceutical user all capsules are of a particular size, type, colour and are printed with a specific matter in a specific manner in specified colour ink as ordered by the pharmaceutical user. If a capsule lot contains any capsule having different size, type, colour or printed matter or style and pattern of printing, or colour of ink than that specified by the customer, such a capsule is termed as a FOREGIN capsule or a STRANGER capsule. Mix-up of such a capsule in a supply lot will damage the image of the product as well as the reputation of its manufacturer and may further lead to legal disputes. It may also create mistrust in the mind of customer. To avoid such an eventuality the user rejects the whole lot, if any foreign capsule is found in it. A FOREIGN capsule is therefore considered as a critical defect in a supply lot.

6.3.5 Maintaining the visual defects affecting accuracy and uniformity of dosage less than the values specified under AQL by empty capsule manufacturer and the control on individual weight of empty capsule for better evaluation of fill weight

Dosages in capsules are expressed in terms of fill weight of medicament in filled capsules. With good performance of the capsule filling machine, with uniform density and proper flow ability of medicament formulation and with body volume of empty capsules remaining within specified limits, accuracy and uniformity of dosage can be achieved in filled capsules.

The body volume of empty capsule is one of the factors responsible for holding the desired content of medicament in filled capsules. Therefore, the defects which affect the body volume of empty capsules are categorized as critical. They are :

(i) Cutting inside body

(ii) Short body

(iii) Dented body

During capsule filling operation, the average fill weight of the medicament in filled capsules, is evaluated at regular intervals by deducting the average weight of empty capsules from the average weight of filled capsules. To achieve uniformity in the weight of fill material in the filled capsules, efforts are made to maintain the individual weight variation of empty capsules in a narrow band with respect to the average weight of that lot of empty capsules.

I.P. monograph does not specify about the limits of individual weight variation of empty capsules, with respect to that of average weight of that lot of empty capsules. The most of the empty capsule manufacturers are able to manufacture empty capsules with the individual capsule weight variation of empty capsule ±8% within ±10% of the average weight. This is specifically mentioned by empty capsule manufactures in their capsule specification document.

6.3.6 Smooth Performance on Various machines of Capsule Usage
6.3.6.1 Strength and Flexibility, and absence of Brittleness

For smooth performance of capsules on various capsule usage machines, the capsules must have good mechanical strength, flexibility and no or minimum brittleness to withstand the various mechanical operations involved in capsule filling and finishing.

The capsules are best suited for these operations, when their moisture content is between 13% to 16% w./w. Therefore it is essential to hold this moisture in capsules throughout the capsules filling and packing operations.

It is important to note that the moisture content of capsule changes depending upon the atmospheric conditions to which it is exposed.

The condition of the air is specified by its dry bulb temperature and relative humidity. With the dry bulb temperature of the air remaining constant, as the percentage relative humidity of the air increases, the moisture content of the capsule shell increases leading to a slight increase in its dimensions (mainly diameter and length). Further increase in relative humidity causes further rise in moisture content and eventually the capsule shell loses its strength, flexibility and shape. The capsule swells and ultimately becomes soft.

Similarly, as the percentage relative humidity of the surrounding air decreases, the moisture content of the capsule decreases, resulting into decrease in dimensions of capsule shell (mainly reduction in its outer diameter and length). With further reduction in relative humidity, the moisture content is further reduced; the capsule shell gets further shrunk and becomes hard and very brittle. Therefore to hold the moisture content of capsules between 13 to 16% w/w, the atmospheric conditions should be such that capsule will remain within this range. This is well achieved throughout the year by keeping the temperature of the air in the capsule filling and packing rooms at 22 to 24°C and its relative humidity between 40 to 50% with the help of air-conditioning system.

Since 13% to 16% of moisture of capsule is ideal for handling capsules, the dimensions of capsules particularly, external diameters of cap and body at cut end are taken as standards for designing the diameters and lengths of cap and body cavities in cap and body bushes respectively.

It is important to note that the basic dimensions of dipping moulds (pins) used by all capsule manufacturers on their capsule manufacturing machines are universally almost identical (except their lock and prelock design features). Thereby the dimensions of all the standard sizes of capsules namely 000, 00, 0, 1, 2, 3, 4 and 5 manufactured by different manufacturers in the world are almost the same.

This has made it possible to make the cap and body bushes of the capsule filling machines of the same dimensions for standard sizes and to get supplies of capsules from different manufacturers which will work on any make of capsule filling machines. For ready reference, the dimensions of standard sizes of capsules and their cap and body bushes diameters, which are functionally important, are given below. Capsules kept in the pan are pressed by the disc for one minute with specific pressure. This action is carried out with the help of pneumatic cylinder. After one minute, disc is moved up and the capsules in the pan are examined.

Fig. 6.1

Table 6.2 : Nominal Dimensions of Capsule

Standard capsule size	Outside φ of cap at cut end in mm	Outside φ of body at the end in mm	Cut length of cap in mm	Cut length of body in mm	Locked length of capsule in mm	Average Wt. of capsule mg.	Body Vol. in c.c.
000	9.96	9.61	13	22.2	25.9	163	1.37
00	8.55	8.22	11.8	20.2	23.5	119	0.95
0	7.66	7.34	10.7	18.5	21.4	96	0.68
1	6.93	6.63	9.8	16.6	19.3	76	0.50
2	6.37	6.08	9.0	15.2	17.8	63	0.37
3	5.85	5.57	8.1	13.6	15.8	50	0.30

| 4 | 5.33 | 5.06 | 7.2 | 12.2 | 14.4 | 39 | 0.21 |
| 5 | 4.91 | 4.65 | 6.2 | 9.3 | 11.4 | 28 | 0.10 |

Fig. 6.2

Standard capsule size in mm	Hole for cap in cap bush in mm	Hole for body in cap bush in mm	Hole for body in body bush in mm	Bottom hole in body bush for push rod in mm
000	10.05	9.65	9.65	9.00
00	8.70	8.28	8.32	7.70
0	7.75	7.42	7.46	6.80
1	7.01	6.72	6.75	6.20
2	6.45	6.15	6.29	5.80
3	5.90	5.64	5.68	5.30
4	5.40	5.14	5.16	4.80
5	5.00	4.71	4.74	4.30

Sometimes, the fracture or breakage of capsule is observed on capsule usage machines, despite the required moisture content in the capsule. Therefore to know whether the capsule would break on capsule usage machines or not, the fracture test or brittleness test is carried out. If capsule passes this test, the capsule is expected not to break or get fractured on capsule usage machines.

The brittleness test was developed by the capsule division of M/s. Eli Lilly and Co. USA. 100 capsules are placed in a flat pan. The pan containing capsules is kept below the pressing disc having a flat surface. It is essential that the surface of the pan and the surface of the pressing disc are perfectly parallel to each other. The pressing disc is fixed to the actuating shaft of a pneumatic cylinder. If more than two capsules are shattered, normally the batch is rejected. The acceptance number of shattered capsules may differ according to the severity of the acceptance standard employed by user. For high output capsule filling machines, even shattering of one capsule is not acceptable to the user.

6.3.6.2 Good Flowability

Good flowability of capsule is one of the requirements for smooth performance of capsule on capsule filling machines. For good flowability the capsule must glide easily. Easy gliding of capsule is possible because of its shape; but it gets affected due to friction between the outer surface of capsules on account of their physical movements during handling. Due to friction, capsule surface develops static electricity. This results into poor flow of capsules. Free flow of capsules is essential for quick filling of capsules into the magazine tubes of capsule filling machines when the magazine block or tubes move up and down mechanically. Failing to do so, magazine tubes will remain empty. If there are no capsules in magazine tubes, the question of loading of capsules in the cavities of the ring or bushes does not arise. Such a situation affects the productivity. Capsule manufacturers now know that surface friction is the main cause of the static charge; some capsule manufacturers treat the capsule surface with very small quantities of carnauba wax and/or sodium lauryl sulphate (powders) in coating pan. By treating the capsule surface in this way, capsule surface gets excellent lubricity and capsules flow well in capsule usage machines.

Instead of giving external treatment to capsules for overcoming the problems of friction, some capsule manufacturers have built flow property into capsule by incorporating fumed silicon-di-oxide (N.F.) in shell composition.

6.3.6.3 Proper Fit for Its Performance

For successful performance of capsules on capsule usage machine, each capsule must have individually proper fit to meet functional requirements of the machine. Requirements are, capsule must

(i) not get partly locked in prelocked state due to mechanical movements of capsules in the hoppers of printing and filling machines.

(ii) not get opened due to vibrations and mechanical movements of capsules in the hoppers of printing and filling machines.

(iii) separate into cap and body by the vacuum as specified by the empty capsule manufacturer. The vacuum pump fitted on the machine is supposed to provide this vacuum.

(iv) not get opened by the vacuum less than specified.

(v) get joined into lock groove of the cap during locking operation at locking station and body should not get dented.

(vi) not pop-off after locking operation is over.

(vii) not get easily opened in locked state.

Those capsules which will not satisfy these needs, may get separated into loose caps and bodies, loose caps may get fixed onto the other capsules, converting that capsule having two caps, leaving body into free state; some capsules may get into semilocked state. All this will happen in the hoppers of printing and filling machines. Such capsules will affect the smooth performance of capsule printing and filling machines resulting into loss of production.

The pulling force required for separation of capsule into cap and body in prelock and lock state can be taken as a measure of the fit of that capsule in that state. It can also be measured quantitatively by force measuring gauge. The force required for separation of body from cap (in unlocked or locked condition of capsule) is measured in grams with the help of this gauge. Similarly the force required for joining the body into the cap for locking can also be measured in grams with the help of this gauge. The force required for separation of capsule in prelock state, is very low; as against this, the force required for rejoining of filled body into the cap for locking is very high. The force required for separation of such locked capsule into cap and body again should be higher than that required for rejoining. If forces required for separation and rejoining of capsule are as per the machine requirements and are in narrow band, the capsule will satisfy all the needs of smooth machine performance. The likely problems arising out of improper fit will be then eliminated.

6.3.6.4 Free from Visual Defects Causing Stoppage of Capsule Usage Machines

The empty capsules have to undergo a number of machine operations till it gets finally packed as a filled capsule. Capsule first is printed on printing machine. It is then filled with medicament on filling machine. Thereafter it is sorted in sorting machine, polished in polishing machine and then packed in bottle, or blister or foil in packing machines. Any hindrance due to defective capsule, results in production loss, thus making the operation uneconomical. The defects in capsules, which hinder smooth performance of capsules on these various machines are therefore considered as critical defects.

These defects are listed below :
1. Flat
2. Mashed
3. Locked capsules
4. Telescoped
5. Large pinch
6. Bad cut edge
7. Trimmings
8. Double caps
9. Loose cap and body
10. Double dip
11. Turned edge
12. Crack.

6.3.6.5 Free from Defects, which have Potential to cause Problems in Capsule usage Machines

"Major" defects in capsules are those which can cause problems in filling such as no proper rectification of empty capsules or non-separation of capsule or no proper rejoining of filled capsule. Because of such defects, it may not be necessary to stop the machine during filling. But during filling operation the machine operator may be required to be alert, constantly watching the filling operation. Moreover the empty capsules with major defects result into rejections in filled capsules. The rejections get mixed up with good filled capsules and it becomes necessary to sort out damaged filled capsules. This is a very time consuming process. Therefore to save the production loss, such defective capsules must not be present in supply lot. Most of the defects likely to cause such problems are given below :

1. String
2. Small pinch
3. Thin ends
4. Long joined
5. Thin spots
6. Weak shoulder
7. Dented ends
8. Long body
9. Long cap
10. Pin grease inside body

6.3.6.6 Aesthetic Appeal

The extent of cosmetic defects in capsule should be within permissible limits. The defects in capsule which affect only the "look" of the capsule are called "minor" defects. These defects are cosmetic in nature and they do not affect dosage, machine performance or product identification.

The minor defects are listed below :

1. Small rough cut
2. Short cap
3. Crimps
4. Very small dents
5. Bubbles
6. Starred ends
7. White and/or dirt specks
8. Pin marks (transparent capsules)
9. Scrapes
10. Dirty capsule
11. Any other defects not affecting dosage, machine performance or product identification.

While describing the standard capsules, mention is made about various types of visual defects in capsules which affect the dosage, stoppage of machines, aesthetic appeal etc. Such defective capsules should be absent in standard capsules. All the efforts are made by capsule manufacturers to eliminate such defects but still some defective capsules remain in the supply lot. To understand their likely level of presence, AQL values for these defects are given in the specification documents. The details are given in Appendix I.

The capsule manufacturer endeavours to make capsules which comply with the essentials of standard capsules. He conveys information about the quality of his capsules through specification document. This information is given in the context of PHARMACOPOEIAL and/or F.D.A. requirements and is furnished in anticipation of customers' general queries regarding quality of the capsules supplied to him.

APPENDIX – I

Capsule Defects :

Capsules are manufactured under controlled conditions through statistical process control to ensure conformance to specifications.

Classification of Capsule Defects :

| Critical defect | It is a defect that affects the performance of a capsule |

	as package for the final product or contributes to a major filling problem.
Major defect	Is a defect that may cause a problem on a filing machine.
Minor defect	Is a defect that has no effect on the performance of a capsule as a package. It is a slight blemish that makes the capsule visually imperfect.

Categorisation of Capsule Defects

Critical defects	Major defects	Minor defects
Holes	Loose pieces	Minor splits
Uncut Cap/Body	Closed capsules	Minor rough cuts
Cracked / Split	Double caps	Minor collet pinches
Short body	Bad join	Minor punched dome
Double dip	Major rough cuts	Bubbles
Telescoped	Major collect pinches	Wrinkles
Mashed	Major punched dome	Star ends
Trims	Thin spots	Specks
	Short cap	Dirt marks
	Long body	Strings
	Long Cap	Scrapes / Scratches
	Grease / Oil rings	

Acceptable Quality Level and Average Outgoing Quality Limit :

Corresponding sampling plans to be used during incoming inspection are as follows :

Categorization of defects	Sample size*	Lot size 500,000 and above			
		Acceptance number	Rejection number	AQL%	AOQL%
CAPSULE DEFECTS					
Critical	1250	0	1	0.01	0.029
Major	1250	1	2	0.04	0.067
Minor	1250	7	8	0.25	0.360

*To be selected from $(\sqrt{K+1})$ cartons where k = number of cartons in the lot.
(With the courtesy of ACG World Wide, Mumbai)

7.
DRUGS OF DIFFERENT MEDICINAL SYSTEMS IN DIFFERENT PHYSICAL FORMS FILLED IN HARD GELATIN CAPSULES

It is estimated that India has produced more than 50 billions of capsules in the year 2007. India is also exporting empty capsules all over the world. Barring exports, the rest of the capsules are used for filling the medicines in India.

Large number of allopathic drugs are filled in hard gelatin capsules. The review was taken from the Indian Journal for allopathic drugs "Current Index for Medical Specialisties (CIMS) July – Oct. 2005". It was noted that over 150 single drugs and around 140 combination drugs are filled in hard gelatin capsules by various pharmaceutical companies and are sold under different brand names.

Recently Ayurvedic drugs manufacturing companies have also started using hard capsules for Ayurvedic products. This market is growing up and will grow faster in times to come.

Market for Neutraceutical products is also growing up very fast all over the world. Many neutraceutical products are being filled in Hard Gelatin Capsules. Good number of Indian companies are filling neutraceutical products in capsule dosage forms and are exporting them to developed countries like U.S.A., U.K., Germany etc.

Normally oil base formulations are filled in "SOFT GELATIN CAPSULES". Soft gelatin capsule manufacturing is a specialized field, hence the soft capsules are manufactured for pharma companies by those specialised companies who have soft capsule making machines and the technology to run them. Therefore, most of the pharmaceutical companies send their oil formulations to these soft capsule manufacturing companies for producing the drugs filled in soft capsules. The pharma companies therefore have no control over the production of soft capsules.

The situation is now changing fast. Empty hard gelatine capsule manufacturers have now developed specially designed empty capsules for filling oils and pastes. Similarly, capsule filling machine manufacturers have also developed and marketed filling and sealing machines suitable for filling oils and pastes and thereafter sealing them to prevent the leakage of filled matter. The pharma companies have therefore now started manufacturing their oil and paste drugs in their own facilities.

Some drugs are formulated in Pellets, as well as in microtablets. They are popularly filled in Hard gelatin capsules.

The combination drugs are also filled in Hard gelatin capsules. The consumption of capsules for filling such combinations are on an increasing scale.

The drugs in various forms, single and in combinations are filled in Hard gelatin capsules. They are illustrated below.

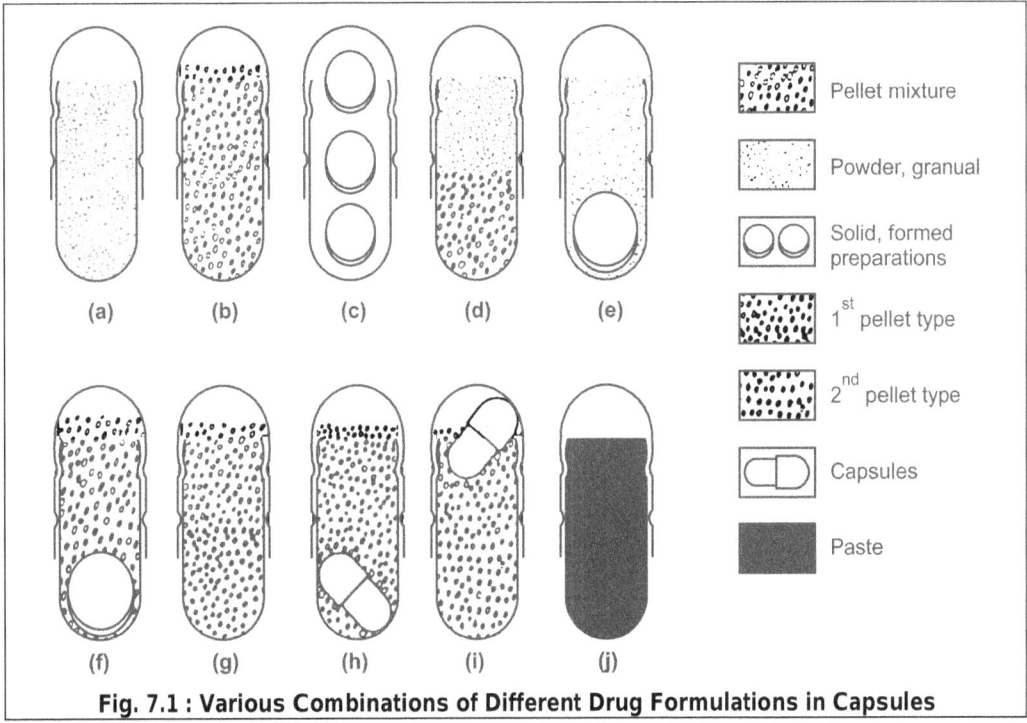

Fig. 7.1 : **Various Combinations of Different Drug Formulations in Capsules**

There are different types of filling machines available for filling the drugs in various forms single and in combination.

All the aspects related to the filling are discussed in the later chapters.

■■■

8.

FORMULATION OF DRUG (POWDER OR GRANULE FORM) FOR CAPSULE FILLING MACHINES

8.1 INTRODUCTION

Drug dose gets converted into capsule dosage form by volumetric filling of the capsule. Different types of Capsule Filling Machines are available, which are working on different filling principles. The particulars of capsule filling machines manufactured by some leading machine manufacturers, working on different filling principles are given in the following table :

Table 8.1 : Machines Working on Different Filling Principles and their Manufacturers

Sr. No.	Filling Principle	The dose is filled in	Type of Machine	Name of Manufacturer
1.	AUGER	Capsule body	Semi-automatic	1. Shionogi Qualicaps (Japan) 2. Pfizer (U.S.A.) 3. Pam Pharmaceutical and Allied Machinery Co. (Pvt.) Ltd. A.C.G. Worldwide, Mumbai 400001
2.	Dosator – Piston	Dosator - Piston assembly	Automatic (a) Intermittent (b) Rotary	1. IMA, Italy 2. mG_2, Italy 3. Pam Pharmaceutical and Allied Machinery Co. (Pvt.) Ltd. A.C.G. Worldwide, Mumbai
3. (a)	Tamping	Capsule body	Hand operated	1. Pam Pharmaceutical and Allied Machinery Co. (Pvt.) Ltd. ACG Worldwide, Mumbai 400001

contd. ...

3. (b)	Tamping	Holes in the dosing disc	Automatic	1. Robart Boush G.m.b.H, Germany 2. Harro Hofliger, Germany 3. Pam Pharmaceutical and Allied Machinery, Co. (Pvt.) Ltd. A.C.G. Worldwide, Mumbai.
4.	Vibratory	Capsule body	Automatic	1. Osaka, Japan (Japan) 2. Shionogi Qualicaps, (Japan)
5.	Vacuum	Dosing tube	Automatic	1. Perry Industries, U.S.A. 2. Romaco, Italy.

8.2 FORMULATION OF DRUGS

Drug in powder or granule form needs various properties to convert it into capsule dosage form. Some specific properties are required for smooth filling on the filling machine; some may be required for good bioavailability while some are required to prevent the undesirable effect on the capsule shell and/or the drug. Merely addition of additives is not enough. It may be required to undergo some process like grinding, granulation etc. All these additions and processings become necessary as the pure drug lacks in having all the desired properties. Converting the Drug to suitable capsule dosage form by addition of required additives and subjecting it to processings, whenever necessary is called 'Formulation of the Drug' in the Pharmacy Parlance.

Selection of the size of capsule for filling the drug in the respective machines is given in the Chapter 10 on filling machines.

8.3 FILLERS OR DILUENTS

Fillers (Diluents) are often needed to increase the volume of the formulation. The most common diluents are starch, lactose, dicalcium phosphate, magnesium oxide etc. Some 3/4 decades back, in India these materials were considered as inert materials, not affecting the disintegration and dissolution of the capsule. It is now found out that these materials do affect the disintegration and dissolution profile of the Drug. Therefore in today's context each filler material used in the formulation is thoroughly evaluated for its performance.

8.4 PROPERTIES OF FORMULATED DRUG REQUIRED FOR SMOOTH PERFORMANCE ON CAPSULE FILLING MACHINE

Different capsule filling machines are available working on different filling principles. The requirement of properties of the formulated drug, therefore, changes from machine to machine.

The properties broadly required in the formulated drug for most of the filling machines are as under :

1. Non-hygroscopicity
2. Homogeneity
3. Uniform Density
4. Flowing Behaviour
5. Cohesiveness
6. Compressibility
7. Lubricity
8. Stickiness
9. Non-Seizing (Seizing due to entrapped powder during rejoining)

The relevance of each property required for capsule filing is described below :

8.4.1 Non-Hygroscopicity

Some of the properties required for filling are closely related to the moisture content of formulation, like flow, stickiness, compressibility etc. Therefore, if the moisture content of the formulation changes for any reason beyond the specified limits, the formulation will have lot of problems in filling of capsules on the machine. The ingredients used in formulation, therefore, should not be hygroscopic in nature. Hygroscopic materials absorb lot of moisture when they are exposed to highly humid areas. Hence, to protect the formulation from moisture, storing and filling of formulation is done in controlled atmospheric conditions. Now-a-days this procedure is very routinely followed.

In certain cases, if the drug to be filled is itself hygroscopic in nature, it is sometimes coated with non-hygroscopic materials. Sometimes the relative humidity of the filling area is reduced to low humidity value. In the latter case care is required to be taken while handling the capsules as capsules are likely to get brittle in the low humidity atmosphere.

8.4.2 Homogeneity

Ingredients mixed together in the drug formulation have different densities. It is therefore, essential to see that the ingredients get thoroughly mixed to form a homogeneous mixture. The homogeneity of the mixture is checked by analyzing contents of the drug to be filled in capsule.

8.4.3 Uniform Density

Where the components of the mixture have the same density and they are mixed together to form a thoroughly homogeneous mixture, there is practically no chance for the components getting separated, even though the mixture is subjected to vibrations. However, where the components, having different densities are mixed together to form a homogenous mixture, on account of their natural tendencies, the chances of the components getting separated when subjected to vibrations are more. The degree of separation would depend upon the difference in densities and the duration and amplitude of vibration. Higher the density difference, faster is the separation. Many a times vibrators are provided on hoppers for improving the flow of formulation. It then becomes essential to watch that the components are not getting separated during vibrations.

8.4.4 Flowing Behaviour

Flow is a very essential property for filling the formulation in the capsule. The filling is mainly carried out in two ways.

(i) Powder (formulation) is conveyed from hopper into capsule body by mechanical device to form a dose.

(ii) The powder is conveyed into the dose forming device and the formed dose is transferred into the capsule body. In this case, the capsule body is used just as a soluble container.

The mechanical device will help to transfer the powder from hopper to the point of filling, but to get filled into the capsule body dosator or piston volume or metering hole or powder tab etc. the powder should have inherent good flow property. Filling otherwise is not possible.

The flow properties in powder can be improved by adding different additives. The additives are as under :

(i) Collidal Silica
(ii) Magnesium Stearate
(iii) Stearic Acid
(iv) Pregelatimized Starch
(v) Spray Processed Lactose
(vi) Dicalcium Phosphate (Unmilled)

It is important to note that if the powder is having fast flowing behaviour, it is difficult to keep the flow under control, thus creating problems while filling.

8.4.5 Cohesiveness

This property is important for a powder which is filled on dosator-piston type machines. The powder having good cohesive property, when compressed in dosator with the piston, forms a firm slug (also called plug). During transfer of slug from dosator to capsule body, dosator has to move from one location to other location. During this movement, a firm slug will hold its powder properly and transfer the full (powder) slug into the capsule. In such a transfer the weight variation of capsule will be within limits.

The dosator has open end at the bottom and if the slug is not cohesive, the powder may fall out from the open end during this travel of the dosator from one location to the other. In such an event, the dose will not get transferred from the dosator to the capsule in full quantity and it will lead to weight variation. This can be avoided by using additives having good cohesive property.

Micro-crystalline cellulose is one of the additives which improves the cohesion to a good extent. Other additives are fine lactose or sprayed lactose.

8.4.6 Compressibility

Compressibility of the powder comes into picture when the powder is to be filled in capsules on dosator-piston type and tamping type machines.

Normally, powder is compressed to :
1. improve its cohesion and
2. improve its density.

Micro-crystalline cellulose improves both cohesiveness as well as compressibility.

The powder is sometimes granulated to get better compressibility.

8.4.7 Lubrication

Lubricants are required in the capsule formulation as :
(i) they ease the ejection of the slug (plug);
(ii) they reduce filming on pistons and adhesion of powder inside the metal surface of the dosator tube.
(iii) and reduce friction between sliding surfaces in contact with the powder.

The common lubricants are :
(i) Magnesium stearate
(ii) Stearic Acid

The lubricants have major role to play in dosator-piston and tamping machines, where the slug (plug) gets formed and delivered into the capsule thereafter. Lubricant facilitates easy delivery of the slug (plug) from the dosator or the tamping hole.

8.4.8 Non-Stickiness

Stickiness of powder to all metal parts of the capsule filling machine leads to weight variations in filled weight. This problem is more serious on tamping type machine. When the dosing disc moves over the bottom metal plate during the tamping operation, the entrapped powder in between the dosing disc and the bottom plate gets heated due to friction. If there are ingredients in the powder which have a low melting point, the melted ingredients alongwith the powder, form a sticky mass with the result that the dosing disc ceases to move and the machine then comes to a grinding halt.

This problem is sorted out by carrying out few changes in the composition of the formulation.

Moisture absorbing excipients are cellulose or starch. It is normally suggested not to mix them with the powder which has a tendency to absorb moisture. In such a case, these excipients are replaced by mannitol or anhydrous lactose.

8.4.9 Filled Capsules Facing Problem During Rejoining and Locking

The particle size of the powder plays an important role in smooth rejoining and locking of filled capsule. The coarse particle size of the powder gives heavy denting of bodies during rejoining and locking. The particle size of the powder is therefore required to be controlled to reduce wastage of dented capsules.

Some additives in the formulation have sometimes seizing properties. Such powder, during filling, get adhered to the external surface of the body and thus offers high resistance during joining. This results into denting of the body. Such dented capsules get rejected. Such additives have therefore to be avoided.

The discussion on formulations for good machine performance is summed up in the following table.

Table 8.2 : Machines using Different Filling Principles and Properties Required in the Formulation for Filling

Sr. No.	Filling Principle	Non-hygroscopicity	Homogeneity	Uniform Density	Flow	Cohesiveness	Compressibility	Lubrication	Stickiness	Non-Seizing
1.	Auger	✓	✓	✓	✓	–	–	✓	✓	✓
2.	Dosator-Piston	✓	✓	✓	✓	✓	✓	✓	✓	✓
3.	(a) Tamping Automatic (b) Tamping Hand Operated	✓	✓	✓	✓	–	✓	–	✓	✓
4.	Vibratory	✓	✓	✓	✓	–	✓	–	✓	✓
5.	Vacuum	✓	✓	✓	✓	–	–	–	✓	✓

For properties refer article 8.4.

✓ = Required

– = Not required

Table 8.3 : Commonly used Additives to Improve Certain Properties

Sr. No.	Name of the property	Name of the additives
1.	Flow	Collidal Silica, Magnesium Stearate, Stearic acid, Pregelatinized starch, Spray processed lactose. Dicalcium phosphate (unmilled)
2.	Lubrication	Magnesium Stearate, Stearic acid
3.	Compression	Micro-crystalline cellulose
4.	Cohesion	Micro-crystalline cellulose
5.	Non-stickness	Magnesium stearate, mannitol, lactose (anhydrous)

8.5 PROPERTIES OF FORMULATED DRUG REQUIRED FOR IMPROVING DISINTEGRATION TIME (D.T.) AND DISSOLUTION

Disintegration of the capsule shell and dissolution of the drug thereafter in the Gastrointestinal fluid are most important factors for absorption of the drug into the G.I. Track, when the capsule is taken by the oral route. This journey of the capsule when orally administered is given in the following schematic diagram.

Action

Step I : Capsule shell gets disintegrated / dissolved.

Step II : Released drug particles get into the gastrointestinal fluid.

Step III : Released drug particles are dissolved in the gastrointestinal fluid.

Step IV : Dissolved drug goes into blood through membrane i.e. membrane permeability.

From the schematic diagram it is seen that to get the drug released in the gastrointestinal fluid, it is essential that the capsule gets thoroughly disintegrated. The drug particles then get dissolved into the G.I. fluid and then get absorbed into blood stream through membrane. Thus, the disintegration of the capsule shell and dissolution of the drug particles into the intestinal fluid assume utmost importance.

The dissolution can be improved by :
(i) Reducing the percentage of additives which come in the way of dissolution.
(ii) Eliminating formaldehyde and or low molecular weight aldehyde from the formulation.
(iii) Adding additives useful for dissolution.

1. The Disintegration Test (D.T.) of empty as well as filled capsule is given in I.P. 1994. The disintegration of filled capsule is given in different pharmacopoeias but the trend is now changing. Instead of D.T. test, they have started giving dissolution test. The test requires testing of the specified quantity of the drug filled in the capsule for its solubility in the specified media in the given length of time as given in the pharmacoepia. To pass the dissolution test, disintegration of the capsule shell is the essential pre-requirement and it thus gets automatically covered in the dissolution test. It is therefore, not prescribed separately.

While carrying out the dissolution test, first thing to be observed is whether the capsule shell is dissolving properly or not. If not, this problem has to be attended first.

The disintegration test is carried out as many products are filled in capsules. It was observed that certain additives in the formulation of the drug affect the D.T. of the capsule. Stearic Acid and/or magnesium stearate, when used in excess quantities in the formulation, the D.T. of the capsule gets affected.

2. Other ingredient which affects the D.T. (disintegration time) of hard gelatine capsule shell is Formaldehyde. This is never added in the formulation as one of the components. But it gets into the formulation through other additives. Sometimes Formaldehyde is present in starch and that starch when added to the formulation the D.T. gets affected. It is therefore necessary to test the additives for the presence of formaldehyde as well as for low molecular aldehyde before using them in the formulation.

An excellent paper has been published on this subject in the year 1994 in the American Journal of Pharmaceutical Sciences - Vol. 83 - No. 7, July 1994 under the title "Cross Linking of Gelatine Capsule and Its Relevance to Their Vitro-in-Vivo Performance". The authors of the Paper are G.A. Digensis, T.B. Gold and Vinod P. Shah.

3. (a) Surface Active Compounds : Surface active compounds are also used in the formulation to secure better drug dissolution. The use of these compounds help expediting the wetting of the surface of the drug particles, thus leading to faster drug dissolution.

The most common surface active compounds used in formulation are :
   (i) Sodium Lauryl Sulfate, and
   (ii) Sodium docusate

They are normally used in concentration of 0.1% to 0.5%.

3. (b) Disintegrants : Disintegrants are mainly used in tablet formulation. Earlier it was a belief that capsule formulation does not need any disintegrants as capsule does not pose any problem of disintegration like tablet. With the introduction of dissolution test, the need for faster disintegration of capsule was felt. Faster release of drug from the capsule shell gives more time to the drug particles to get dissolved into the G.I. solution. In the light of this, new disintegrants are finding a place in the drug formulation. The new disintegrants are :

    (i) Cross camellose sodium type A (AcDisol, F.M.C. Corporation, Food and Pharmaceutical Products P.A. U.S.A.).

    (ii) Sodium Starch Glycolate (Primajel, Generichem Corporation., Little falls, N.J. USA)

    (iii) Crospovidone (Polyplasdone XL.ISP Corporation Wayne NI USA).

They are normally used between 4% to 6%. But this percentage changes, depending upon other additives used in the formulation.

The disintegrants used in the formulation have a characteristic to absorb the moisture in the G.I. fluid at a rate faster than the capsule shell and they swell inside. With the pressure created inside, the capsule shell bursts open. The pressure inside and the force with which the shell bursts open lead to breaking of formulation ingredients into smaller particles and thus help faster solubalization of the drug in the G.I. fluid.

4. Hydrophilization : Another way to improve the wettability of the poorly soluble drugs is to treat the drug with a solution of hydrophilic polymer.In this process the solution of hydrophylic polymer is spread on the formulation in a high shear mixer and the resultant mixture is dried and screened. This process is called "Hydrophilization".

By using this process Mr. Lerke treated phenytoin drug by hydrophilization with methyl cellulose. The processesd drug was filled on tamping machine. The drug showed fastest dissolution than the same drug without carrying the process of hydrophilization. This work was published by C.E. Lerke and others in the Journal of Pharmaceutical Sciences 67, 935 (1978) under the title "Effect of Hydrophilization of hydrophobic drug on release rate from capsule".

8.6 REQUIREMENTS OF FORMULATION FOR EMPTY CAPSULE

    1. **Aldehyde Reaction :** It is a known thing that formaldehyde reacts with gelatine and gets cross-linked. Such cross-linked gelatine is insoluble in water at 37°C. It only swells and because of this the drug does not get released and the bioavailability of the drug gets affected. If by any chance, any ingredient filled in the capsule has traces of formaldehyde present in it, the filled capsule fails to the D.T. and the Dissolution tests. Initially when the capsules are freshly filled, the problem of D.T. and Dissolution may not be seen; but the problem surfaces with the passage of time and gradually gets aggravated and finally the product fails to pass the D.T. and Dissolution Test.

2. **Millard Reaction :** In Millard Reaction, the amino group of amino acids, peptides or protein react with "glycoside" hydroxyl groups of sugars, ultimately resulting into formation of brown pigments.

   Therefore drugs having such structures, when filled in capsule react with gelatin and the effect of brown pigment formation is seen. In transparent capsule such pigmentation is seen from outside. Such capsules are considered as defective and hence rejected.

3. **Fading of Capsule Colour :** It is known in capsule industry that certain colours do get faded due to oxidizing and reducing agents present in the gelatine or formulation. Care, therefore, has to be taken that gelatin or formulation does not contain either oxidizing and or reducing agents beyond certain limits. Fading of the colour is a slow process and the effect of fading is not seen immediately but after sometime. The faded capsules get rejected.

4. **Black spot formation due to Vitamin 'C' in Formulation :** It is known in the pharmaceutical industry that Vitamin 'C' interacts with gelatine and forms black spots on the capsule shell. Such interaction takes place in humid atmosphere. Black spot formation is avoided by filling the Vitamin 'C' formulation in dry area – R.H. less than 40% and temperature of the room between 20-25°C. After filling, the filled capsules are cleaned and polished and packed in airtight bags in the same dry atmosphere.

5. **Perforations :** It is observed that certain drugs filled in hard gelatine capsule have small percentage of organic solvent present in them. Such filled capsules develop perforations in the shell in a short period of time.

8.7 CONCLUSION

From the above discussion, it can be seen that development of capsule dosage form is a very complex process. The drug is put into the market only when the manufacturer gets the confidence that the capsule dosage form developed satisfies all the requirements of F.D.A. and the Market and that it will continue to do so consistently from batch after batch, for all the time to come. This confidence gets generated only after innumerable trials are taken over a considerable period of time, involving untiring efforts of the dedicated research minded people, receiving unstinted support, financial and otherwise from the manufacturer. This work is therefore handled by very senior and experienced pharmacists.

■■■

9. DIFFERENT MECHANISMS USED ON CAPSULE FILLING MACHINES TO OPERATE CAPSULES FOR FILLING DRUGS

9.1 INTRODUCTION

Filling the drug manually in the capsule is a three-step operation. It is as follows :

(i) Separating the cap and body of the capsule.

(ii) Filling the drug in the opened body.

(iii) Joining the body filled with the drug with the cap.

Filling of drug in the capsule mechanically on the filling machine involves number of steps as stated below :

1. Rectification or orientation of capsule.

2. Opening the capsule and separating cap and body.

3. Filling the drug in the opened body.

4. Joining the filled body with cap and locking the capsule, and

5. "Ejecting" the filled capsule.

The diagram given below depicts the above operations.

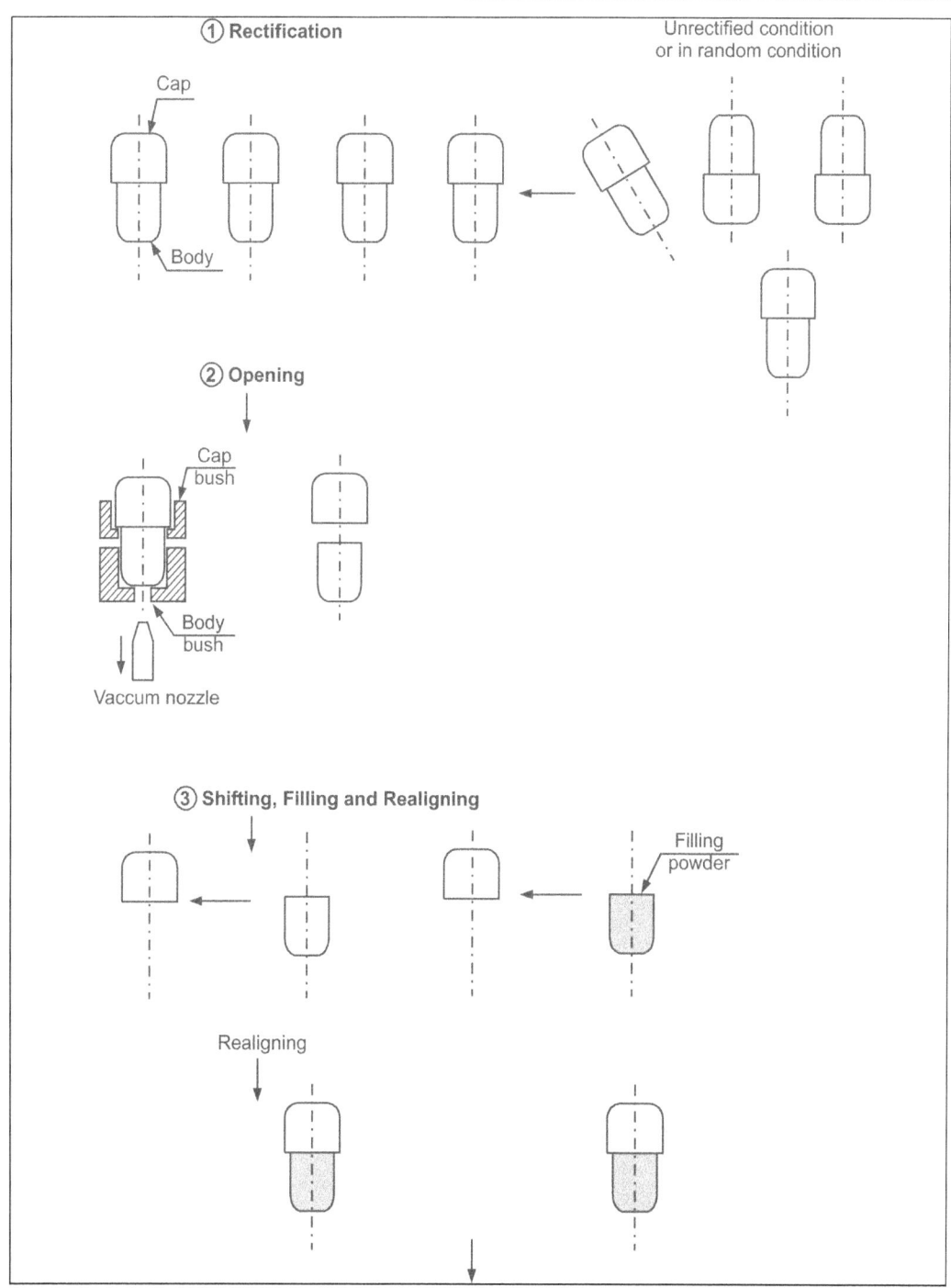

contd. ...

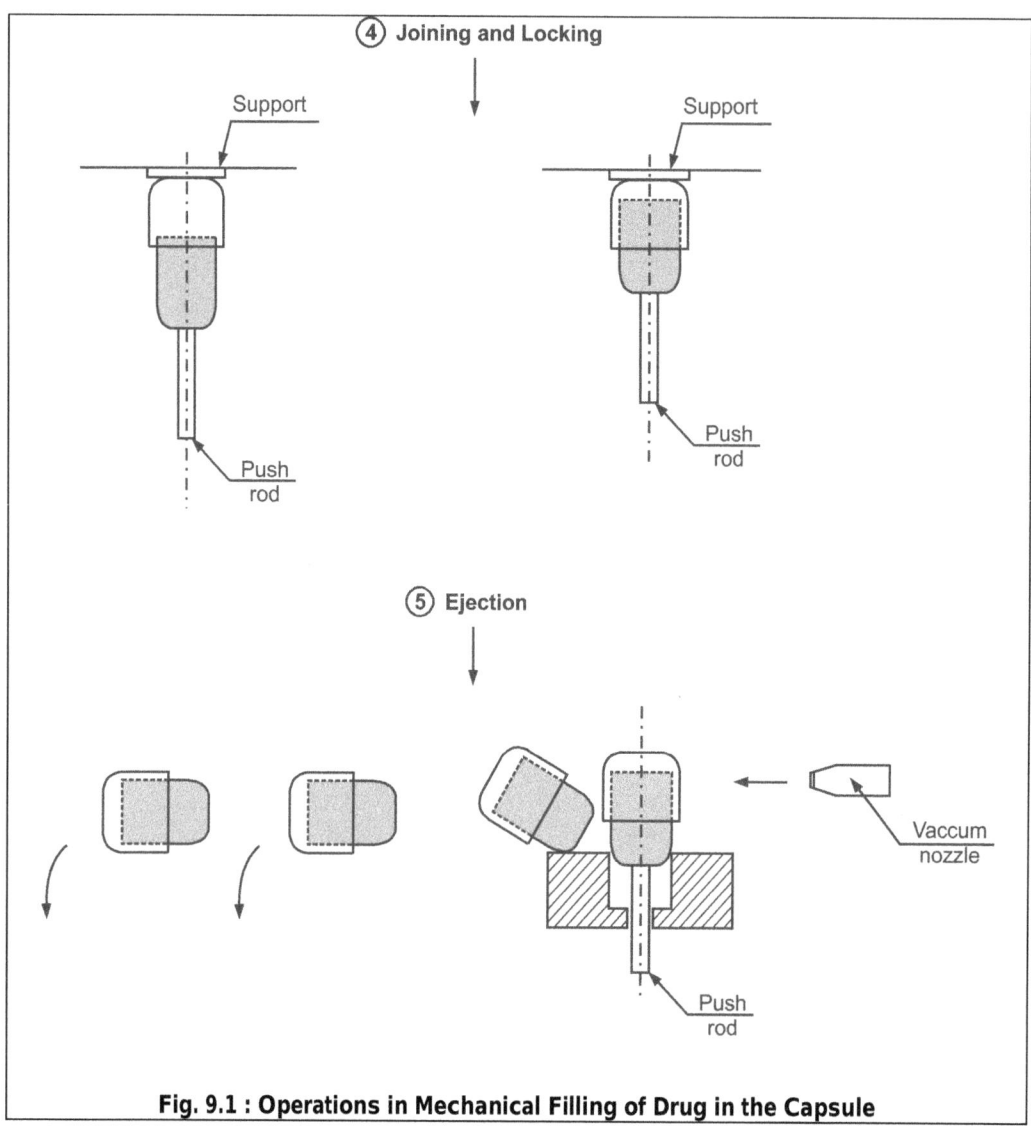

Fig. 9.1 : Operations in Mechanical Filling of Drug in the Capsule

Several types of capsule filling machines are in use in the pharmaceutical industry. They can be classified in four categories :

1. Hand operated.
2. Semi-automatic (ring type).
3. Automatic (intermittent).
4. Automatic (rotary).

Every capsule filling machine for filling the drugs in capsules has to handle two components, namely capsules and drugs. The suitable mechanisms are fitted on the machines to handle them. These mechanisms carry all the operations of capsule filling step wise in an orderly fashion. The mechanisms used for filling drugs in powder or granule forms are discussed separately.

The mechanisms used for handling the empty capsules are discussed below.

9.2 RECTIFICATION OF CAPSULES

Rectification of capsules is also described as orientation of capsules. Rectification of capsules means, arranging the capsules from disorderly manner into an orderly manner. In disorderly manner, capsules are lying in such a fashion that their cap and body ends are pointing out in any direction. In orderly manner, capsules in disorderly state are arranged in such a way that their cap ends get pointing out in one direction and body ends get pointing out in opposite direction.

In rectification process, the capsules lying in disorderly manner in the capsule hopper of the filling machine, are brought into rectified condition by a rectifying mechanism before they are further processed for filling.

On hand operated capsule filling machine, capsule is first manually rectified and then it is loaded in the hole of the loading plate manually. Now, separate machines are manufactured to carry out this operation. On these machines capsules are first oriented and then they are loaded automatically in the capsule loading plate of the hand operated capsule filing machine (See Fig. 9.2).

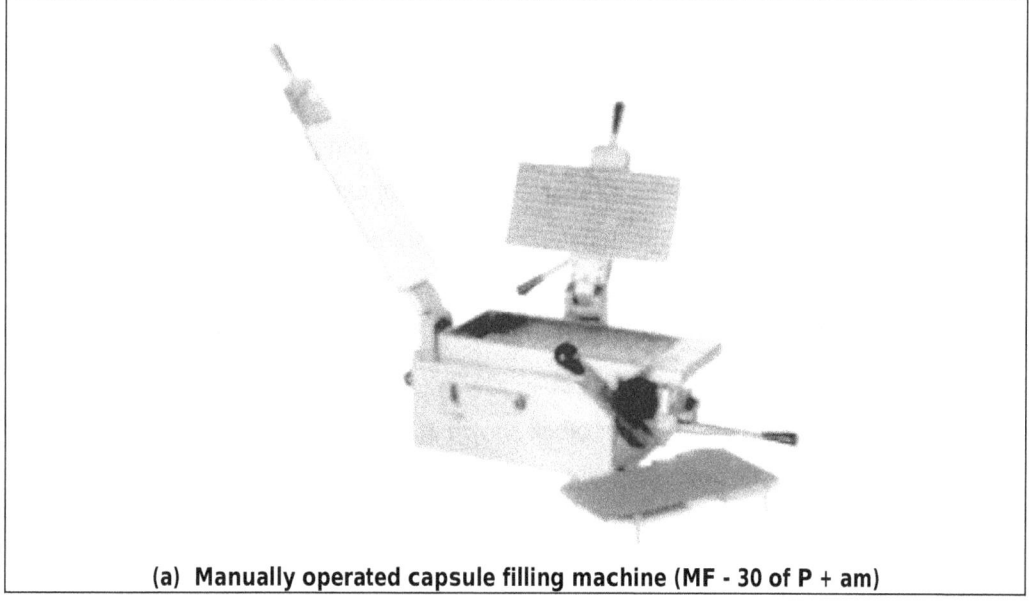

(a) Manually operated capsule filling machine (MF - 30 of P + am)

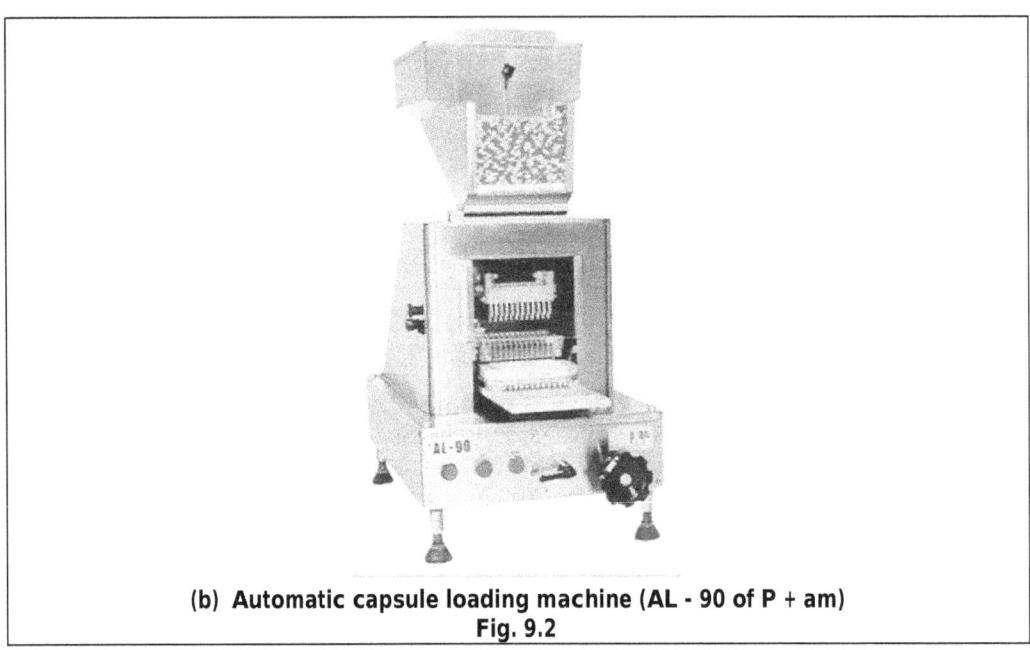

(b) Automatic capsule loading machine (AL - 90 of P + am)
Fig. 9.2

---

*With the courtesy of ACG Worldwide, Mumbai.

There are two types of mechanisms used for orientation/rectification of capsules.

(a) Conventional mechanism and

(b) Drum orientation mechanism (patented by Shionogi Qualicaps).

(a) Conventional Orientation Mechanism :

Most of the automatic capsule filling machine manufacturers have employed conventional mechanism for orientation or rectification of capsules.

The three important parts used in this mechanism are as follows :

(i) Rectifier block.

(ii) Horizontal blade also known as Horizontal push blade or horizontal push finger.

(iii) Vertical finger.

(i) Rectifier Block : The rectifier block shown in the Fig. 9.3 is of the machine which is designed to work with four capsules at a time. Therefore, the rectifier block in the figure is provided with 4 slotted vertical cylindrical holes, having closed bottom. The bottom of the holes is closed so that the capsules received into the holes should not slip from the bottom.

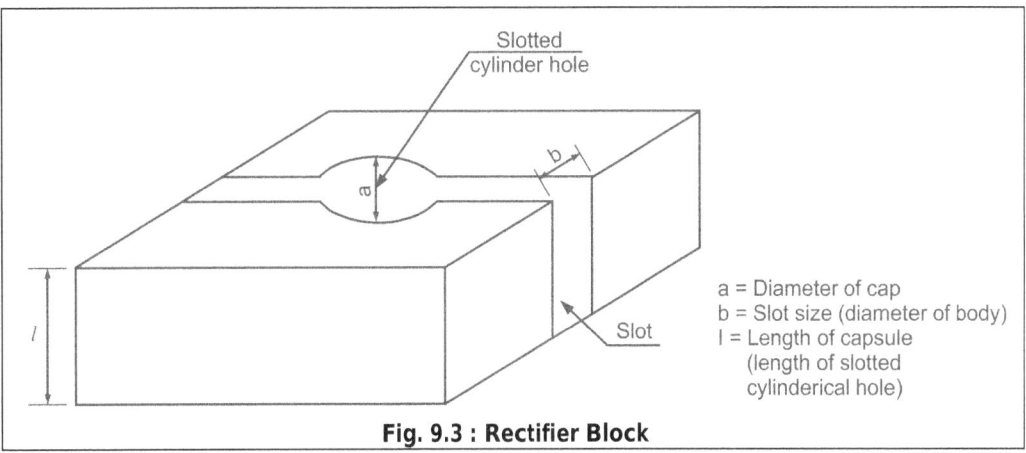

Fig. 9.3 : Rectifier Block

a = Diameter of cap
b = Slot size (diameter of body)
l = Length of capsule (length of slotted cylinderical hole)

The length of the slotted cylindrical hole corresponds to the length of the size of the capsule for which the machine is designed. The diameter of the cylindrical hole is slightly bigger than the cap diameter of the size of the capsule. Due to these dimensions of cylindrical holes, capsules delivered from magazine tubes get into the cylindrical holes easily and remain in the vertical position. One cylindrical hole accommodates only one capsule at a time. The capsules are delivered into the slotted cylindrical holes from the magazine tubes in a random fashion.

The size of the slot passing through the cylindrical hole right upto the forward end of the block, is slightly bigger than the diameter of body at the cut end. But it is smaller than the diameter of cap at cut end. Therefore cap part of capsule offers a higher resistance than body when capsule is pushed forward into the slot. The job of pushing the capsule forward from the hole and then further through the slot to final location is carried out by horizontal push finger or horizontal push blade.

(ii) Horizontal push finger or blade : There are four horizontal push fingers fitted to the plate called horizontal push fingers assembly. Finger assembly moves horizontally forward and backward in the slotted holes and slots in the rectifier block. For sake of convenience only one push finger, one hole and one slot is described along with its working. The rest of the three fingers do the same function. The horizontal push finger is shown in Fig. 9.4. The profile of the push finger looks like an anchor shape. It has two arcs with a protruding taper portion inbetween. The protruding part between two arcs is called pinnacle of horizontal push finger / blade.

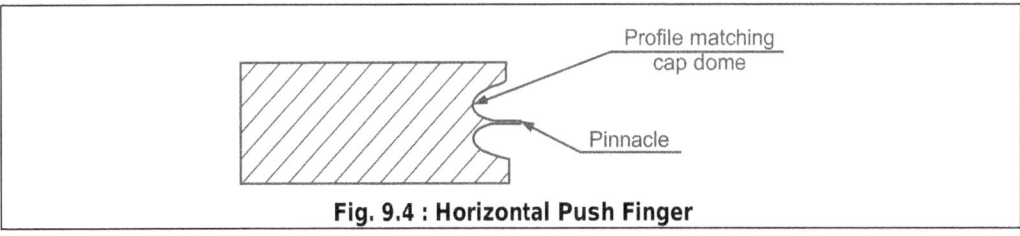

Fig. 9.4 : Horizontal Push Finger

The protruding part is designed such that, it will touch the centre line of capsule when it touches the capsule in the rectifier hole during its forward motion for rectification.

During the forward stroke of horizontal push finger, passing through the slot of cylindrical hole, the pinnacle being protruded, always comes first in contact with the centre line of the capsule.

The centre line of plain capsule is at the cut end of cap, whereas in locking type of capsule, it is located on the body, slightly below the cut end of cap.

Orientation in the rectifier block : The pinnacle point of horizontal finger with its forward stroke pushes the capsule forward from the cylindrical hole by striking over the centre of the capsule. During forward movement of capsule in the slot, the dome base of cap gets wedged inbetween the slides of the slot at the entry point. This is because dome diameter of cap is bigger than the width of the slot. Similarly cap dome base being most rigid portion of the capsule offers the highest resistance while going through the slot. The cut end of cap gets pressed into the slot at two opposite points, but being less rigid than the dome base offers much less resistance. The body portion of capsule offers no resistance while passing through the slot.

Because of the types of resistance offered by different parts of capsules, the following things take place sequentially when the capsule is pushed forward by the horizontal finger in the slot.

1. Cap gets wedged into slot.
2. Capsule gets turned from vertical to horizontal position. The turning of capsule takes place at dome base of cap.
3. Cap dome gets into grip of anchor arc.
4. Capsule is moved forward upto a specific location in horizontal position.

This is essential because the vertical finger has to touch the capsule at specific point to turn the capsule from horizontal position to vertical position with body dome pointing downward.

In the process of orientation, cap dome of capsule always offers a high resistance, therefore, it remains at the back and it moves forward only when it comes in the grip of arch of the anchor. In case of body, it offers very little resistance, therefore it moves earlier than cap.

In short, capsule may get into cylindrical hole of the rectifier block in any random fashion, but when the capsule is moved forward through slot of the rectifier block, capsule gets rectified. This complete process as described above is called the rectification process. Please See Fig. 9.5.

At the end of the forward stroke of the horizontal finger, capsule is taken forward in the horizontal position upto a specific point. It remains into that position in the slot and the horizontal finger comes back to its original position for the next stroke.

(iii) Vertical Finger : The profile of the vertical finger is shown in the Fig. 9.6. The vertical finger turns the rectified capsule from horizontal position into vertical position with cap up and body down position and drops the capsule into bush assembly.

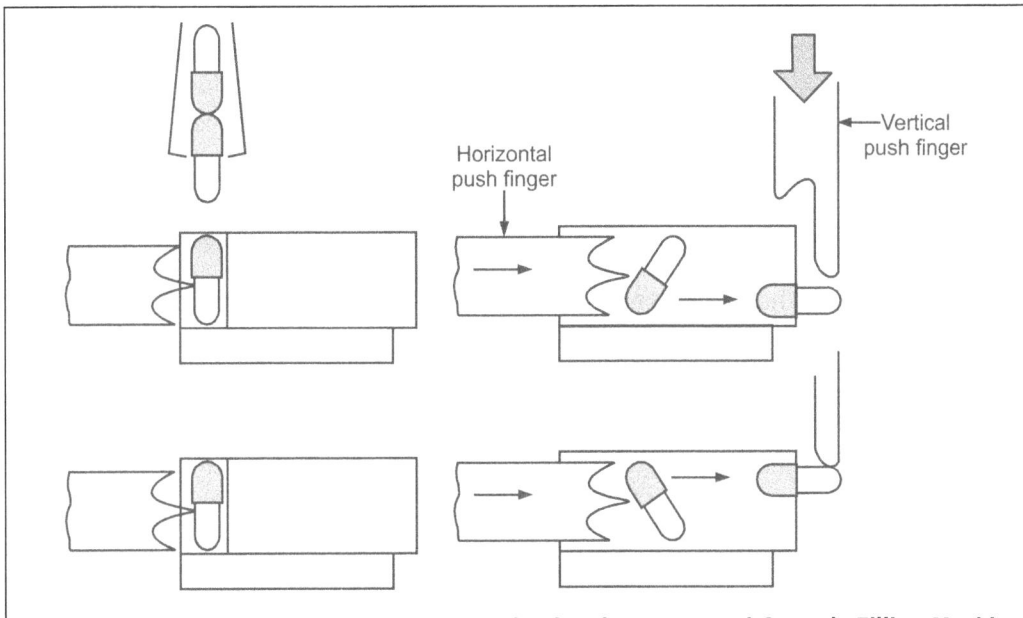

Fig. 9.5 : Standard Capsule Rectification Mechanism in Automated Capsule Filling Machine

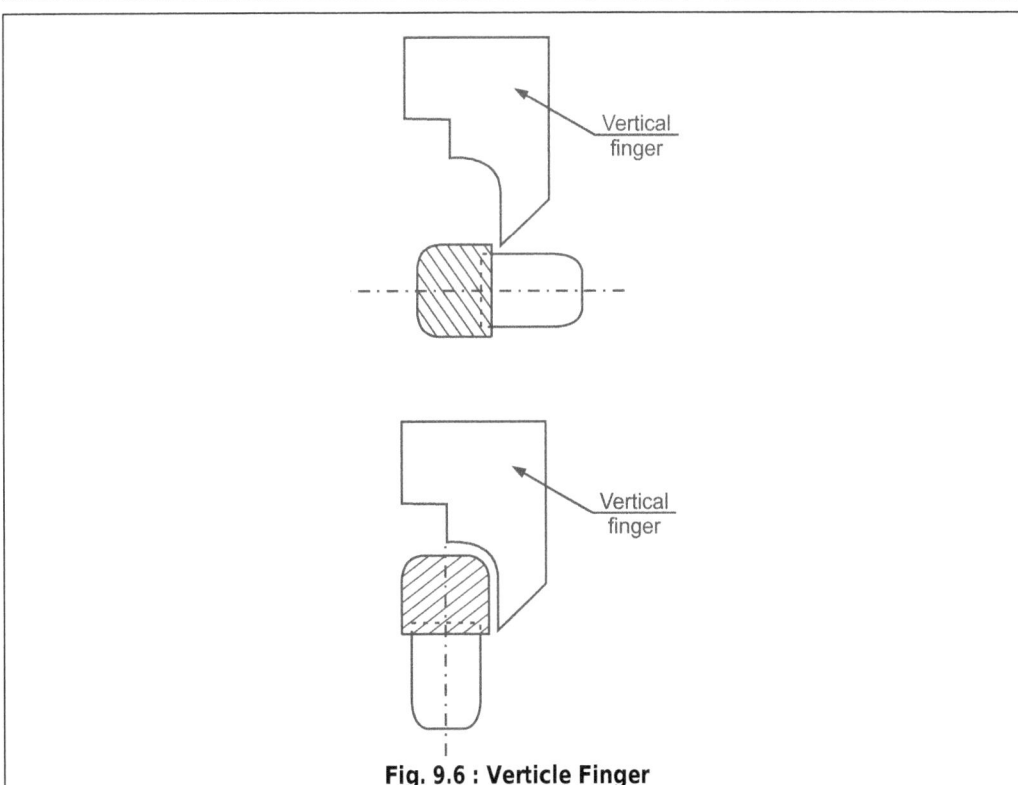

Fig. 9.6 : Verticle Finger

The vertical finger has only one arc. It is because it has only to turn the axis of capsule from horizontal position to vertical position. The rectification action has been already carried out in rectifier block by horizontal finger. Here the turning of capsule takes place at the dome base of cap. This action is similar to the action taking place in the rectifier block.

When the capsule is turned into vertical position, its vertical axis gets exactly aligned with the vertical axis of bush assembly. Because of this, when capsule is pushed down by the vertical finger from the rectifier block slot, in the vertical position, capsule gets easily loaded into the bush assembly.

(b) Drum Orientation Mechanism (Patented by Shionogi Qualicaps)

This process of orientation has been patented by M/s Shionogi Qualicaps (Japan). It is described in U.S. Patent No. 4,731, 979, March 22, 1988.

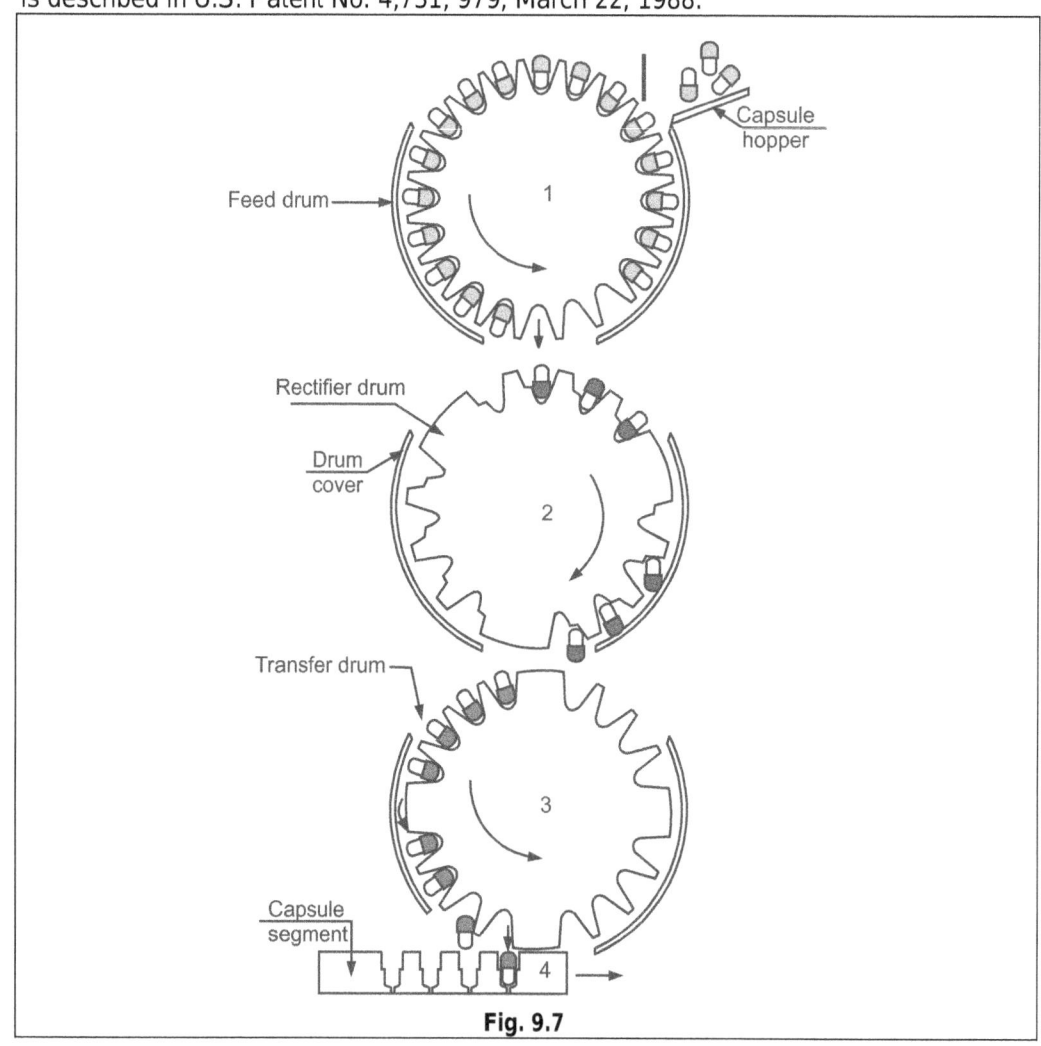

Fig. 9.7

(i) Drum arrangements : The schematic drum arrangement is shown in Fig. 9.7. There are three drums located one over the other. The top drum is called "FEED DRUM" and it is indicated by number 1. The middle drum is called "RECTIFIER ROLLER OR RECTIFIER DRUM", indicated by number 2. The third drum is called "TRANSFER ROLLER or TRANSFER DRUM" and it is indicated by number 3. Below this drum is capsule segment and it is indicated by number 4. After the rectification, capsules in the rectified condition are received in the capsule segment. The direction of rotation of the drums is shown in Fig. 9.7 by arrows. For synchronizing the movements of capsule transfer from one drum into another all the three drums have same pheripheral speed.

(ii) Cavities in drums : The cavities in the 1st drum are slightly bigger in diameter than the diameter of cap of the capsule for which the machine is designed. The depth of the cavity is slightly more than the length of the capsule. Therefore capsules will get fully into the cavities and the capsules will not protrude out from the drum surface. The dimensions of cavities are such that :

(1) Capsules can get into the cavities with Cap dome facing – Body dome facing down or Body dome facing up – Cap dome facing down i.e. in any random fashion.
(2) Capsules can get easily loaded from capsule hopper into the cavities and
(3) Capsules can also get transferred easily from the cavities of the 1st drum into cavities of the second drum. This is shown in Fig. 9.7.

The cavities in the rectifier drum i.e. drum no. 2, have a different design.

Each cavity in the rectifier drum is such that it is vertical and also extended horizontally on the circumferences of the drum to accommodate the body part of the capsule. The hole in the upper part of vertical cavity will accommodate the cap whether capsule is kept in the cavity in vertical or horizontal position. In short, the upper part of vertical hole is common between vertical and horizontal cavity.

The upper half part of each vertical cavity has the diameter slightly bigger than the cap diameter of capsule. The lower half part of this cavity has diameter slightly bigger than the body diameter of capsule. Therefore in this cavity, if capsule is received with body dome facing downwards, it will get into the cavity perfectly well. But if it is received in reverse way, i.e. cap dome facing downwards, the capsule will not get accommodated fully in the cavity. Cap dome will rest over the body hole and body will be protruding out of the drum surface. To accommodate the protruded body part into the horizontal slot, it needs to be pushed into horizontal slot by some mechanism. Such mechanism is fitted on the rectifier drum.

The cavities in all the three drums are positioned such that at meeting points of the drums, capsules can get transferred easily from top drum to bottom drum.

The cavities in the 3rd drum, i.e. 'Transfer Roller' are same as in case of drum no. 1. Therefore, capsules from the rectifier roller will get fully into the cavities of transfer roller. Capsules will not protrude out from the cavities. From transfer roller, the capsules in rectified condition get easily loaded into capsule segment.

(iii) Rectification : Cavities in the Feed Drum (drum no. 1) during its rotation pick-up capsules from capsule hopper in a random fashion. During rotation, when the cavities in the drum face the downward direction, capsules will start falling out from the cavities. To overcome this problem, the drum is protected with the cover so that capsules will not fall out. The cover is not provided where the two drums meet. This is required for allowing the transfer of capsule from first drum into the cavities of the rectifier drum (drum no. 2).

When the capsules are received into cavities of rotating rectifier drum, they will get into the rectifier drum into two ways :
1. Some capsules will be facing their body dome in the downward direction and
2. Others will be facing their cap domes in the downward direction. See Fig. 9.8 for rectification of such capsules.

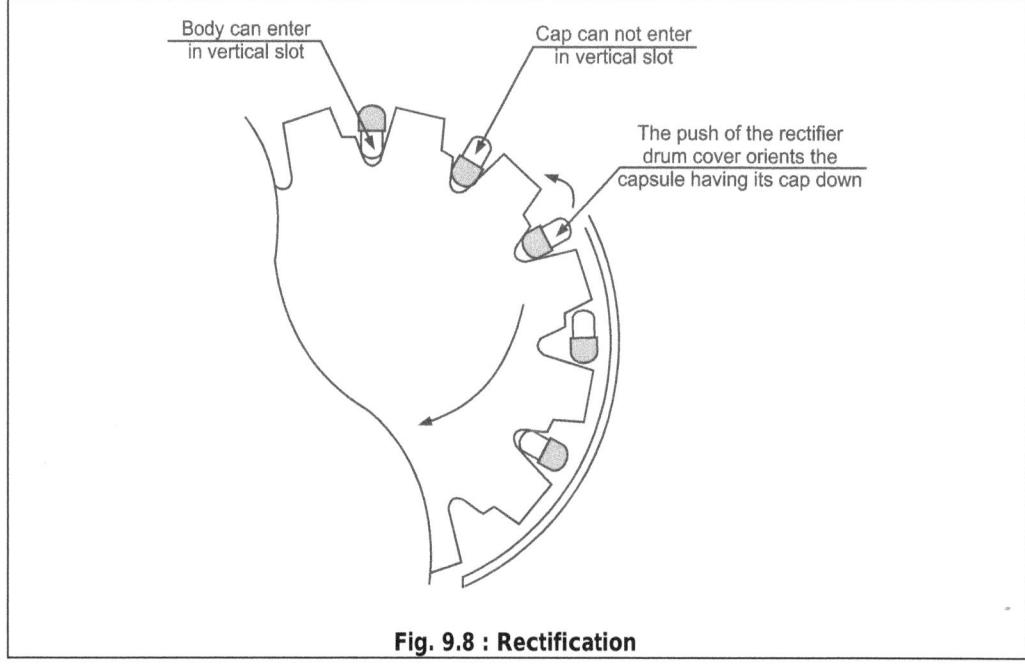

Fig. 9.8 : Rectification

The capsules facing their body domes in the downward direction will go fully into the vertical cavities of the rectifier drum and will not protrude out from the cavities. However, the capsules facing their cap domes in the downward direction, will not get fully into the vertical slot and the bodies of such capsules will protrude out of cavities. The cover is provided to the rectifier drum as shown in Fig. 9.7. The rectifier drum rotates in the opposite direction of the horizontal cavities.

During rotation of the rectifier drum, when protruded bodies come in contact with the edge of the cover of the rectifier drum, the capsules turn their axis, because of the push offered by the edge of this cover and body part of the capsules gets pushed into horizontal cavities, thereby the capsules remain in the horizontal position partly in horizontal cavity and partly in vertical cavity. However, this does not apply to the capsules which are fully gone into the vertical cavities of the rectifier drum with their body domes facing downward.

When the rectifier drum rotates more than 90° from the meeting point of feed drum and rectifier drum, at that position capsules will remain in slots as described below. The capsules which were received in the cavities of the rectifier drum with body domes pointing downwards, would remain in the vertical cavities, as they were received. However, the capsules which were received with cap domes pointing downwards would turn and remain partly in horizontal and partly in vertical cavities together.

As the rectifier drum rotates further it comes in contact with rotating transfer drum. The caps portions of the horizontal capsules first come in contact with the cavities of transfer drum, thereby capsules go into the cavities of transfer drum with cap domes facing downward position.

The capsules in vertical cavities, changes their direction facing cap domes pointing downward when rectifier drum rotates through 180° for coming in contact with transfer drum. At that point of meeting, capsules simply drop down with caps pointing in downward direction.

Therefore, when the capsules are received in transfer drum, they are fully oriented. When the transfer drum rotates through 180° from receiving point, for delivering the capsules into capsule segments, the capsules are delivered with body domes pointing in downward direction and cap domes pointing out in the upward direction.

The drums are provided with the covers wherever required.

9.3 OPENING THE CAPSULE AND SEPARATING CAP AND BODY

The conditions required for separation and joining of the capsules are described below :

Cap and body have common vertical axis in joined condition. For opening the capsule into cap and body, body has to be taken out from the cap by following the same axis.

Similarly for joining the cap and body to form a capsule, the open ends of cap and body should face each other and their vertical axis should be matched. Body should follow the same vertical axis for joining. Conditions required for opening and joining of capsule on capsule filling machine are met with the help of pair of cap and body bushes or pair of cap and body segments or pair of cap and body rings. For the sake of convenience, working of only cap and body bush assembly is described. Same is applicable for segments and rings assemblies.

In the assembled condition of cap and body bushes :
1. Cap bush always remains over the body bush.
2. The hole in the cap bush always remains concentric with hole in the body bush and
3. The holes have common axis.

Therefore, when the capsule remains in the holes of the bush assembly, cap and body remain concentric with each other and they share the common axis. Both these conditions are essential for opening and joining of capsules.

The capsule is loaded into the concentric holes of the bush assembly from the rectifier with cap up – body down position. Due to this, cap remains into the cap hole in cap bush and the unopened part of body gets partly into body hole in body bush. Once the loading is complete, the bush assembly moves to the next station. At this point, vacuum is applied at the bottom part of the body bush. Due to Vacuum, body gets separated from the cap and gets fully into hole of the body bush. If the capsule fit is loose, body comes down fast and dome portion of the body hits the bottom of the body hole. The body sometimes get cracks on this account. To avoid this, body is provided the support of push rod, which moves downward slowly thereby allowing the body to come down slowly.

On some machine, vacuum is applied on the loading station itself, instead of applying the vacuum on the next station.

On all the capsule filling machines, (except hand operated machine) the capsule separation is done by vacuum.

On hand operated capsule filling machine, the body is held by clamping mechanism and after the body is clamped, cap is removed. After removal of cap, body is declamped. Being elastic, body gets its original round shape and sits properly in the hole. Thereafter drug is filled into the body.

After separation of cap from the body, for filling the drug powder into the body, it is essential to shift the cap away from body. The shifting of cap will allow the filling mechanism to fill the drug powder into the body. The lateral shifting of cap bush from the body bush is carried out by the mechanism fitted on the filling machine.

9.4 FILLING THE DRUG INTO THE OPENED BODY

The drug is filled into the opened body by filling mechanism. The different mechanisms working on different filling principles are separately given in the chapter on "Capsule Filling Principles and Filling Machines".

9.5 JOINING THE FILLED BODY WITH CAP AND LOCKING THE CAPSULE

After filling the drug powder into the body in the body bush, cap bush is reassembled with the body bush. Cap bush is provided with the support of rod or plate on the top of cap bush to hold the cap in position for joining. The body push rod, pushes the filled body into the cap thereby capsule gets joined and locked. On some machines, two stations are provided one for joining and next one for locking. On the last station, joined and locked capsule is ejected from the bush assembly into the container.

9.6 EJECTING THE FILLED CAPSULE

On the last station, top support on cap bush is removed and joined capsule is ejected from the cap side of the assembly with the help of push rod which actuates from the bottom hole of the body bush.

■■■

10.
FILLING MACHINES

10.1 INTRODUCTION

Drugs are available in various forms as follows :

1. Powder and granules
2. Pellets
3. Micro tablets (ready dosage form)
4. Tablets (ready dosage form)
5. Oils and pastes

All these forms are filled in Hard Gelatin Capsules. Even the combinations of these forms are filled in hard gelatin capsules.

A number of filling machines are available for filling powders and granules as most of the drugs are available in this form.

(For filling the drugs in other forms [other than powder and granules] special machines are designed, manufactured and marketed as special purpose filling machines).

Manufacture of capsule filling machine is a specialized field. There is limited number of capsule filling machine manufacturers in the world. Till recent past only very few companies located in Germany, Italy and USA manufactured these machines.

The picture is now changing; these machines are also manufactured in other countries like India, Korea, China, Japan etc.

Over the period of time, different capsule filling machine manufacturers developed machines fitted with different filling mechanisms working on different filling principles. These filling principles are as under :

1. Auger
2. Dosator-Piston
3. Tamping
4. Vibrator
5. Vacuum

The machines working on Auger and Dosator-piston principles are described below :

10.2 AUGER FILL MACHINES

10.2.1 Principle

In auger fill principle machine, the empty body is filled with powder or granules by moving auger screw. The auger screw rotates with constant speed in the powder hopper and the powder in the hopper is conveyed and filled into empty body positioned below the hopper.

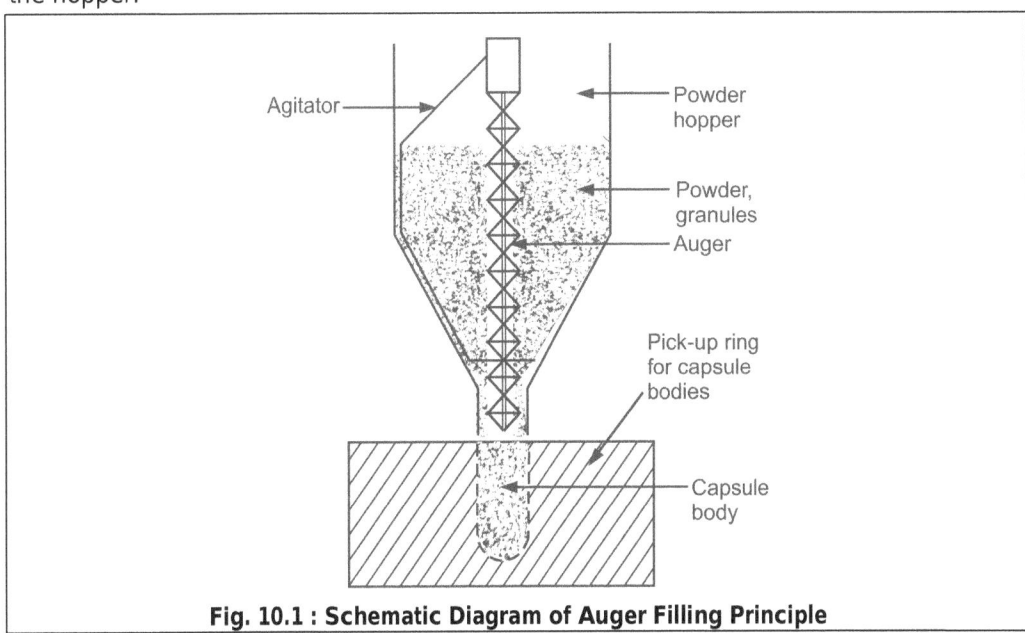

Fig. 10.1 : Schematic Diagram of Auger Filling Principle

10.2.2 Calculation of the Volumetric Capacity to Determine the Capsule Size for Filling the Unit Drug Dosage

Normally, size of capsule is decided in such a way that it will accommodate the drug volume to be filled along with the volume of additives, leaving extra capacity available for adjustment in the variation of drug additives, volumes arising out of bulk density variations. In short, the size of the capsule selected for filling has bigger volumetric capacity than the volume of the materials to be filled in. The following example will make the concept clear.

Example : The drug to be filled in the capsule is 250 milligrams with bulk density 0.700 gms/cc. Find out the volume of the drug so that size of the capsule can be selected for filling.

Solution : The volume required to occupy 250 milligrams drug is found out in the following equation.

$$\frac{\text{Mass}}{\text{Volume}} = \text{Density}$$

$$\therefore \frac{\text{Mass}}{\text{Density}} = \text{Volume}$$

$$\therefore \frac{0.250 \text{ gms}}{0.700 \text{ gms/c.c.}} = \text{Volume}$$

$$\therefore 0.357 \text{ c.c.} = \text{Volume}$$

Thus, 0.357 c.c. volume is required to fill drug of 0.250 milligrams.

Normally 10% additional volume is kept to accommodate the additives. However, it may differ from formulation to formulation.

Thus, in the present example we require 0.3927 c.c of the volume arrived as under:

```
    0.357   c.c   Volume of the drug
+   0.0357  c.c.  Volume for additives
    0.3927  c.c
```

Therefore, we have to fill 0.3927 c.c. volume of powder.

Table 10.1 : The Volumetric Capacities of the Standard Size Capsules

Size	Volume c.c capacity
00	0.95 c.c.
0	0.68 c.c.
1	0.50 c.c.
2	0.37 c.c.

In the case under consideration, size no. 1 capsule will be suitable because it has bigger volume available for filling the volume of the drug as well as additives, still leaving 0.100 c.c. volume extra. This extra volume becoming available is normally filled with filler materials also known as diluents. This is the normal process to select the size for initial trials of capsules for filling.

10.2.3 Historical Development

Mr. A. Colton (USA) is the inventor of semi-automatic (ring type) capsule filling machine working on this principle. His company marketed this machine as 'COLTON 8'. This machine was designed to rotate the body ring with eight different speeds to fill different powder weights; therefore, it was named as 'COLTON 8' machine. In or around 1960, Ms. Colton and Co. was closed down. It resulted into non-availability of this machine in the market.

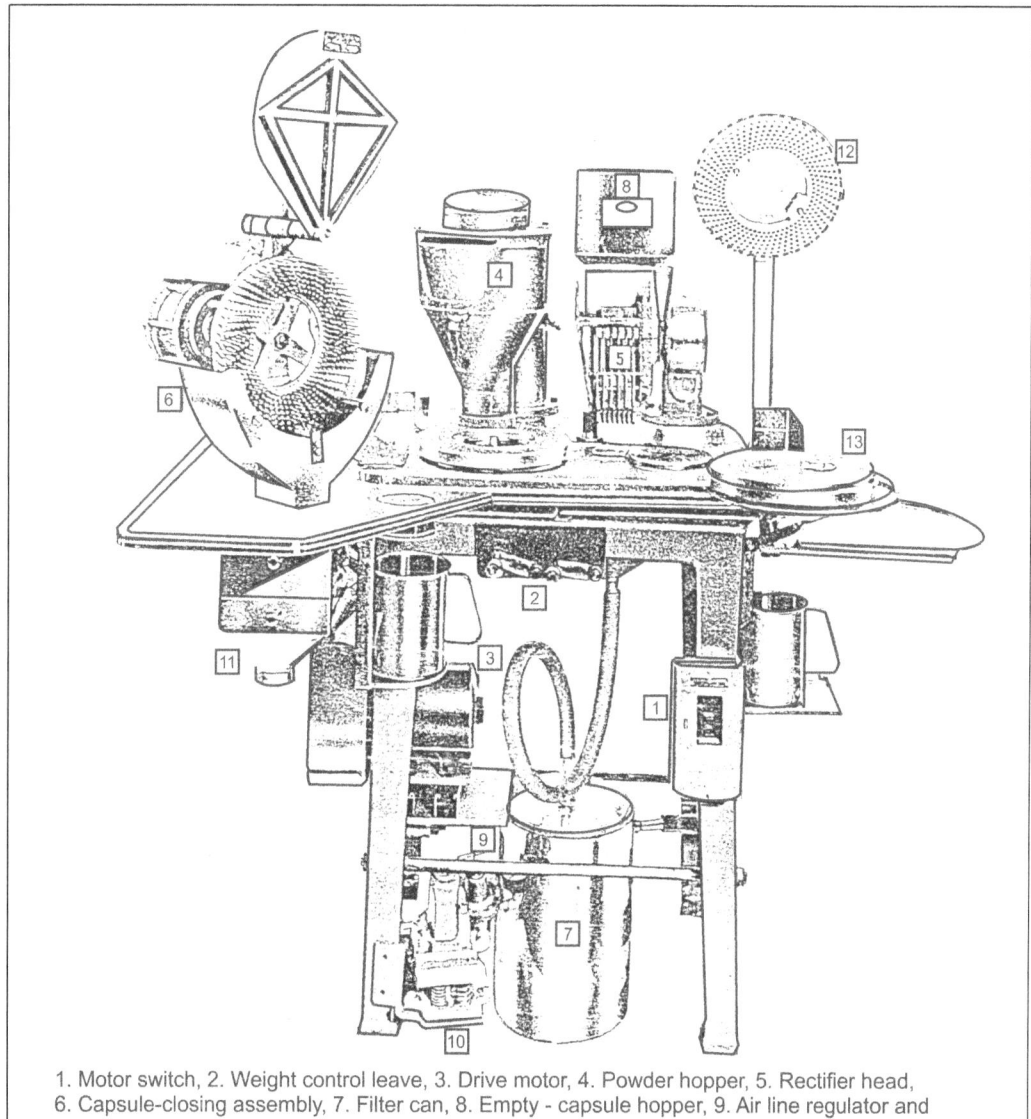

1. Motor switch, 2. Weight control leave, 3. Drive motor, 4. Powder hopper, 5. Rectifier head, 6. Capsule-closing assembly, 7. Filter can, 8. Empty - capsule hopper, 9. Air line regulator and pressure gauge, 10. Foot-control valve for closing, 11. Receptacle box, 12. Filling ring (cap section), 13. Filling ring (cap and body section)

Fig. 10.2 : The Lilly Version of the 'Colton 8' semi-automatic capsule filling machine

M/s. Parke Davis and Company, USA and M/s Eli Lilly & Company, USA came out with a similar version of the machine and marketed them as P.D.8 and Lilly 8 machines respectively.

Recently capsule divisions of both these companies have changed their management and are working under the names of M/s Pfizer and M/s Shionogi respectively (only capsule division of Eli Lilly and company is taken over by M/s Shionogi of Japan).

By the end of 20th century, M/s Eli Lilly (capsule division) now known as ' Quali cap'- Shionogi of Japan, has come out with variation of new auger type filling machine. This machine is more versatile than the earlier model.

M/S HOFLIGER and KARG produced first fully automatic (intermittent) machine working on this principle. In this machine when the body was positioned below the hopper, the auger screw in the hopper would start rotating. The timing control on the auger rotation used to regulate the fill weight of powder in the capsule body.

In this machine, the hopper position was fixed and the capsule bodies were moved below the hopper by the intermittent rotating disc.

There were two disadvantages in this machine :

(i) After opening of cap and body, same cap was not joined to the same body; therefore rejection wastage of capsule was high at the time of joining of filled body into the cap.

(ii) The powder to be filled was required to be very free flowing.

In or around 1965, Indian Drugs and Pharmaceuticals Ltd. Rishikesh, India, were having such 4-5 machines working in the formulation division to fill capsules. They are no more in operation.

'Colton 8' of semi-automatic ring type machines are now manufactured by different machinery manufacturers of the world. All these machines may have minor differences, but the working principle is the same.

Since 1977, 'COLTON 8' type filling machines were manufactured in India by Ms. P + AM (Pharmaceutical and Allied Machinery Company Pvt. Ltd), one of the group of companies of ACG Worldwide, Mumbai.

10.2.4 Description and Working of Machine (Working on the same Filling Principle)

M/s. P + AM marketed Auger filling principle machine as SA-9 machine. This is also known as SA-9 ring type filing machine. The detailed working of this SA-9 ring type filling machine is given below. The overview of the machine is shown in Fig.10.3. The sections of (a) loading of capsules in ring assembly (b) filling of powder in body ring and (c) capsule closing are shown in figures 4, 5 and 6 respectively.

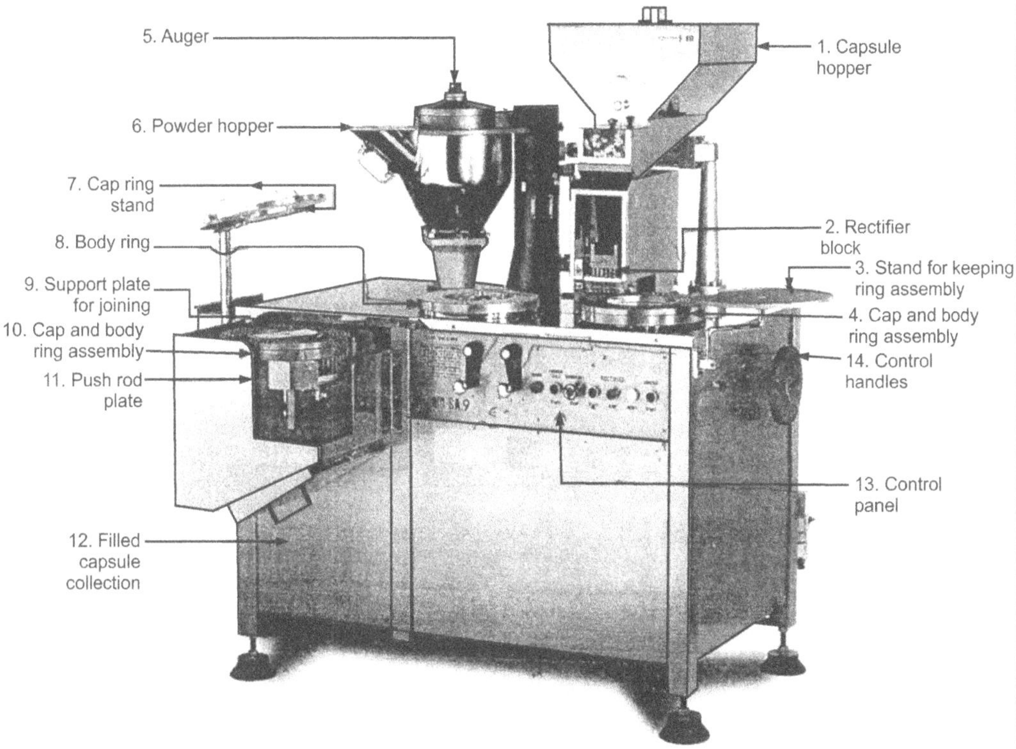

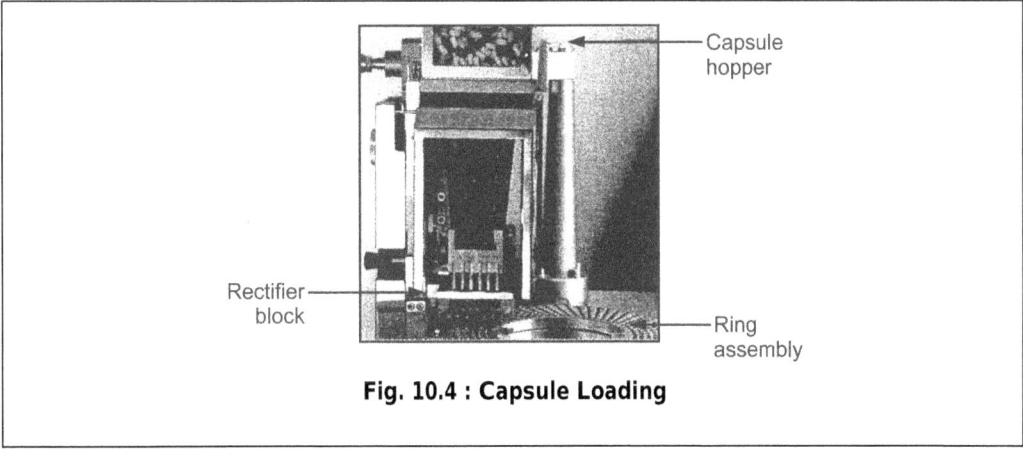

Fig. 10.3 : Filling Machine

Fig. 10.4 : Capsule Loading

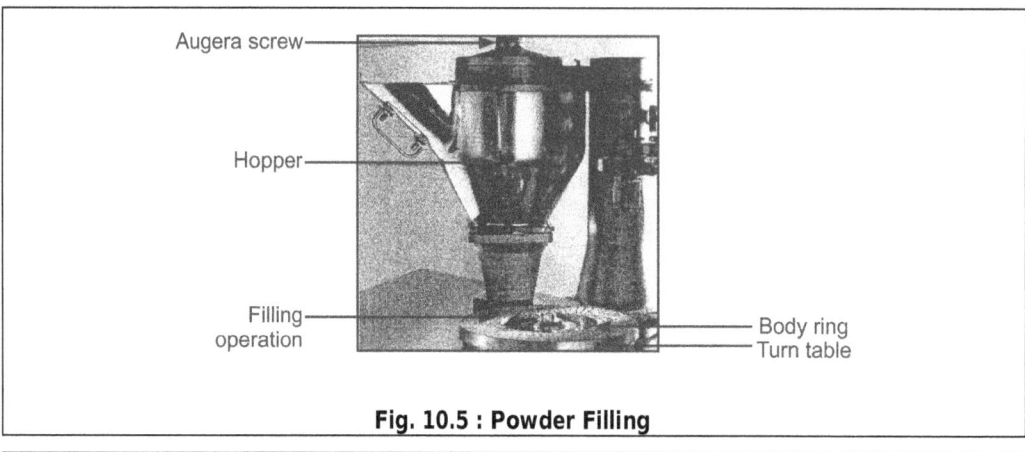

Fig. 10.5 : Powder Filling

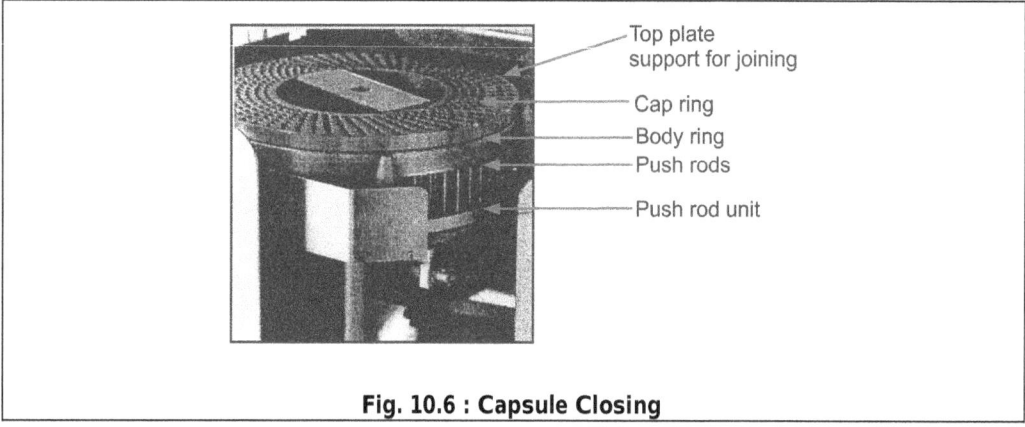

Fig. 10.6 : Capsule Closing

All figures with the courtesy of ACG World Wide, Mumbai

10.2.4.1 Machine Parts Handling Capsules

(a) **Capsule hopper :** For holding the empty capsules.

(b) **Magazine tubes :** For carrying the capsules from hopper to the Rectifier.

(c) **Rectifier / orientation mechanism :** The mechanism, which orients the capsules with cap up, and body down.

(d) **Aluminium-ring assembly :** For holding the oriented capsules.

Note : The detailed rectification process is given in Chapter No 9.

10.2.4.2 Machine Parts Handling Powder

(a) **Powder hopper :** For holding the powder/granules to be filled in the capsules.

(b) **Auger :** Fitted inside the hopper delivers during the rotation, powder from the hopper into the capsule bodies located in the aluminium ring. Auger has two speeds viz. fast and slow (now-a-days variable speed Augers are also in use).

(c) Turn table : It moves the body aluminium ring below the hopper and it has 9 different speeds which can be selected as per the requirement.

(d) Body aluminium ring : For holding the capsule bodies for filling the powder.

Augers with different twist angles are given below :

1. **Standard Auger or Single Flute Auger :** The name itself indicates that it is used for most of the powders and hence it is named as standard auger. Unless specified, normally machines are dispatched with this auger pre-fitted. The degree of flute is 180°.

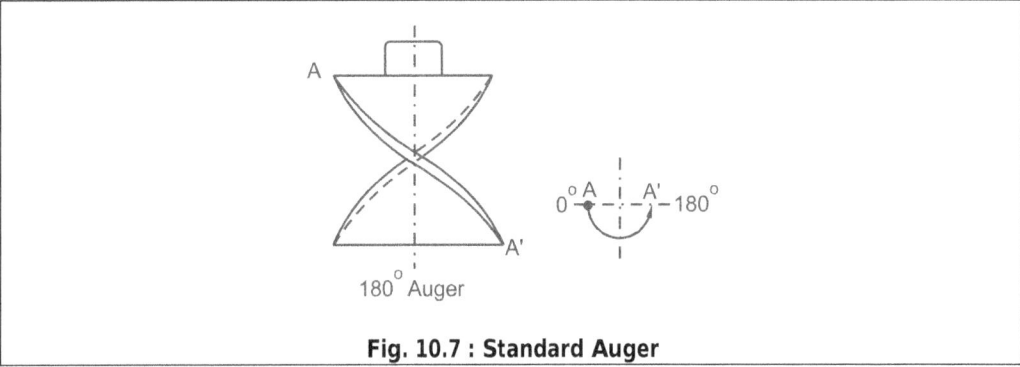

Fig. 10.7 : Standard Auger

2. **Spiral Auger or Double Flute Auger :** It is used when bulk density is low or powder is fluffy or for the powder which shows resistance to flow down. It is used when you get low weight than the desired weight even at the slowest speed of the filling table. The flute degree is (Approx.) 270°. This Auger presses more powder than standard Auger.

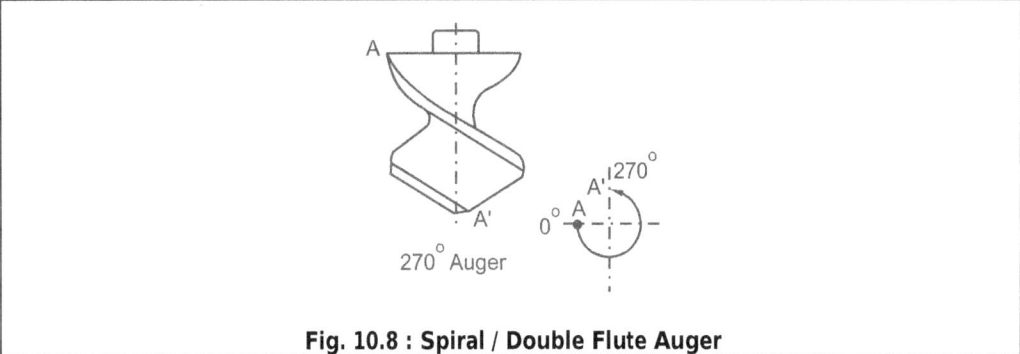

Fig. 10.8 : Spiral / Double Flute Auger

3. **Four Flute Auger or Flower Auger :** It is used for the powder having high bulk density. It is used when you get higher weight with standard auger even at the highest RPM of the filling table.

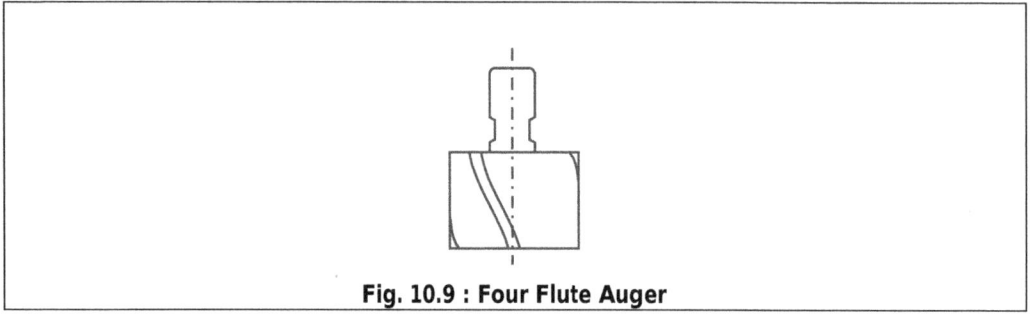

Fig. 10.9 : Four Flute Auger

4. **90° Auger :** Looks similar to standard auger. Presses less powder than the standard auger. If you get higher weight with the standard auger and lower weight with the four-flute auger than the desired weight, shift to 90° auger is done.

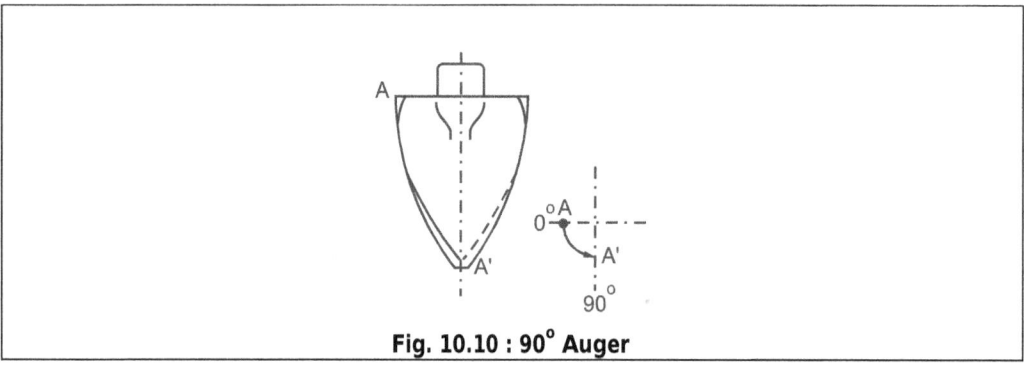

Fig. 10.10 : 90° Auger

5. **225° Auger :** Looks similar to spiral auger. Presses less powder than spiral auger and higher powder than the standard auger.

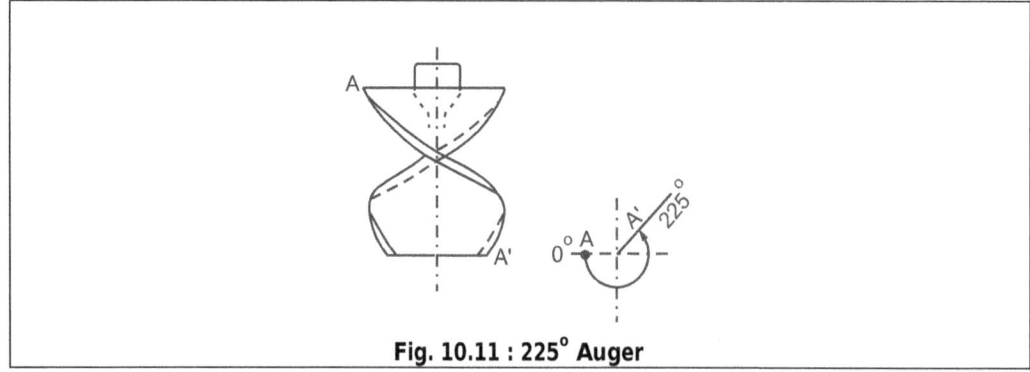

Fig. 10.11 : 225° Auger

6. T-Shape Auger : We have this auger for the powder having very nature of granules and only needs the distribution or heavy power. It is used when even four flute auger gives more weight at higher speed of the table.

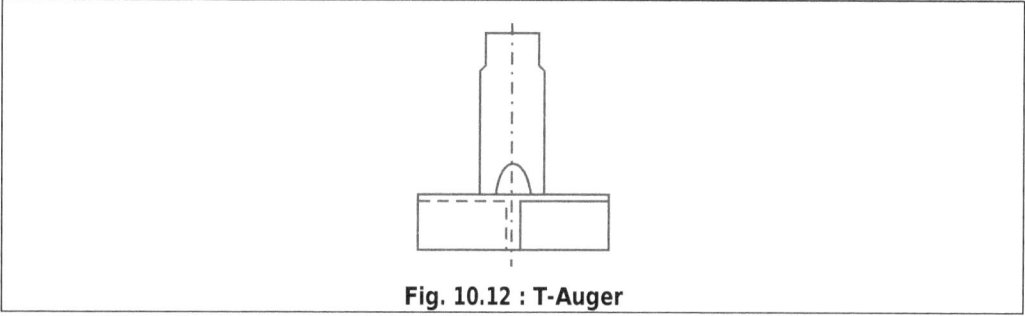

Fig. 10.12 : T-Auger

10.2.4.3 Powder Filling Process

The empty capsules are fed from hopper in the rectifier block. In rectifier block, capsules are rectified and loaded in capsule holes in ring assembly. In this way, loading ring is fully filled with empty capsules in one complete rotation of the ring. The vacuum applied at the bottom of the ring assembly facilitates the loading of capsules in ring assembly. Due to this vacuum, capsules loaded in ring assembly are separated into caps and bodies and remain in cap holes and body holes in the respective rings. There after, the cap ring is separated from the body ring and kept on the cap ring stand. The body ring is kept on the turntable. The turntable can be rotated with 9 different speed levers, which are provided on this machine. With the help of the control levers any one speed out of nine speeds can be selected to rotate the turntable. Any suitable screw can be fitted in the hopper depending on the powder characteristics. In the old machine only one fixed speed was provided to rotate the auger. In this machine two speeds are provided to rotate the auger. Any one speed can be selected for rotation of auger. This flexibility is provided to get the desired fill weight in a narrow band.

Except speeds of turntable, no other provision was available on the earlier Colton 8 type machine for achieving the full weight.

The movements of auger for filling operation and starting and closing of rotation of auger for filling are fully automated. Starting the electrical switch fitted on the machine activates these movements.

Before starting the filling operation, powder is filled in the hopper. When the hopper is actuated by electric switch, the powder hopper automatically moves over the body ring and at the same time body ring starts its rotation and auger screw also starts its rotation with respective set speed. Once the hopper is moved over the body ring, it remains in the steady position till body ring completes its one round. During rotation of body ring, powder is filled into the bodies from the hopper by the rotating auger. At the end of full rotation, three things happen automatically and simultaneously; (1) Hopper returns back to its home position (2) auger screw stops its rotation and (3) body ring stops its rotation. This is very essential to stop the damage of filling machine.

After filling the powder, cap ring is kept over the body ring and both rings are aligned. The ring assembly is now removed from the turntable. It is then kept over the push rods in the closing section (See Fig. 10.6). Capsule holes in the ring assembly and push rods are aligned before they are pushed into joining box. Top plate of the joining box (See Fig. 10.6) gives a support to cap ring plate from the top. Due to this, caps remain in the Cap holes in steady position without getting thrown out during the joining operation. Filled bodies get into respective caps smoothly. After ring assembly and push rod plate are pushed into the joining box, the push rod plate is actuated by pneumatic cylinder fitted below the push rod plate shaft. Push rods join the filled bodies in caps in the ring assembly and get the capsules locked. Thereafter, the ring assembly is moved out from the joining box. Once the ring assembly is brought back to home position, it is turned down by 180° and the filled capsules come out from the ring; they pass over the screen to remove the powder adhered and fairly clean filled capsules are collected in a box. On SA9 machine, once the ring assembly is put over the push rod in aligned conditions and electric button is pressed, all the above actions are done automatically.

10.2.5 Weight Control

The factors controlling the fill weight are given below.

1. Level of the powder in the hopper.
2. Speed of the turntable.
3. Type of auger.
4. Speed of auger.

Higher level of powder in the powder hopper, lower speed of the turn table, lower speed of the auger and higher twist angle give more fill weight.

10.3 DOSATOR-PISTON MACHINE

The Dosator-Piston filling machine is available in two types.

(A) Intermittent type.
(B) Rotary type.

10.3.1 Dosator-Piston Machine Intermittent Type
10.3.1.1 Principle

In dosator piston filling machine, the powder is filled into the cylindrical tube by dipping the open end of the tube into the powder bed. The volume of the powder filled in the tube is controlled by the inner diameter of the cylindrical tube and by the piston height set from the open end of the tube. The schematic diagram of dosator-piston filling is shown below.

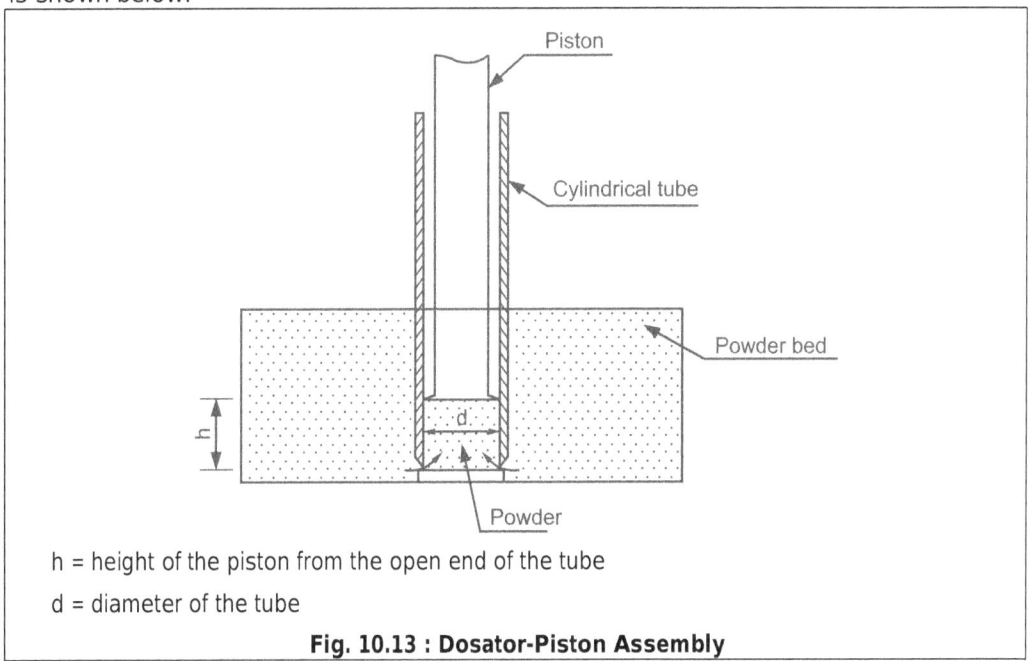

h = height of the piston from the open end of the tube

d = diameter of the tube

Fig. 10.13 : Dosator-Piston Assembly

10.3.1.2 Calculation of Volumetric Capacity to Determine the Capsule Size for Filling the Unit Drug Dose

The dose is formed in the cylindrical tube of dosator-piston assembly by dipping it into powder bed in powder tub, which is fitted in powder filling device.

To get the dose of required weight, it is essential to know its equivalent volume of powder required to be filled in dosator-piston assembly. This is calculated on the basis of equation of cylinder volume.

The weight of the powder dose to be filled in capsule is fixed to calculate the volume of the powder (drug). The equivalent weight of powder can be calculated from tap density of the powder. Tap density is found out experimentally. Once the tap density is worked out, the volume is calculated as follows :

Mass = Volume / Density (tap)

Therefore, Mass of powder to be filled / Tap density = Volume of powder

Once the volume is calculated, the piston height of the dosator from the open end (h) is calculated by the equation :

Volume = $\pi r \times r \times h$ (since the capsule is of cylindrical shape)

h can be calculated from the above equation since we know the volume and "r " which is the capsule body radius.

Once the 'h' is calculated, the piston height can be set accordingly to get the required volume of the powder to have the required fill weight.

Therefore, before starting the filling trials the piston heights of all dosators are set.

The capsule size is fixed based on the volume of the powder to be filled in.

10.3.1.3 Historical Development

Filling Machines Working on Dosator-Piston Principle :

When the compounder dispenses the drug powder in a capsule, he puts the drug powder over a glass plate or a ceramic tile and forms a heap of it. Thereafter he opens the required size of capsule and dips the open end of the body into heap of drug powder for a couple of times, till he gets the powder properly filled in the body. Thereafter he puts the cap over the filled body to form a filled capsule. It appears that the concept of dosator-piston filling must have been derived from seeing this operation.

Mr. A. Colton was the first person who made a fully automatic machine (intermittent type) to fill drug into empty capsule. This was designed to work exactly on the same lines as compounder dispenses the drug in the capsule. In this machine, the closed end of the body shell (dome of the body) is held by the collet and open end of the body is dipped in the powder bed in the powder tub couple of times to fill the body with the powder. In this machine, body acts like a dosator-piston. This machine had a capacity of filling 3000 capsules per hour.

There were two such machines working in India :

1. M/s. Alembic Chemicals Baroda.
2. M/s. Deys Medical Stores, Kolkatta.

10.3.1.4 Description and Working of Machine
(Working on Dosator-Piston Intermittent type Filling Principle)

The working of the Dosator-Piston type machine (Intermittent type), AF 40 machine manufactured in India by P + am of ACG worldwide is described below Fig. 10.14.

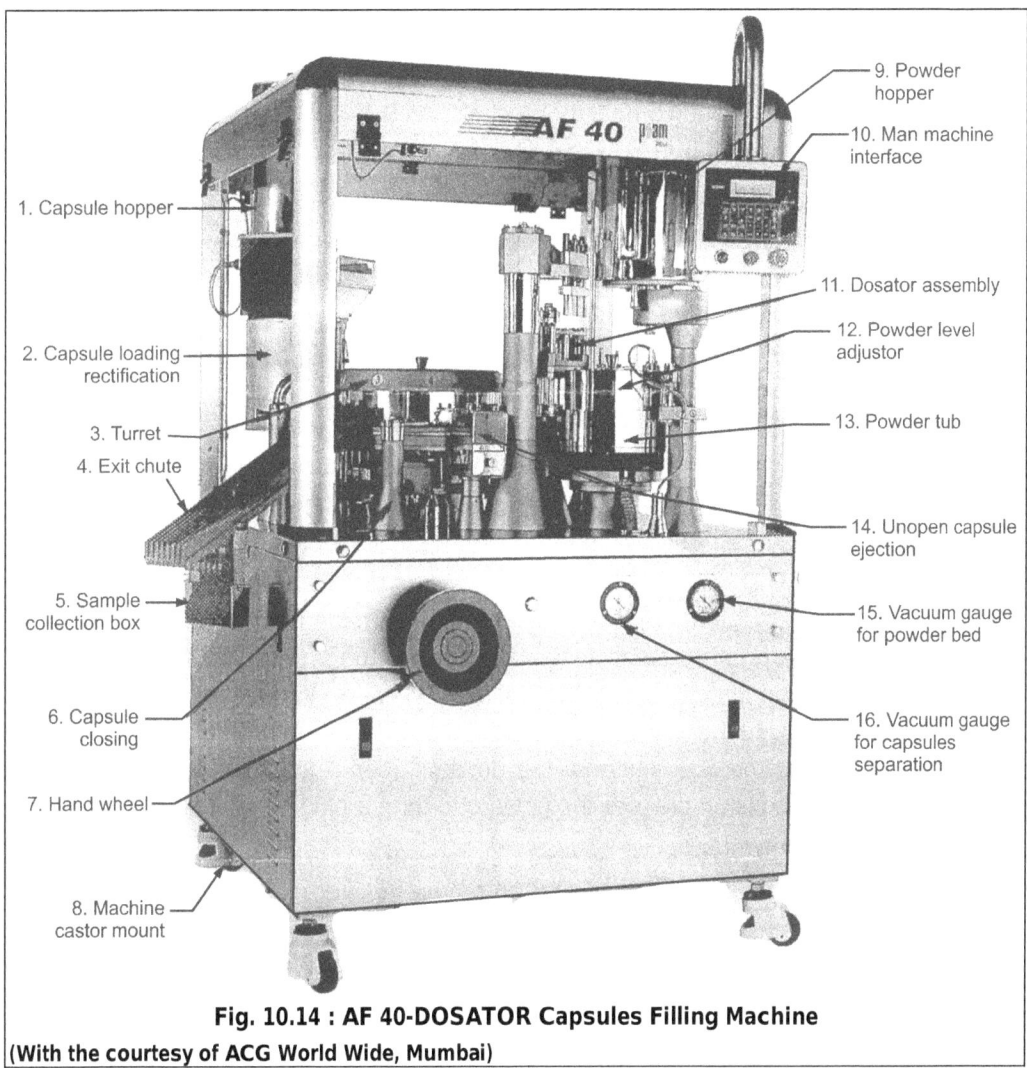

Fig. 10.14 : AF 40-DOSATOR Capsules Filling Machine
(With the courtesy of ACG World Wide, Mumbai)

10.3.1.4 (A) Machine Parts Handling Capsule
1. Capsule Segment.
2. Body Segment.
3. Vacuum arrangement for Cap-Body separation.
4. Cap Segment Supporting Plate.
5. Push Rod for ejecting filled and locked capsule.

10.3.1.4 (B) Machine Parts Handling Powder
The powder filling device consists of :
1. Powder hopper, powder stirrer, powder gate and plastic tube
2. Powder tub

3. Powder level controller
4. Reforming of powder bed and powder level adjuster
5. Dosator assembly and compactor bracket

1. Powder Hopper, Powder Stirrer, Powder Gate and Plastic Tube :

Powder hopper is a stainless steel container fitted with acrylic window; the powder stirrer is mounted centrally in the hopper and driven by a separate motor. At the delivery end of the hopper, adjustable gate is provided to control the rate of flow and to facilitate the removal of powder at the end of shift. Plastic tube is fitted to the gate to convey the powder into powder tub.

2. Powder Tub :

The function of powder tub is to create a uniform powder bed of a constant height. Vacuum is provided at the bottom so that bed formation becomes better. But vacuum will suck the powder. To minimize this, 5 micron filter is fixed in the tub to prevent the excess powder from being sucked out by the vacuum. This is essential for plug formation and good fill weight control.

At the bottom of the tub there are 35 round buttons made from stainless steel (S.S). With each 180° rotation of dosator assembly, powder tub is indexed by 72° and S.S. buttons are positioned directly below the dosator cylinders. When the dosator cylinder enters the powder inside the powder tub, the dosator cylinder gets filled with powder and forms a plug against the S.S. buttons; the dosator open end is set 0.1 mm from the bottom face when the piston presses the powder to form a plug.

3. Power Level Controller :

Every time when the powder is picked up by the dosator-piston assembly, the level of the powder in the tub goes down. When the powder level goes below the set level, it is sensed by a capacitive type proximity switch which sends a signal to the PLC (programmable logic circuit). Now, the PLC starts the powder feed motor to feed powder into the powder tub. This arrangement maintains the required quantity of powder in the tub to rebuild the powder bed.

4. Reforming of Powder Bed and Powder Level Adjuster :

When the powder is picked up by the dosator-piston assembly, void is created in the powder bed. To rebuild the bed without voids, the bed with the voids is cut, ploughed and thereafter uniform bed is formed by mechanical devices and vacuum arrangement provided in the tub. When the good bed is formed, the required height of the bed is maintained with the help of the level adjuster. The height of the bed is normally kept 2½ times the plug height. With this arrangement, every time dosator-piston units dip in the powder bed, they always get a uniform bed of proper density for forming the dose.

5. Dosator Assembly and Compactor Bracket :

In this model, there are 14 dosators in dosator assembly. There are 7 dosators on one side (1 to 7) and 7 dosators on the other side (8 to 14).

Dosator assembly during dosing process moves up and down as well as indexes 180°. This means that while one side of dosators is forming the plugs in the dosators when they are dipped in the tub, other side of dosators is ejecting the previously formed dose in the body of the capsule.

Compactor bracket performs two functions.
(i) Moving dosator-piston assembly up and down.
(ii) Compacting the powder when dosators' open ends are 0.1 mm distance from button surface.

10.3.1.4 (C) Working of the Machine (Powder Filling Process)

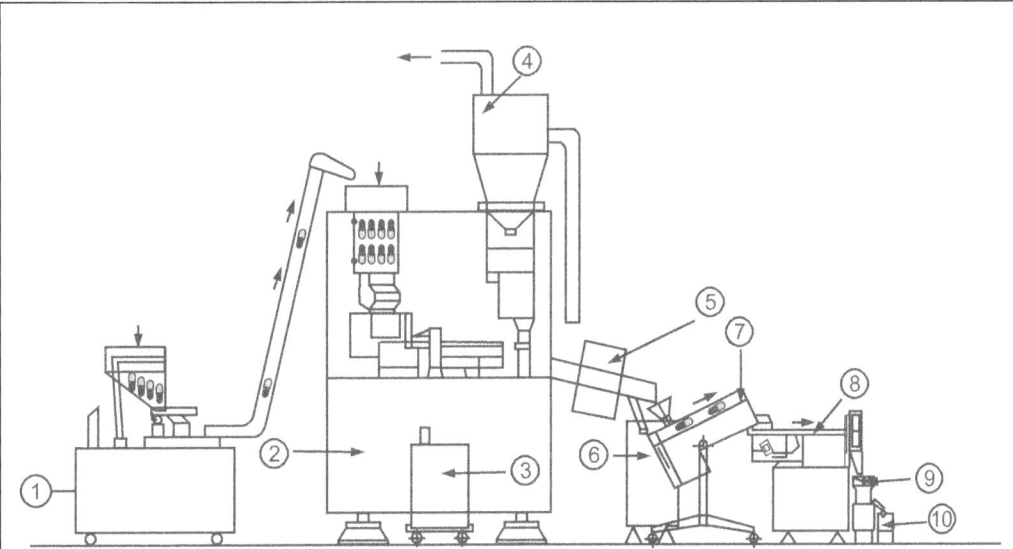

1. Empty Capsule Sorter Elevator – SE-100
2. Automatic Capsule Filling Machine
3. Air Displacement Unit – ADU
4. Automatic Product Conveying System – PCS-200
5. One Line Metal Detection System
6. On Line Check Weigher – CW-10
7. Dedusting and Polishing Machine – DP-100
8. Mini Capsule Sorter – MCS-100
9. Empty Capsule Eliminator – ECS-100
10. Capsules reading for blister packing

(Approximate dimensions of the Line are L × W × H = 3900 mm × 3200 mm × 2000 mm)

Fig. 10.15 : Automatic Capsule Filling Transfer Line - Ready to Blister Pack

(With the courtesy of ACG World Wide, Mumbai)

The machine and the schematic diagram are given in Fig. 10.14 and Fig. 10.15 respectively. Before describing the general working of AF-40 machine, some terms, which are commonly used, are given below :

1. **Pair of segments :**

They are two separate components. One is called cap segment and another is called body segment. In assembled conditions they are called PAIR OF SEGMENTS. On AF-40 machine, pair of segments always move out as one unit. Only at two stations the cap and the body segments move out horizontally from one another for carrying out two different operations.

   1. Filling the medicine in body.
   2. Ejecting the unopened capsule.

Cap segment is fitted with 7 capsule bushes and body segment is also fitted with 7 body bushes. In each cap bush, there is a hole for cap and in each body bush there is a hole for body. In assembled condition, the each pair of cap and body shares a common vertical axis. When cap or body segment moves vertically up or down, the respective capsule and body hole still shares a common vertical axis. Sharing the common axis is important for :

   1. Loading the capsules in the holes in cap segment.
   2. Separation of cap and body.
   3. Rejoining of capsule.
   4. Ejection of filled capsule.

(For the sake of convenience, every time instead of stating, cap hole in cap bush and body hole in body bush, it will be stated as cap and body respectively.)

2. **Working of AF-40 machine :**

There are 10 stations provided on the machine. Each station is provided to carry out a specific operation. The pairs of segments are fitted on the mechanism, which rotate these segments intermittently through each station. During rotation, each pair of segments stops on the station for a specific time. During the stoppage, specific operation is carried out. In this way, during one rotation each pair of segments move through all the stations.

On each station, specific filling operation is carried out.

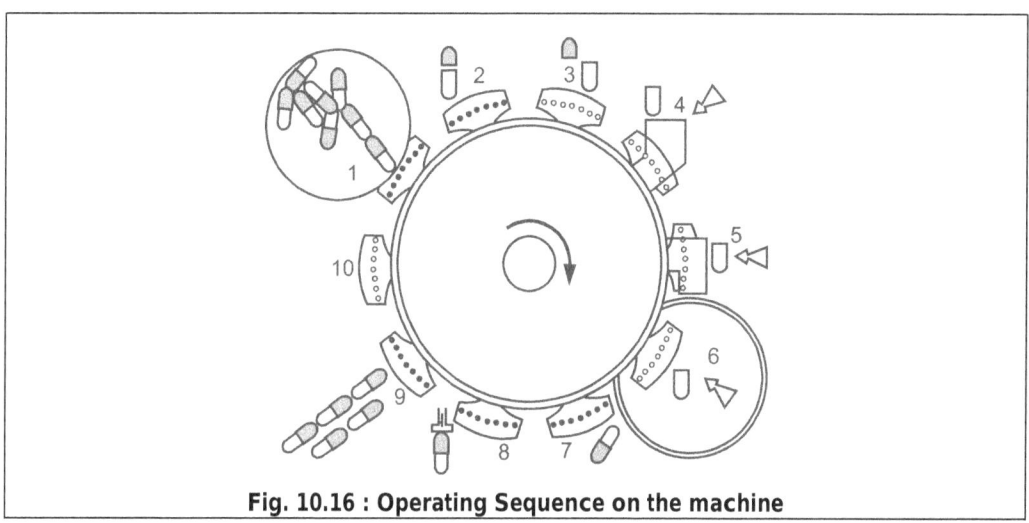

Fig. 10.16 : Operating Sequence on the machine

Station No.1 : On this station 7 empty capsules in rectified condition are loaded into 7 cap bushes in the pair of segments. Capsules are separated into caps and bodies by vacuum.

Station No. 2 : No operation takes place. The pair of segments moves to Station No. 3. While moving towards station 3, two things happen; cap segment first moves up and then gets horizontally shifted. This avoids crushing of unopened capsule.

Station No. 3 : On this station the bodies in the body segments are exposed for carrying out the filling operation.

Stations No. 4 and 5 : They are provided for filling tables and pellets.

Station No. 6 : It is for filling powder or granules in capsules. (The powder filling device is described separately).

Station No.7 : This is for ejecting the unopened capsule. The ejected capsule is normally collected in a box connected to this station.

Station No. 8 : On this station, cap and body segments come together to form a pair of segments. Cap segment is supported at the top by supporting plate. With the help of push rods, filled bodies are joined into caps to form filled capsules and capsules are locked.

Station No. 9 : While going from station 8 to 9, cap support plate is moved away and 7 joined and locked capsules are ejected out from the pair of segments.

Station No. 10 : On this station, bushes are cleaned with vacuum and pairs of segments are ready for the second round.

10.3.1.5 Powder Filling Device

The powder filling device is fixed close to Station No. 6. It consists of a hopper, stirrer, feed tube, telescopic tube, powder level sensing device, powder tub, level adjuster, replensishing devices, dosator assembly and compactor bracket.

Fig. 10.17 : Powder Filling Section of the Automatic Capsule Filling Machine
(With the courtesy of ACG World Wide, Mumbai)

The mechanism provided in the machine facilitates very accurate fill weights, even for partial filling of capsule.

While describing the device, only the process of powder filling in the capsule body is covered. The following factors control the fill weight :

(a) Uniform density of the powder bed where the dose is formed in the dosator. To form a bed of uniform density, powder must have good flow properties.

(b) Constant powder bed height as per the requirement.

(c) Cohesive properties of the blend. This is required so that the plug can be taken from tub to capsule body without loss of powder from the open end of the dosator. If the plug is not cohesive, loose powder may fall out from the open end of the dosator. This will lead to weight variation.

(d) Adhesive property of the plug. If the plug gets stuck to the dosator wall from inside, the plug will not get fully transferred into the body, resulting in less powder getting filled. This will lead to weight variation.

10.3.1.6 List of Few Machine Manufacturers (Intermittent Machines)

Three main companies who are manufacturing dosator-piston-intermittent-type machines are :

1. M/s. IMA, Italy
2. M/s. Romao Macofar, Italy
3. P+AM, India.

M/s. IMA markets these machines under the trade name Zanasi and Zanasi plus.

Zanasi has many models. They are Zansai 6, 12, 25 and 40. The production capacity in each model is different. It ranges from 6000 to 40000 capsules per hour. Zanasi plus capsule models have production capacity ranging from 8000 to 85000 capsules/ hour.

There are few other companies in Europe who are manufacturing dosator-piston type machines. One of them is Romaco Macofar, Italy.

M/s Pam Pharmaceutical and Allied Machinery Co. Pvt. Ltd. (P + AM), a member of the ACG worldwide, Mumbai is the first to manufacture dosator-piston (intermittent) type machine in India in around 1990. This machine is marketed as AF-40.

Table 10.2 : List of Intermittent Dosator-Piston Capsule Filling Machines Manufactured by Some Leading Machine Manufacturing Companies.

Sr. No.	Series Model No.	Production rate per hour	Special Features
1.	Pam Pharmaceutical and Allied Machinery Co. Pvt Ltd. ACG World Wide (India) Machine : AF-40	40,000	Powder, Granules/Pellets/oil and pastes with help of special attachments.
2.	IMA (Italy) Machine : ZANASI 6 ZANASI 12 ZANASI 25 ZANASI 40 ZANASI plus, Various models	6,000 12,000 25,000 40,000 8,000 to 85,000	(1) All the models are available in F and E versions. F : available in standard fittings. E : provided with automatic sampling with check weight units. (2) Samples are drawn on statistical basis and piston setting is done automatically. (3) With several capsule weights out of limits, machine stops automatically. (4) With attachments, pellets, tablets and particle filling is done.
3.	Romaco Macofar (Italy) Machine : CD 25 CD 40 CD 60	25,000 40,000 60,000	(1) Can fill sizes 00-0-1-2-3-4 and 5. (2) Can fill many combinations like powder, granules, tablets, small capsules, pellets etc.

10.3.2 Rotary Machines

10.3.2.1 Principle

There is no difference in the principle used in intermittent and rotary machines for filling the capsules. In both the machines, the dosator piston assembly is dipped into the powder bed, and the dose is picked up. In other words, the principle used is identical. The only difference is that here the action of filling is carried out while the machine is in rotation.

10.3.2.2 Calculation of Volumetric Capacity to Determine the Capsule Size For Filling the Unit Drug Dose

Same as that for Dosator intermittent type

10.3.2.3 Historical Development

Dosator-piston rotary machines are also described as continuous dosator machines. These machines are comparable with those of rotary tablet machines. They are designed to give higher outputs.

MG2 company is the first company who introduced the first dosator piston rotary machine and marketed three machines as Model G 36. The capsule filling operations on this machine were carried out on capsule bushes which were fitted on continuous rotating chain. In the new models, chain is not used as carrier of bushes.

Upto few years back, there were only three Italian companies who were manufacturing rotary machines. They were :

(i) MG2
(ii) ZANASI
(iii) IMA S.P.A.

In industry, rotary machines are also known as 3 turret, 2 turret and 1 turret machines.

MG2 machines have 3 turrets. One turret is for rectification of capsules, second turret is for transferring of rectified capsules into the third turret and the third turret is for all the rest of operations of filling.

Zanasi rotary machines have 2 turrets, one for rectification and transfer of capsules into the second turret and second turret is meant for carrying out all the rest of the filling operations - i.e. opening of capsules, filling the drug and closing and locking the capsules and discharging them.

IMA machines have single turret. All the operations are carried out at different horizontal levels on a revolving common shaft.

In IMA machine the filling of capsule is a totally dust free operation. Therefore, it is considered to be very safe from operator's point of view. This they have achieved by carrying out the powder filling operations in completely covered area. For an outsider, when he sees the operation from outside, he does not understand where the capsule filling operations are carried out.

10.3.2.4 Working of Rotary Machine

(Working on Dosator-Piston Rotary Type Filling Principle)

The latest Dosator-Piston rotary type machine marketed is described below to understand working of the rotary filling machine.

Single turret machine, manufactured by M/s IMA Co. (Italy) is considered to be the latest and most approved machine in rotary series. The basic working of this machine is described below :

The overview of the machine is given in the figure below.

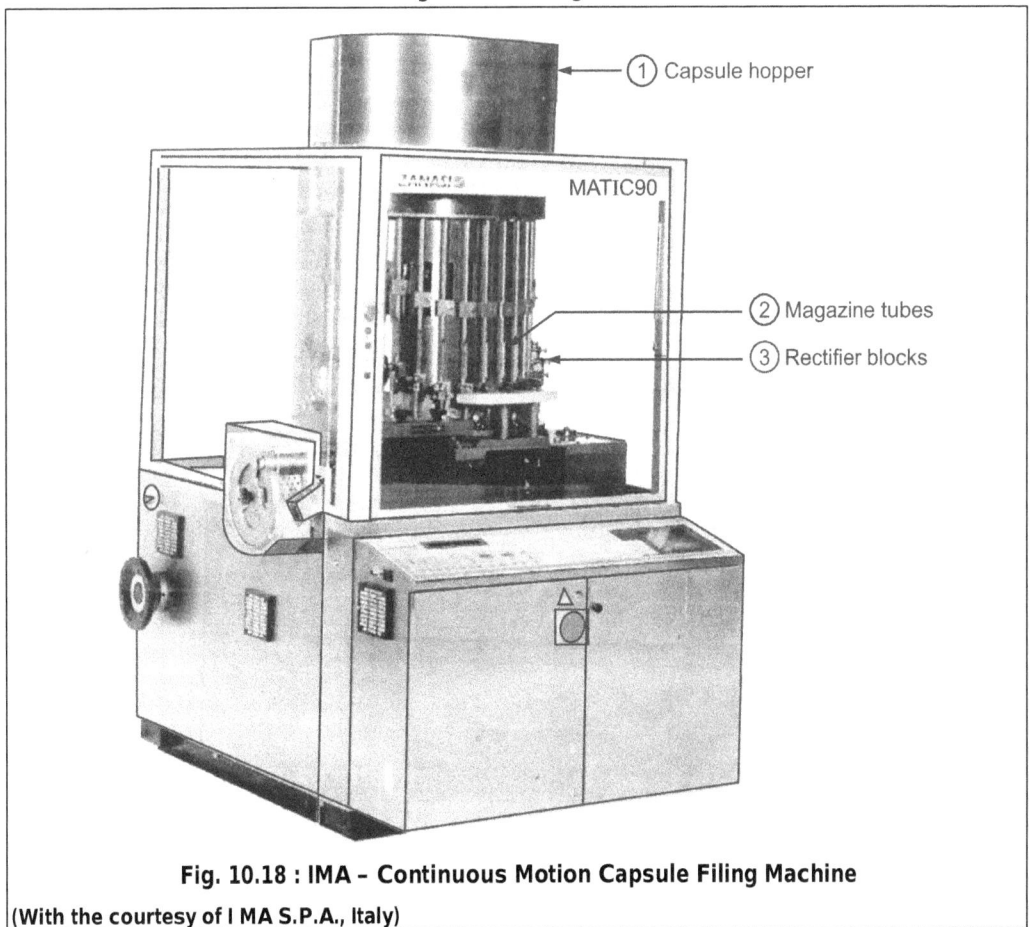

Fig. 10.18 : IMA – Continuous Motion Capsule Filing Machine
(With the courtesy of I MA S.P.A., Italy)

The machine has following parts :-

10.3.2.4 (A) Machine Parts Handling Capsule
1. Capsule hopper.
2. Magazine tubes fitted with rectification mechanism.
3. Cap bushes fitted in a ring.
4. Body bushes.
5. Body push rods having vacuum arrangements to suck the body from capsule into body bushes.

10.3.2.4 (B) Machine Parts Handling Powder
1. Rotating powder tub.
2. Dosator-piston assemblies.
3. Body bushes below the cap bushes for loading separation, rejoining, locking and ejection.

Except parts 1 and 2, the rest of the parts are not seen in the overview of the machine. These parts are shown and described with figures, given to explain the working of the machine.

10.3.2.4 (C) Working of the Machine
All the parts stated above are fitted on the main turret shaft. The main turret shaft rotates constantly through 360° during working. While rotating, all the capsule filling operations are carried out. For carrying out the filling operation from receiving the capsule from capsule hopper till the filled capsule is delivered, shaft has to turn through 810, i.e. 810/360 = 81/36 = 2 and ¼ rounds. Within these 2¼ rounds, the capsule is oriented in the first round; in the 2nd round, capsule is transferred into cap bush, separated in cap and body, un-opened capsule is discharged, the separated body is filled with the powder in the dosater circuit, filled body is rejoined and locked in the cap and in the remaining 90° round, the filled capsule is discharged.

(The movement of capsules in the vertical plane are shown in Fig. 10.19 and Fig. 10.20).

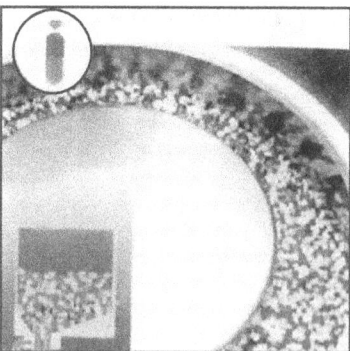

The capsules are contained in a top hopper. Feed tubes gently penetrate the layer of capsules and transfer them to the positioning station.

Fig. 10.19 : Capsule Feed

The capsules are positioned first horizontally and then vertically so that the bottom points downwards. They are them placed in the transport bushings

Fig. 10.20 : Positioning

The empty capsule hopper is at the top of the machine. The magazine tubes are fitted with rectification mechanisms; (overview Fig. 10.18). Magazine tube is the tube which carries the capsule. They move up and down in the hopper and capsules get loaded into magazine tubes. On higher output machines more number of magazine tubes are provided.

Capsules are rectified in rectification mechanism. i.e. cap up and body down position. This mechanism is similar to conventional mechanism. The rectified capsules are loaded in the cap bushes fitted on the rotating discs, (see Fig. 10.21 the inner view) from the rectifier mechanism fitted into the magazine tubes; they move up and down and rotate further.

The pushers move upwards so as to open the capsule, sucking the bottom into the mower transport bush

(a) Opening

The lower bushing moves toward the inside to perform product dosing and a pusher eliminates any un-open capsules from the cover bushings

(b) Elimination of defective capsules

Fig. 10.21

Exactly below the cap bush, body bush is provided and when the body bush is below the cap bush, both the bushes are concentric with one another. This is essential for 1) perfect loading and separation of body in the body bushes 2) joining and locking and 3) ejection of the filled capsules.

Body bush only moves from its original position away from the cap bush i.e. towards centre shaft for receiving the powder plug from the dosator as the powder tub is fitted towards the main shaft. Once this operation is completed, body bush returns back to its original position for carrying out joining, locking and discharge operations. When the body bush moves away from the cap bush for filling, the body push rod moves up and goes in the cap bush. The unopened capsule in the cap bush, if any, get ejected from the cap bush and such capsules are collected in a separate box. Body push rod comes down to its original position, this allows the body bush to occupy its original position.

After body bush occupies its original position, the body push rod moves up, joins the filled body into the cap and locks it, and the joined and locked capsule is ejected from the cap bush. Ejected capsules are collected in the finished capsule container.

The bottom bushing moves towards the outside and realigns with the cover bushing. The capsules are closed.

Fig. 10.22 : Realignment and Closing

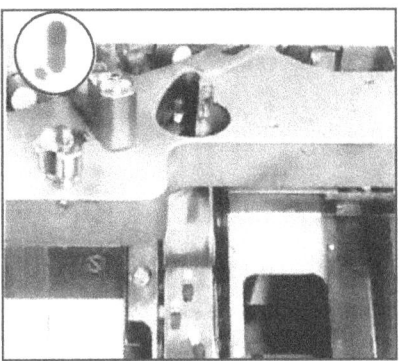
The filled capsules are pushed toward the discharge chute.
Fig. 10.23 : Expulsion

Powder Filling Operation : The powder tub and cap bush circuit plate move in two circuits having two different radii. To understand this, the top view is given. (Fig. 10.23)

Fig. 10.24 : Powder and Pellet Dosing

The powder tub where the powder bed is formed also rotates. Before the dosator-piston assembly dips inside the powder bed, powder bed of required height, uniform density is made available for dipping the dosator to get the plug of uniform weight.

The reformation of the powder bed is done exactly in a same way as that of intermittent machine.

10.3.2.5 Weight Control

Same as that for dosator intermittent type. In rotary machines many devices are provided like facility to check the full weight on-line and accordingly incorrect weight filled capsules are separated automatically.

Mechanical sorting of faulty empty capsules, mechanically sorting of faulty filled capsules are carried out automatically. (Manufacturers of machines have developed the capsule filling totally automatic to the extent that no man is needed to run the line).

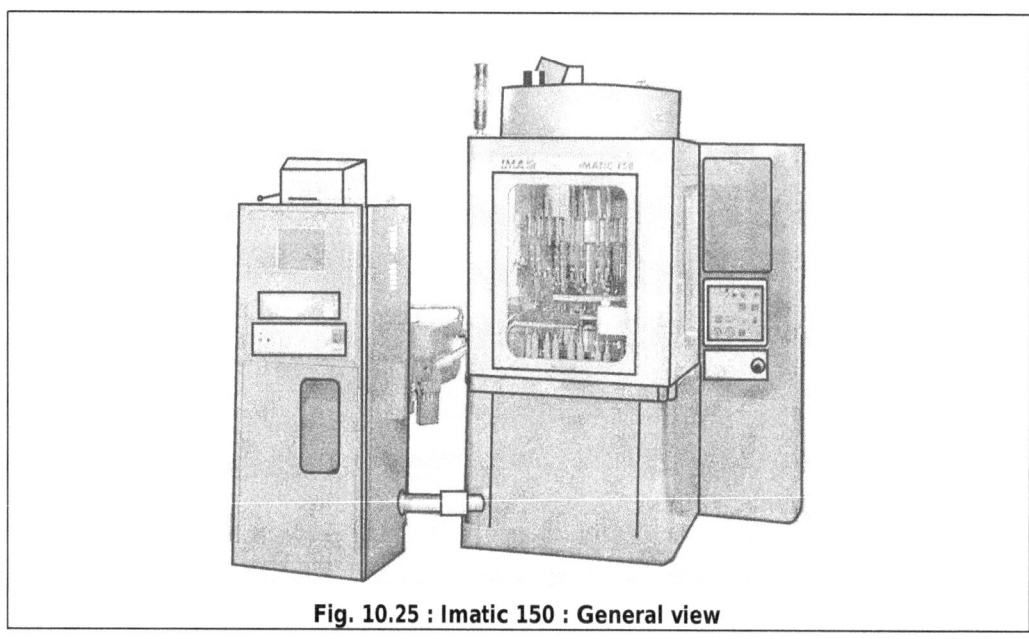

Fig. 10.25 : Imatic 150 : General view

M/s IMA have recently introduced a new machine called IMATIC 150 which uses the same working principles of the old machine (rotary turret) but with a more advanced technology. (Fig. 10.25).

10.3.2.6 List of Manufacturers of Rotary Machines

A list of the machinery manufacturers of rotary machines and models they have marketed is given below.

Table 10.3

Sr. No.	Series Model No.	Production per hour	Special Features
1.	MG2 machines (Italy) (A) Supermaa Different models	24,000 to 48,000	All capsule sizes 000 to 5 can be filled on MG2 machine.
	(B) Futura with different number of dosator-piston units	6000 ; 12000 ; 24000 ; 48000; 96000	G 100 and G 140 are provided with Automatic capsule weight control system.
	(C) G series (1) G 38/N and G 60	Upto 60,000	
	(2) G 37 N and G 100	Upto 1,00,000	
	(3) G 120/N and G 140	Upto 1,20,000	

contd. ...

2.	Harro Hofliger, KFM 3 Series	24,000	Capsule size from 00 to 5 can be filled.
3.	IMA (Italy) (A) MATIC with different dosator-piston units.	60,000 90,000 1,20,000	A statistical weight control system tests all capsules from each dosator in turn and is able to self adjust all working parameters on the machine automatically.
	(B) IMATIC with different number and dosator piston units	1,00,000 1,50,000 2,00,0090	These machines are equipped with automatic clean in place system, which performs pre-washing, washing with detergent, rinsing with deionized water and drying with hot air. In place, cleaning is enabled by a complete sealing of the powder dosing area from the rest of the machine.

■■■

11.
FINISHING OPERATIONS

11.1 CAPSULE CLEANING AND POLISHING

While filling the drug in capsules, some powder is likely to stick to capsules because semi-automatic filling machine has an inherent property whereby powder always remains on the loading ring. And in the case of fully automatic capsule filling machine, although the drug to be filled is made in the form of slug which enters directly into the body of the capsule, the loose powder sometimes can get mixed or spread on good capsules on account of some capsules whose caps got separated or damaged during closing operation.

This necessitates cleaning and polishing of filled capsules.

In older days, people used to polish/clean the capsules with Turkish Towel manually to get clean and polished capsules. Sometime they used to spread few drop of glycerin on towel to get a glossy finish.

To get higher output, industry started using automatic polishing / cleaning machines.

There are two types of polishing machines being used :

(a) Belt Type Polishing Machine : Machine as shown in Fig. 11.1 where capsules are passed between two polishing belts. Generally, belts are made from wool or now-a-days synthetic wool. The two counter rotating belts clean and polish the capsule. The lower belt is running faster than the upper belt in order to transport the product. Dust is continuously removed from polishing fleece by vacuum.

Fig. 11.1 : Belt Type Polishing Machine
(With the courtesy of ACG World Wide, Mumbai)

(b) Spiral Brush Type Polishing Machine : The machine uses the rotating brush concept to clean the capsules on a continuous basis (Fig. 11.2).

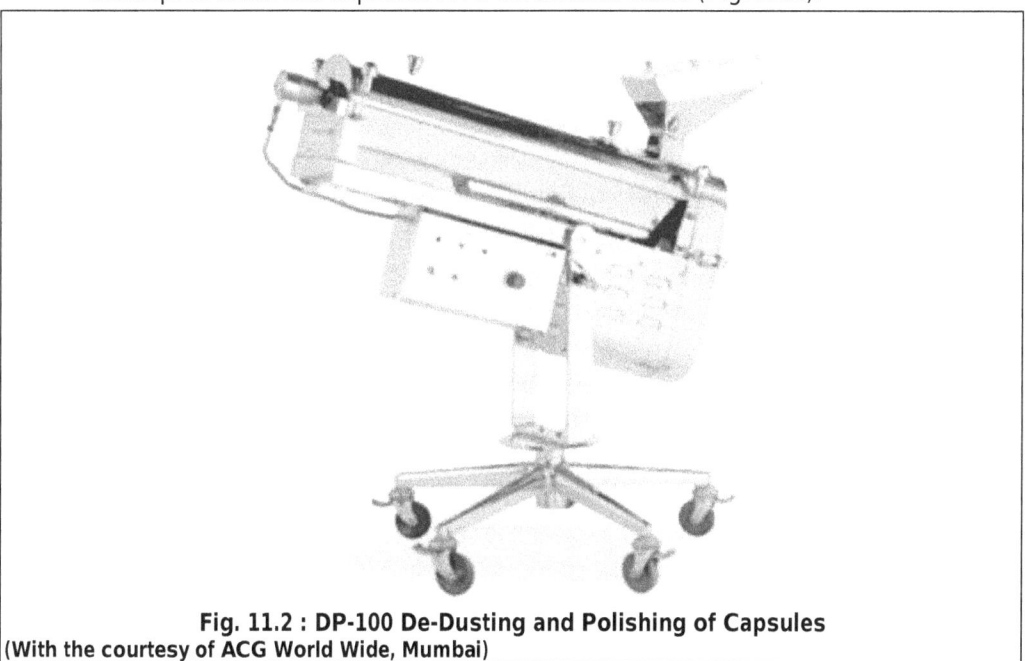

Fig. 11.2 : DP-100 De-Dusting and Polishing of Capsules
(With the courtesy of ACG World Wide, Mumbai)

Capsules are fed into a cylindrical chamber (polishing chamber) where a rotating spiral brush removes the powder particles sticking to the outer surface of capsules and at the same time transports the capsules forward.

A vacuum cleaner, the suction side of which is used for cleaning purpose is used to suck the deducted particles on a continuous basis.

As the capsules are fed into the polishing chamber from the infeed hopper, the spiral brush pushes the capsules towards the delivery chute against the force of gravity. During this process, the capsules undergo a rubbing action against the nylon bristles and surface powder gets removed and gets sucked by the vacuum cleaner. The continuous rubbing of capsules against the rotating brush ensures complete polishing of the capsules.

For effective polishing of the capsules, a vacuum cleaner must be used. A flow of 2500 - 3000 litres/min and maximum vacuum 500 m of water is recommended.

Also a uniform carpet flow of the capsules is to be ensured at the infeed.

Now-a-days, this type of polishing machines are widely used by industry.

This type of machine is made by M/s. Pam Pharmaceutical and Allied Machinery Company Pvt. Ltd., Mumbai.

11.2 CAPSULE SORTING

All capsules coming from filling machine are not always in good condition, there may be some damaged such as telescopic / loose caps and bodies / dents at dome of capsule etc., during the closing operation due to either machine problem or capsule quality problem.

These capsules need to be separated out; hence capsule sorter is required to eliminate manual sorting.

One of the examples of sorting machine is Pam's MCS - 100, where diametrically distorted capsules are sorted out by hexagonal plate sorter, which does not allow to pass diametrically distorted capsules. Passed capsules get carried by vibrator sorter to specially designed sorting plates, which remove loose caps and bodies and then alongwith good capsules get transferred to polishing machine or collection box (Fig. 11.3).

Fig. 11.3 : MCS – 100, Mini Capsule Sorter
(With the courtesy of ACG World Wide, Mumbai)

Capsules sorted out on above machine do not sort out empty or partially filled capsules. These capsules are passed through empty or partially filled capsules sorter. Here the air in the confined circular container blows off, on account of its whirling action the empty or partially filled capsules fed from the sorter and the heavy i.e. correctly filled capsules get collected through the discharge chute.

Air volume and velocity is adjusted as per weight of the filled capsules. Machine does not sort out if weight variation is small (Fig. 11.4).

Fig. 11.4 : Empty Capsule Eliminator
(With the courtesy of ACG World Wide, Mumbai)

Finally all capsules are passed through visual inspection, where defective capsules like foreign, dented or with any other visual defect, not detected on previous machine get manually sorted on the conveyor belt of the feeder sorter machine.

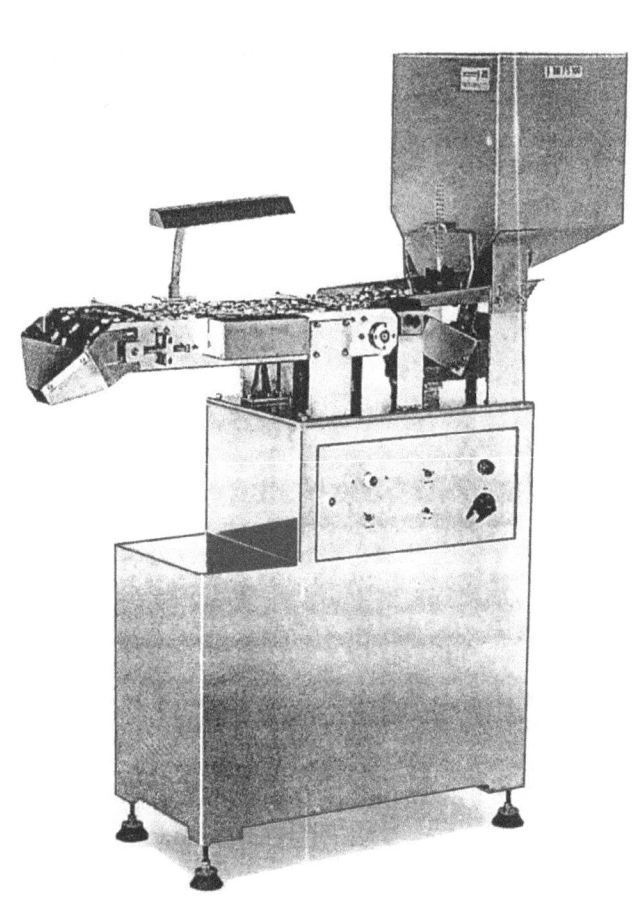

Feeder Sorter :
FS-100 :
Output : 60,000 Capsule/hr.
Removal of loose powder by vibration;
Manual sorting of capsules on conveyor belt.

Fig. 11.5 : Visual Capsule Sorter

(With the courtesy of ACG World Wide, Mumbai)

11.3 CAPSULE BAND SEALING

1. One of the reasons that prevented use of hard gelatin capsules for liquid filling in the past was the propensity for leakage of the formulation through the gap between the cap and the body of the capsule. The leakage problem got eliminated by introduction of providing band sealing at the junction of the cap and

body of the capsule. Band sealing is an operation where, at the cap and body junction, gelatin band is applied throughout its circumference, generally with a colour different than that of the cap and the body. This provides easy identification of the tampering of the capsule. The Tylenol case necessitated such a tamper evident method to protect the drug filled inside the capsule. In USA tamper evident packaging of the capsules is a requirement of the F.D.A. for over-the-counter human drug products.

2. **Advantages of band sealing :** The sealed hard gelatin capsules help drug formulator to extend or add many types of products that can be made and filled. Sealed capsule ensures leak-proof hermetic seal of cap to the body.

   Sealed capsule reduces the transmission of gases i.e. oxygen into the shell thus reducing the potential for oxidation. Moreover, the sealed capsule prevents the escape of odours from inside the capsule, which helps better administration of the drug.

3. **Band Sealing Machine :** The Band Sealing Machine was first introduced in 1950 by Parke Davis & Company, for Sealing with gelatin solution and then by Shionogi with the hermetic sealing in the year 1987. In India, PAM of ACG World Wide Group produced Automatic Band Sealing Machine. (Fig. 11.6).

Fig. 11.6 : Automatic Band Sealing Machine
(With the courtesy of ACG World Wide, Mumbai)

Sealing Mechanism :

Here, capsules are fed to the conveyor belt in oriented manner through their patented single drum rectification system. Capsules are transported through slots provided in carrier links to the sealing station, where two seals are applied to each capsule. This ensures that there is no air bubble or unevenness after applying the second band.

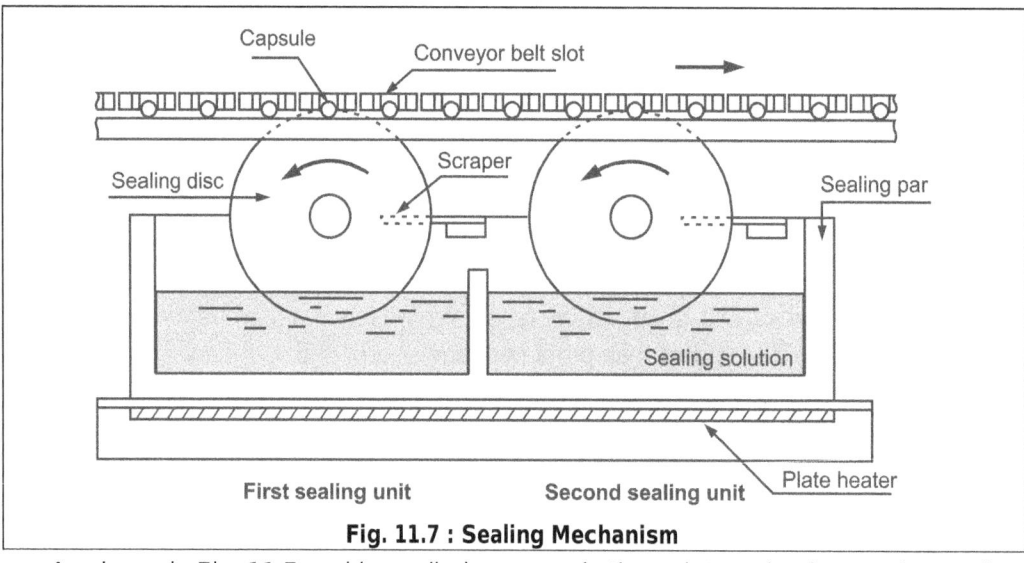

Fig. 11.7 : Sealing Mechanism

As shown in Fig. 11.7 seal is applied on capsule through two circular rotating sealing wheels. Sealing solution is picked up by rotating sealing wheels, which are having grooves to hold sealing solution. Scraper plate scraps the excessive sealing solution and solution further applied on capsule through circumference. Second sealing disc removes air bubble and unevenness in first band applied.

The wet bands of material are dried by using filtered air at room temperature or slightly heating air by heater provided in air system. In this process, loss of moisture from capsule shell is reduced to the minimum to avoid brittleness.

Drying cycle takes approximate 8 to 9 minutes and sealed dried capsules are discharged through discharge chute.

Above sealing method is widely used and similar machines are made by IMA (Italy) and Qualicaps (USA) also.

Another type of band sealing machine made by M/s. Capsugel is called 'LEMS'. In this type of machine there is no band provided.

LEMS Sealing Process :
- Sealing fluid is sprayed onto the joint between the cap and body, lowering the melting point of gelatin in the wetted area.
- Sealing fluid contains approximately 50% water and 50% ethanol resulting in a lower surface tension than water alone. The fluid thus penetrates the cap/body overlap more easily and a better seal is established.
- Approximately 50 microliters of fluid is sprayed during a one second cycle, followed by suction to remove excess fluid.
- Air heated to 40-60°C is gently blown across the capsule during the cycle to complete the melting and fusion of the two gelatin layers.
- Gelatin setting is completed while the product returns to room temperature.

In this process, we cannot see the sealing band applied on capsule. The capsule aesthetically looks good, but we cannot predict the sealing quality as no visual band is seen. (Refer Fig. 11.8)

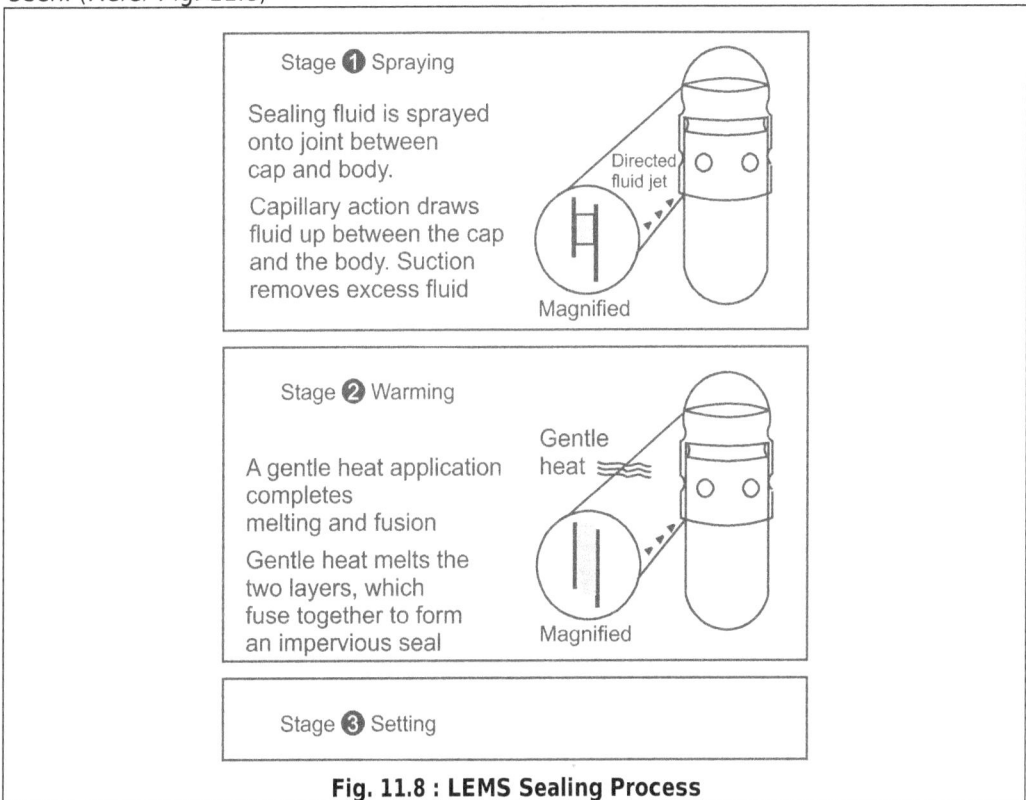

Fig. 11.8 : LEMS Sealing Process

11.4 WEIGHING OF CAPSULES AND CHECK WEIGHING MACHINES

During and at the time of post filling of capsules with various formulations, it is necessary to check the weight of the filled capsules. This is done to ensure that the net weight of the formulation filled in capsules is as per the desired fill weight for that particular product and batch.

For Manual filling and on Semi-automatic capsule filling machines, Operator and Quality control officer are checking filled capsules at a set time interval on stand along weighing balance. He keeps the records of sample weighed capsules with respect to the time, date, batch and other related information.

For Automatic capsule filling machines, the above operation is made automated using Programmable Logic Controller, Weighing balance, Printer and necessary feeding and weighing system for capsules. These machines are known as Check Weighing Machines.

There are two types of Check Weighing Machines available in the market.
1. Sample Automatic Check Weighing Machines.
2. 100 % Check Weighing Machines.

11.4.1 Sample Automatic Check Weighing Machine

These machines are generally used with Automatic Capsule Filling Machines and attached to the outlet chute of the Capsules Filling Machines. They are having either common or separate Programmable logic controller and Data display unit.

At the set time interval during operation of filling machine, desired number of filled capsule samples are taken from the Outlet chute of the Capsule filling machine. These filled capsules are collected in a vibratory feeder and then they are fed one by one to the weighing balance. On weighing balance, each capsule's weight is checked precisely and recorded. Once the capsule weight is completed, capsule is ejected out using air blast from the weighing pan of the weighing balance. Based on the set weight variation limit on Average fill weight, capsules are accepted or rejected and respective weight is printed accordingly. The cycle continues till the desired sample readings are recorded.

The readings are printed along with the other statistical data for the sample weighed, such as maximum weight, minimum weight, standard deviation, (% + / –) weight variation of individual capsules, average weight of the sample, accepted capsules, rejected capsules, capsules recorded beyond the set limits along with the standard recipe of that batch such as time, date, product name, operator name, capsule size etc.

Once the above cycle is completed for desired sample of capsules, the balance capsules in the vibratory feeder are purged out without weighing and recording these capsules.

The check weighing machine also has provision to give feedback to the Capsule filling machine as follows :

(a) Providing alarms and display for samples weighed beyond set Average weight of the capsules.
(b) Stopping the Capsule filling machine if consecutive samples are found beyond set tolerance limits.
(c) Correcting the Capsule filling machine settings automatically and with or without stopping the filling machine so that average weight can be adjusted according to the set fill weight.

This machine does the sample check weighing of the batch filled on the Automatic capsule filling machine and ensures no manual intervention required for weighing and recording of filled samples.

Pam Pharmaceuticals and Allied Machinery Company Limited manufactures this type of Weighing machines known as 'Check Weigher Model CW 10'. Other manufacturers of these machines are Macofar, IMA and Harro Hoffliger.

11.4.2 100% Check Weighing Machine

In this type of Check Weighing machine, each and every filled capsule of the batch is weighed, recorded and sorted out for capsules, which are beyond required limits of average total weight of the capsules. This machine either can be attached to the Automatic capsules filling machine or used as a stand-alone. This Check weighing machine is having different versions for checking capsules and tablets.

This 100% Check Weighing machine consists of Capsule/Tablet hopper, Feeding mechanism, Load cell bank (Multiple load cells), Accepted and Rejected capsules flaps, Industrial Programmable Computer, Printer and High end electronic controls.

Products (Filled Capsules/Tablets) are fed in the hopper of this machine and with the help of feeding mechanism, individual product is placed gently on the each load cell of the machine. Within fraction of a second, each product is weighed, recorded and decisions are taken to accept or reject the weighed capsule as per it's reading and set limits for accepting the product. The weighed capsules are ejected out from the outlet chute and rejected capsules are removed from the outlet chute using quick operating flaps. This operation continues till the batch is completed.

The recorded weight of the accepted and rejected products is printed with various statistical data and analysis of the weighed product, graphs and recipe of the batch.

These 100% Check Weighing machines can be used for various sizes of capsules and tablets using change parts of feeding and ejecting mechanism. These machines are equipped with latest electronics technology for getting the higher production and accurate checking of the products. It gives accuracy as well as repeatability of +/− 2 milligrams. Various models are available with output upto 60,000, 120,000 and 180,000 capsules per hour.

Pam Pharmaceuticals and Allied Machinery Company Limited manufactures this type of Weighing machines` known as '100% Check Weigher'. Other manufacturers of these machines are Anritsu, Bosch, Harro Hoffliger and IMA.

Fig. 11.9 : 100% Check Weighing Machine
(With the courtesy of ACG World Wide, Mumbai)

■■■

12.
PACKAGING OF FILLED CAPSULES

12.1 INTRODUCTION

In general terms, packaging can be described as a specific method of preparing goods for transport, warehousing, logistics, sale, and end use.

By extension, packaging is the science, art and technology of enclosing, carrying or protecting products for distribution, storage, sale and use.

The basic functions of a packaging can thus be listed as follows:

1. Containment;
2. Protection;
3. Preservation;
4. Transportation;
5. Conveys relevant information;
6. Helps in selling.

12.2 HISTORY OF PACKAGING

The history of packaging can be traced along the progress that mankind has made through the years. It starts with the use of natural resources in the earliest days and progresses through the times resulting in the present system where polymeric films are being extensively used for various applications either independently or in combination.

The first packages used the natural materials available at the time like baskets; wooden material like barrels, pallets or boxes; ceramics; the woven bags etc. The later range of packaging materials were used to form packages for example, glass and bronze containers and plastic films. The development in the packaging materials has been done and continues to be focused on improving the efficiency in terms of usage, performance, economies and more importantly functionality. In the true sense functionality decided the application and more importantly the source of raw material to be used for packaging application.

In 2003, the packaging industry was still in the early stages and accounted for only two per cent of the gross national product even in the developing countries. Most of this, consisted of food packaging which was of prime importance. This has witnessed a rapid growth since then and this promises to grow further, in developed countries and mostly in developing countries.

Pharma packaging has similarly undergone a sea change in the past few years, coming out with solutions that are consumer friendly besides being safe and also aesthetic in nature. Some of the common forms include strip packing and blister packing to Alu packing. The other packaging options available now also include plastic, glass, aluminium, PET bottles or paper packages. The Indian pharmaceutical packaging industry itself has matured into a major business, worth more than ₹ 28,000 Crore and growing at a rate of around 12-14 per cent annually.

The rules and regulations governing the pharmaceutical packaging Industry have also developed along with the basic Pharmaceutical Industry. Thus, the facilities manufacturing pharma packaging are now required to fulfill strict norms, especially for the primary packaging. Since consumer safety is of utmost importance, issues like expiry date, manufacturing date on the pack, right packaging, child resistant packaging, information about the medication have to be printed on the primary packaging units. Also these processing companies have to follow international standards of hygiene, qualification and competency level of workers, and record keeping besides following GMP guidelines. There are similar guidelines for the secondary and tertiary packaging, which also cover storage and distribution areas.

12.3 FOCUS ON QUALITY

Incoming and in-process quality checks are done on raw material like foils, ink, adhesives and polymers which continue through the primary and secondary packaging stages. The units should conform to cGMP and clean room facility norms and IP and USP regulatory norms. There is regulation for product packaging and labelling though there are no standards for labels. Just like the container and products, labels and leaflets are also of utmost importance. The label and leaflet serve the purpose of informing the patient, the pharmacist, the distribution channel and manufacturer; in short it takes care of communication of necessary information to all concerned.

We will now study the basic functions of packaging which can thus be listed as follows:

1. Protection physical and barrier;
2. Containment;
3. Conveys relevant information;
4. Marketing;
5. Security;
6. Convenience for handling and transportation;

Physical protection : The objects enclosed in the package may require protection from, among other things, mechanical damage, electrostatic discharge, compression, temperature etc. The package is designed to address the basic need of protecting the medicine and retain it in its form as packed.

Barrier protection : It is necessary that in order to avoid degradation of a medicine in packed condition, a barrier from oxygen, water vapour, dust etc., is often required. The need is primarily dependant on the formulation involved. Thus, permeability becomes a critical factor in design. Keeping the contents clean, fresh, sterile and safe for the intended shelf life is a primary function in this regard. Some of the recent technological developments are seen in food packages where modified atmospheres or controlled atmospheres are also maintained, while some packages contain desiccants or oxygen absorbers to help extend shelf life.

Containment : In some packages, small objects are typically grouped together in one package for reasons of efficiency. For example, a single box of 1000 pencils requires less physical handling than 1000 single pencils. Liquids, powders, and granular materials need containment. Tabletting of powders or capsulation are also used for grouping.

Information communication : Packages and labels communicate how to use, transport, recycle, or dispose of the package or product. With pharmaceuticals, food, medical, and chemical products, some types of information are required by governments. Some packages and labels also are used for track and trace purposes.

Marketing : The packaging and labels can be used by marketers to encourage potential buyers to purchase the product. Package graphic design and physical design have been important and constantly evolving phenomenon for several decades. Marketing communications and graphic design are applied to the surface of the package and (in many cases) the point of sale display.

Security : Packaging can play an important role in reducing the security risks of shipment. Packages can be made with improved tamper resistance to avoid tampering or to help indicate tampering. Packages can be designed to help reduce the risks of package pilferage. Some package constructions are more resistant to pilferage and some have pilfer indicating seals. Packages may include features like authentication seals and use security printing to help indicate that the package and contents are not counterfeit. Packages also can include RFID tags and the like. Using packaging in this way is a means of loss prevention and is becoming popular.

Convenience : Packages can help to introduce features that add convenience in distribution, handling, stacking, display, sale, opening, reclosing, use, dispensing, and reuse.

In addition to this, in specific packaging for pharma purposes, portion control is an additional feature that needs to be addressed.

Portion control : Single serving or single dosage packaging has a precise amount of contents to control usage. Bulk commodities (such as salt) can be divided into packages that are a more suitable size for individual households. It also helps in control of inventory.

12.4 TYPES OF PACKAGING

Packaging may be looked at as being of several different types. For example a transport package or distribution package can be the shipping container used to ship, store, and handle the product or inner packages. Some identify a consumer package as one which is directed toward a consumer or household.

Packaging may be described in relation to the type of product being packaged: medical device packaging, bulk chemical packaging, over-the-counter drug packaging, retail food packaging, military material packaging, pharmaceutical packaging etc.

It is sometimes convenient to categorize packages by layer or function: "primary", "secondary" etc.

- Primary packaging is the material that first envelops the product or is in direct contact with it and holds it. This usually is the smallest unit of distribution or use and is the package which is in direct contact with the contents.
- Secondary packaging is outside the primary packaging, perhaps used to group primary packages together for e.g. an individual carton or carton of five units.
- Tertiary packaging is used for bulk handling, warehouse storage and transport shipping. The most common form is a palletized unit load that packs tightly into containers.

These broad categories can be somewhat arbitrary and need to be studied in context with their specific area of application to decide whether the packing is primary or secondary in nature. For example, depending on the use, a shrink wrap can be primary packaging when applied directly to the product, secondary packaging when combining smaller packages, and tertiary packaging on some distribution packs.

12.4.1 Major Types of Packaging Materials

The following are the major materials used for pharmaceutical packaging at the present.

1. **Glass :** While the use of this material for pharmaceutical packaging is fast reducing, glass containers like bottles continue to be a regular form of packaging for liquids, tablets and capsules. Ampoules and injection syringes are also other commonly used glass containers. Apart from the usage of appropriate containers other important factors include conformance to industrial norms, and adherence to European and United States Pharmacopeia. Some of the common tests conducted for this include the light transmission and hydrolytic resistance.

2. **Paper :** This is mostly and widely used as a secondary packaging material in the form of cartons. However, applications of processed – i.e. paper in the laminated and / or coated paper are also known though in small quantities. Also, paper is used in the form of multilayer laminates particularly in the form of pouches. Characteristics like bursting strength etc. are of prime importance. Printability is also an important feature. A major shortcoming is the lack of barrier and can only be used as a primary packaging material in a limited way and only after processing with other substrates or coating.

3. **Metal :** This was once a major type of packaging material mostly used in the form of cans, aerosol containers etc. and aluminium and stainless steel continue to be in use for the purpose. Metals are near absolute on the scale of impermeability to moisture and gases, and in unison with their strength, they are still the ideal packaging material. The high costs are a limitation. The packaging of individual solid dosages in aluminum blisters and strips has been popular for long.

4. **Plastics :** This form of packaging is fast growing and popular with the fast developing field of plastics in general and is today widely used as blisters and containers. Their ease of handling, light weight characteristic and unbreakable nature are major positives. Not all plastics have all these virtues of their own and it is common to coat or combine more than one type to get a combination of characteristics. Common structures are well defined and accepted.

12.4.2 Closures and Containers

As discussed above, containers are mostly made of metal, glass and plastics, and are required to be inert as possible. There is a definite need to avoid any unwanted interaction between the contents and the make of the material of the container and closure. Closures could also be of rubber particularly where they have to be pierced with needles.

Closures and containers, as primary packaging components, are of critical importance and hence an inseparable part of the drug preparation.

Rubber closures, caps, seals etc. are special form of closures and are used to ensure that the containers maintain their seal integrity under standard or specified conditions of storage, handling and transportation through the life cycle of the drug packed. These could be further strengthened by plastic or metal straps for different reasons including one of security.

There are different types of speciality closures depending upon their intended function. Some of the most important are as mentioned below.

Child resistant types provide safety against unintended use by children, while the tamper evident closures seek to provide safety against intended pilferage, alteration or the like of the packed formulations. The latter are a means of anti counterfeiting, to address a fast developing challenge in pharmaceutical packaging.

12.4.3 Package Development Considerations

Package design and development are often thought of as an integral part of the new product development process. Very often, development of a package (or component) can be a separate process, but must be linked closely with the product to be packaged.

Some of the important requirements considered for determination of appropriate package design are an extension of the basic packaging requirements and include the following: structural design, marketing, shelf life, quality assurance, logistics, legal, regulatory, graphic design, end-use, environmental etc. The design criteria, performance (specified by package testing), completion time targets, resources, and cost constraints need to be established and agreed upon.

Transport packaging needs to be matched to its logistics system which takes into consideration the local aspects including availability and infrastructure apart from local rules and regulations, if any. This is mostly required in secondary and tertiary packaging.

With some types of products, the design process of a package involves detailed regulatory requirements for the package. For example with packaging foods, any package components that may contact the food are food contact materials. Toxicologists and food scientists need to verify that the packaging materials are allowed by applicable regulations. Packaging engineers need to verify that the completed package will keep the product safe for its intended shelf life with normal usage. Packaging processes, labelling, distribution, and sale need to be validated to comply with regulations and have the well being of the consumer in mind.

Sometimes the objectives of package development seem contradictory. For example, regulations for an over-the-counter drug might require the package to be tamper-evident and child resistant. These intentionally make the package difficult to open. The intended consumer, however, might be handicapped or elderly and be unable to readily open the package. Thus, meeting all these goals is a challenge.

Package design may take place within a company or with various degrees of external packaging engineering: independent contractors, consultants, vendor evaluations, independent laboratories, contract packagers, total outsourcing etc. It is necessary that effective quality management system along with verification and validation protocols be used for specific types of packaging and is certainly recommended for all.

Since consumer safety is of utmost importance, expiry date and information about the medication are some of the most important criteria to be taken care of.

12.5 PACKAGING OF FILLED CAPSULES

12.5.1 Introduction

Packaging is basically defined as 'the collection of different components which surround the pharmaceutical product from the time of production until its use'.

12.5.2 Importance of Packing in Pharmaceutical Manufacture

An effective packaging should be able :
1. To protect against all adverse external influences that can alter product properties.
2. To protect against biological contamination.
3. To protect against physical damage.
4. To carry the correct information and identification of the product.
5. To tamper evident/child resistance/Anti-counterfeiting.

12.5.3 Functions of Packaging Containment

1. Not to leak, nor allow diffusion and permeation.
2. Strong enough to hold the contents during handling.
3. Protection from : Light, Moisture, Oxygen, Biological contamination, Mechanical damage, Counterfeiting

12.5.4 Material Characteristics

Quality of material should follow following characteristics :
1. It must preserve the physical properties of all dosage forms and protect them against damage or breakage.
2. It must not alter the identity of the product.

3. It must preserve the characteristic properties of the product to comply specifications.
4. It must protect product against undesirable or adulterating chemical, biological or physical entities.

Choosing Appropriate Primary Pack :

Product characteristics/sensitivity to :
1. Hygroscopicity
2. Physical degradation
3. Chemical degradation
4. Drug release properties
5. Mechanical properties
6. Photosensitivity
7. Gas liberation tendency
8. Dimensional aspects

Selection of packaging material :
1. Moisture barrier requirements
2. Light barrier requirements
3. Gas barrier requirements
4. Chemical properties

12.5.5 Testing and Stability

Critical parameters during screening :
1. Release of chemicals from components of packaging material.
2. Release of visible and / or sub-visible particles.
3. Adsorption or absorption of pharmaceutical components by packaging material.
4. Chemical reaction between pharmaceutical product and packaging material.
5. Degradation of packaging component in contact with pharmaceutical products.
6. Influence of manufacturing process on the container.

QC Plus (Qualification) :
1. What need to be looked in
2. WVTR (Water Vapour Transmission Rate)
   - Flat film
   - Formed blister
3. OTR
4. Extractables and Leachables
   - Periodic review and re-equalification in case of major change and source change.

Packaging Integrity :

A failure in an impervious container closure system can occur due to the failure in their seal integrity at the interface, which may effect the drug product stability due to ingress of moisture, oxygen or microbial contamination.

1. Forming - can have impact on WVTR.
2. Sealing - pressure, temperature and dwell time - leads to increased permeability.

Integrity Testing :

1. Bubble Test - Blister / Strip pack, Liquid bottles / cap.
2. Pressure decay test - Vials, Ampoules, Blister, Pouches, IV bag.
3. Vacuum decay test - Vial, Ampoules etc.

12.6 PACKAGING MATERIALS FOR BLISTER PACKING OF H. G. CAPSULES

12.6.1 Main Considerations When Selecting Blister Packing Materials

The choice of forming and sealing materials used depends on the degree to which the product needs to be protected from light, heat and moisture. Each material has different resistance to each of these elements and all will affect the shelf life and storage conditions of the packaged drugs. Tests are usually carried out during a drug's development (stability studies) to identify which materials are most suitable; bearing in mind the differing cost implications. The plastic forming films such as polyvinyl chloride (PVC), polypropylene (PP) and polyester (PET) are thermoformed, and are usually colourless and transparent. However for child-proof packs, or if the drug must be protected from light, forming films can also be opaque.

12.6.2 Forming Films

The forming film is the packaging component that receives the product in deep drawn pockets. Plastic forming films such as polypropylene (PP), Polyvinyl Chloride (PVC) can be thermoformed, but support materials containing aluminum are cold formed. The forming film and lidding materials are an integrated package and must match one another precisely. The forming film is usually colourless and transparent. However, if the manufacturer wishes to make a childproof package, or if the drug must be protected from light, then forming films can also be opaque.

PVC (Polyvinyl Chloride) : PVC used as a forming film is called rigid PVC because it is almost free of softening agents. Currently it is the most widely used forming film and displays ideal forming characteristics. Its water-vapour permeability is very low.

However, PVC was widely criticized because its combustion results in hydrochloride emissions and if combustion takes place under certain conditions it can produce dioxins. New studies have shown that in today's incineration plants PVC doesn't create any problem and energy recovery of plastics including PVC is a sustainable operation.

PVDC (Polyvinylidene Chloride) : PVDC-coated PVC has characteristics similar to those of uncoated PVC except that the water vapour permeability of films coated in this way is reduced by a factor of 5-10. The coating is applied on one side and usually faces the product and the lidding material.

PVC and ACLAR (CTFE) : PVC-CTFE films made from PVC and ACLAR (CTFE) have the lowest water-vapour permeability of all the films used for blister packaging. The environmental concerns raised about PVC also apply to PVC-CTFE film.

PP (Polypropylene) : There is an increasing trend towards the use of PP as a support material for blister packages. The water-vapour permeability of uncoated PP is lower than that of PVC and is comparable to the water-vapour permeability of PVDC coated PVC. One problem posed by PP processing is thermoforming. The temperature required for thermoforming PP and the temperature of the subsequent cooling process must be precisely controlled. Another problem is warping of package - often resulting in the requirement for PP formed packages to be straightened before cartoning.

New High Barrier Thermoforming Film : There is a new high barrier thermoforming film based on a new type of plastic granules called COC (Cyclo-olefine copolymer). The COC films are solvent-free laminated to both sides with 30 micron PP films; consequently the laminate is free from solvents. The packaging system in combination with PP-sealable aluminium push-thru lidding foils guarantees a high seal integrity. Peel and peel-push laminates are also available.

PS (Polystyrene) : PS is perfectly suitable for thermoforming but its high water-vapour permeability does not permit its use as a blister material for pharmaceutical purposes.

Coldform Film (Biaxally Orientated Polyamide) (OPA) : Normally the permeability of plastic forming films increases with rising temperature. This is not true for aluminium formed packaging. Forming plastic film also causes a noticeable reduction in the thickness of the material. However, when comparing the water-vapour transmission rates of the base material with that of the finished package there is not always a direct relationship between the thickness of the film and the water-vapour barrier effect.

The following table shows the water-vapour transmission rate of various packing materials.

Table 12.1

Material	Water Vapour Transmission Rate
PVC	3.1
PVC/PVDC 40 gsm	0.75
Triplex	0.45
Aclar (Suprex 900)	0.23
Aclar (Ultrex 2000)	0.12
OPA/ALU/PVC (cold form)	Zero Transmission

12.6.3 Lidding Material

The lidding material consists of support material e.g. aluminium that has a printed primer on one side and a sealing agent e.g. a heat-sealing lacquer on the other side. The sealing agent side faces the product and the forming films.

After the tablets or capsules have been properly fed to the performed support materials the lidding material is sealed onto the support material. Temperatures for this, can range from 140-300°C. There are two sealing techniques : intermittent sealing with sealing plates and continuous sealing with sealing rollers. Intermittent sealing machines are operated at lower sealing temperatures than are continuous sealing machines. Intermittent sealing machines also have a longer sealing time. An essential component of lidding material is the sealing coating. The side of the lidding material that faces the product and the forming film must be provided with a coating material suitable for heat sealing. This is usually accomplished by means of a heat sealing lacquer which must comply with FDA standards and must precisely match the respective forming films. Precisely match means that with predetermined sealing parameter, a permanent sealing effect between the lidding material and the forming film must be guaranteed under any climatic conditions. An additional requirement is that the sealing strength must fall within a predetermined tolerance.

Hard Aluminium : Hard Aluminium is the push through lidding material that is most widely used in Europe. The foil usually has a thickness of about 25 micron. However, this may in time be reduced to 15 micron. The hardness of the aluminium facilitates push through opening. Usually only the print-primer side features a printed design, but occasionally the side with the heat-sealing lacquer can also be printed. A double coat of heat-sealing lacquer (a heat sealing primer and the actual heat-sealing lacquer) has become the standard for lidding materials. The heat-sealing primer ensures optimum adhesion of the heat-sealing lacquer to the aluminium foil. Then the heat-sealing lacquer can be perfectly matched to the formed films. If the heat sealing primers are coloured then the heat-sealing lacquer applied over the primer can protect the packaged product from coming into contact with the pigments. If additional printing is required on the side of the heat sealing lacquer, the only alternative is to apply two coats of the lacquer. This is necessary because the printing inks must be between the heat-sealing primer and the actual heat-sealing lacquer.

Soft Aluminium : This is frequently used for child-proof push-thru foils. With the exception of the type of aluminium used, the structure of this lidding material corresponds to that of hard aluminium. The softness and thickness of this type of aluminium help to prevent children from pushing tablets through it. The lidding material is also provided with a perforation along the sealed seams to prevent the lidding material from being peeled off the form film in one piece.

Paper-Aluminium : For a combination of paper and aluminium the weight of the paper amounts to 45-50 g/m^2. In the USA, the thickness of the aluminium is greater than in Europe. The reason for this is that in Europe this lidding material is used for childproof push-thru packages. Therefore, the aluminium foil is relatively thin. In the USA, this type of material is used as a peel-off foil and for effective peeling the aluminium foil must be relatively thick. Printing can take place directly on to the paper surface.

Paper-Pet-Aluminium : Lidding material made of a paper-polyester-aluminium laminate is often called peel-off-push-thru foil. This kind of material is used predominantly in the USA and is virtually unknown in Europe. The concept is to first peel off the paper-PET laminate from the aluminium and then the tablet is pushed through the aluminium.

Requirements for Lidding Components : The basic lidding material must meet requirements for elasticity or inelasticity specific to the type of machine used. It must guarantee water-vapour transmission rate that is atleast as low as that of the forming films and it must be suitable for the type of opening appropriate to the package e.g. push-thru or peel-off. The heat-sealing coat must be compatible with the plastic material of the form films and it must ensure constant sealing for any given sealing parameter. The sealing strength must be suitable for push-thru or peel-off opening and of course it must comply with FDA recommendations.

Eye Marks : The eye marks must be carefully adjusted to the type of machine used. If the machine is controlled by a feed mechanism, the eye marks must have extremely close tolerances. The total deviation across a distance of 1000 mm must not exceed +/− 0.4 mm. If the machine is controlled by a straightening mechanism that carries a roller with the lidding material, the distances between the eye marks are deliberately printed in the negative range because the lidding material is stretched to correspond to the speed of the machine.

12.7 PACKAGING MACHINERIES

12.7.1 Basic Operations Involved in Packing

1. Feeding of product in a hopper.
2. Feeding Station - Counting Disk / Feeding Shoot.
3. Alu/PVC/PVDC Feeding Station - Slotted Rollers.
4. Forming Mechanism - Blister in case of Blister Packing.
5. Filling Operation Station.
6. Hot Sealing Station.
7. No-Fill Detection station.
8. Strips Cutting Station.
9. No-Fill Rejection Station.
10. Collating Strips Station.

12.7.2 Types of Packing

12.7.2.1 Bulk Packing in Glass/HDPE Bottles

Fully Automatic Capsule Counting and Filling Machine : Here the product is spread over a rotating disc with exact number of slots on the surface as required for one container fill. The container is moving on a belt below the disc. As the disc reaches its bottom position, the magnetic solenoid is actuated by a micro switch and fills the capsules into the bottle. The Container moves further on the belt and the cap is sealed and Label is fixed on the container manually or through automatic cap sealing machine and labelling machine respectively. The filled and sealed containers are collated into a corrugated carton and secondary labelling is done.

A typical Counting and Filling machine is shown below :

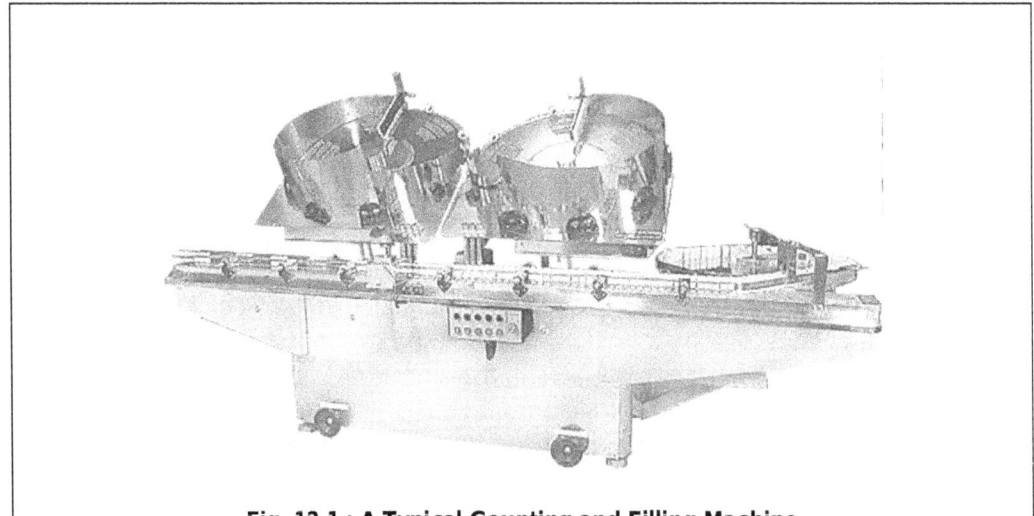

Fig. 12.1 : A Typical Counting and Filling Machine

The salient features of Capsule Counting and Filling machine :

- Fully Automatic Double Disc.
- 36' Unscrambler with Mechanical vary speed drive to feed the bottles.
- 120" Independent drive, two SS 304 Slots Conveyor with Mechanical vary speed drive for carrying the containers.
- 36' Independent drive disc with SS 304 Hopper to store and count the products.
- 220 V solenoid coil with plunger system to stop the bottles while Filling the products.
- Height alignment mounts to align with existing machine height.

12.7.2.2 Strip Packing Machine

Strip Packaging machines are designed to handle a wide range of products with utmost precision and speed upto 2400 units per minute. The products from the hopper passes through a stainless steel feeding system and goes to sealing roller cavities where laminated foils, drawn from two rollers, packs and seals the products in a continuous strip. The strip then passes through vertical and horizontal cutter assemblies to deliver the desired sizes of strip packages.

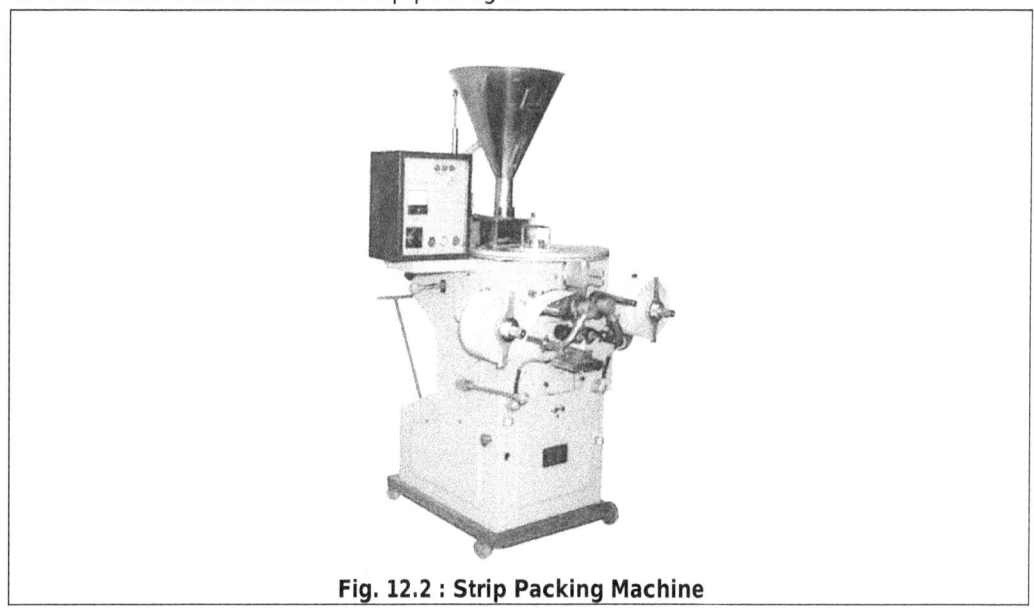

Fig. 12.2 : Strip Packing Machine

The filled and sealed strips are fed to a conveyor belt wherein the strips are collated and packed in a pre-printed inner carton, closed and then are collated into a corrugated carton and secondary labelling is done.

Machine also comes with optional features such as Electronic temperature control system with indicator to read foil sealing temperature and Strip counter and Batch coding attachment.

Strip Packaging Machines are :

(i) Suitable for packing tablets, soft capsules and hard gelatine capsules,

(ii) Available in different models of 2, 4, 6, 8, 10 and 12 track having capacities to pack 400 to 3000 tablets per minute with maximum sealing width of 250 mm.

(iii) Suitable for most heat sealable foils like Paper Poly, Aluminium Poly, Cello Polly, Cellophane, Glassine Poly.

(iv) Capable of ensuring air-tight leak-proof packing.

These machines have standardized, quickly interchangeable parts, including adjustable foil cutting and slitting devices. The machines are provided with vibratory feed control for higher output and cartridge type heaters and thermostatic temperature control suitable for all types of packing materials.

12.7.2.3 Blister Packing Machine

Blister Packing Machines are designed to handle a wide range of products of various different sizes with the variety of forming films like PVC/PVDC/ACLAR/ALU etc.

The production flow of a thermoforming machine encompasses a number of functioning steps that can be found in all types. In the initial step the formation of the receiving pocket cavities for the capsules take place. The moulded blister cavities inside the base web are then filled with the capsules and subsequently sealed and closed. Embossing and perforating follows, with the blisters being die cut before being packed into folded boxes.

Blister packing machines are available with a range of performances. The maximum machine output depends upon the attributes of the thermoforming film, the capsule composition and size, the product in-feed and the performance characteristics of any successive machines.

In India ACG Worldwide, one of the largest groups in the world, besides manufacturing and marketing empty hand gelatine capsules, is also manufacturing a wide range of blister packing machines handling a variety of films and laminates. One such machine is their B-45', a servo driven continuous motion blister machine where flat bed forming of PVC, PVDC, ACLAR and Aluminium films is done with rotary sealing. Forming is done with compressed air.

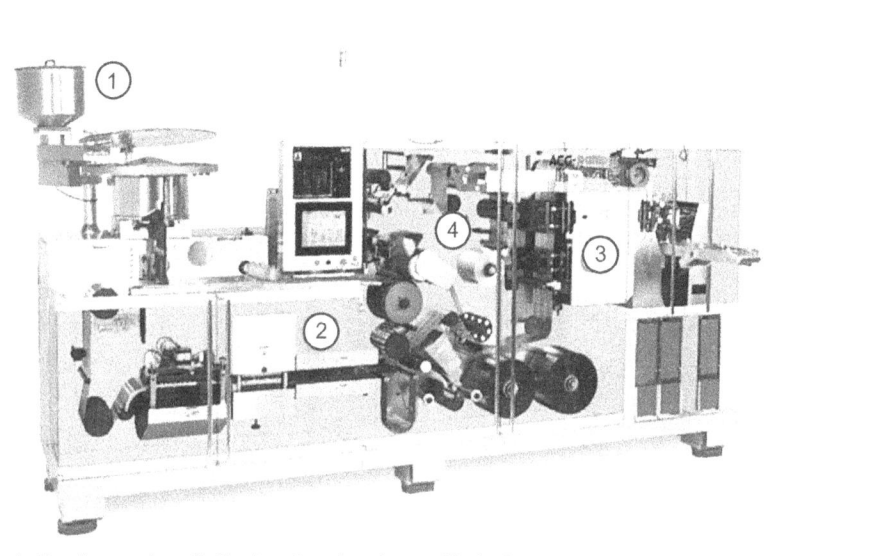

1. Feeding system 2. Pre-heating, forming and indexing
3. Embossing, perforation and punching 4. Over printing unit and registration control

Fig. 12.3 : Blister Packing Machine
(With the courtesy of ACG Worldwide, Mumbai)

www.ingramcontent.com/pod-product-compliance
Lightning Source LLC
Chambersburg PA
CBHW081915180426
43198CB00038B/2682